Parenting Our Schools

ALSO BY JILL BLOOM

Help Me to Help My Child:
A Sourcebook for Parents of
Learning Disabled Children

Parenting Our Schools

A Hands-On Guide to Education Reform

JILL BLOOM

With a Foreword by Howard Gardner, Ph.D.
Professor of Education, Harvard University

LITTLE, BROWN AND COMPANY
BOSTON • TORONTO • LONDON

First Edition

Library of Congress Cataloging-in-Publication Data

Bloom, Jill.
    Parenting our schools : a hands-on guide to education reform / Jill Bloom ; with a foreword by Howard Gardner.—1st ed.
      p. cm.
    Includes bibliographical references and index.
    ISBN 0-316-09984-8
    1. Home and school—United States.   2. Education—United States—Parent participation.   3. Educational change—United States.   I. Title
LC225.3.B56 1992
370.19'31'0973—dc20   91-41533

10 9 8 7 6 5 4 3 2 1

RRD-VA

Published simultaneously in Canada by
Little, Brown & Company (Canada) Limited

Printed in the United States of America

To Ron,
my staunchest advocate and best love
and
to Mom and Dad,
who taught me that teaching
is a political statement
and that loving children is
the most political act of all

Contents

Foreword

*T*HE achievement of high-quality education for our children is a formidable challenge, and never more so than today. It requires the vigilant and caring attention of various groups in our society, with parents having special opportunities as well as special obligations. Jill Bloom's impressive achievement in this book is to master the complex and often crazy-quilt world of school practices in America today, arming parents with the information we need to understand and to take the lead in education reform. In one comprehensive chapter after another, she demystifies the public education system, providing enough information for any reader to master the topic under discussion, whether it be budgeting practices, the operation of parental councils, procedures of teacher certification, or the role of basic skills in the work world of the future. Anyone who reads this book will be able to pick up today's newspaper — and tomorrow's as well — and understand the discussion of educational issues; and anyone who is willing to devote time and effort to advocacy will develop the skills necessary to pursue his or her goal. The author clearly outlines the steps that parents can take to bring about needed or desired changes.

While making us masters of the educational terrain, Ms. Bloom goes well beyond this daunting task. She keeps steadily in mind the *reasons* why it is necessary to understand these issues, and she never lets the details overwhelm the big picture. She provides vivid examples of programs and approaches that work and helps us to understand *why* they are effective. Most importantly, she places at the forefront the position of parents: our need to understand the options that are available, the steps necessary to achieve our goals, and the optimal ways to help our own children, our neighbors' children, and indeed all children. While the author expects much of parents, she is also able to view us in perspective, recognizing our limitations, our anxieties, and, at times, our provinciality.

I came to know Jill Bloom during the last year of her life — perhaps fittingly, in our roles as parents of kindergartners at the Graham and Parks Alternative Public School in Cambridge, Massachusetts. Jill was an individual of great energy and magnetism, and, like countless others, I immediately took a liking to her. We discussed our many mutual interests in education, parenting, psychology, writing, life in Cambridge; we exchanged writings; we found ourselves at the same professional and family settings. I knew that she was working on a major book in the area of education, and once I had the opportunity to read it, I was overwhelmed by her achievement.

In the person of Jill Bloom, quality American education had an advocate of rare talent and vision. Armed with this book, we can continue to advocate for change, as she so ably did in her own heroic life. I am honored to have the opportunity to introduce *Parenting Our Schools* to the wide audience it deserves.

Howard Gardner, Ph.D.
Professor of Education
Harvard University

Parenting Our Schools

Introduction

*M*Y daughters' public school works. It looks good on the outside — neat and clean, with no graffiti and a quietly effective security procedure. Judging by statewide test scores, a lot of learning is taking place on the inside, with an emphasis on basic skills and a reverence for creative ways to teach them. The staff is committed to a coherent curriculum with social as well as academic merit. The principal knows all 360 students by name.

The children — who come from a variety of racial, ethnic, and economic backgrounds in our mid-sized city — are fairly well behaved and seem, by and large, to be enjoying their education. There's a lot of noise, but a lot of curiosity, too, and the hallways are plastered with an ever-changing display of individual and class efforts. Most important, the curriculum at the school meets my daughters' particular needs as well my own expectations of what those needs are. In other words, each of my children is learning what she needs to learn in the way I think she should learn it.

It's not a perfect place — the concept of parental choice seems to break down every once in a while, and there's concern that the Haitian bilingual students are not being mainstreamed as effectively as they could be — but it works. And it works because parents are actively involved everywhere in the school, from fund-raising to curriculum development, from staff hiring to grant writing.

They're involved because they are solicited by the principal and welcomed by the staff. A full-time parent liaison has her own office in the building to facilitate the parents' needs and answer any questions. Even though it's not always easy, parents, teachers, and administrators work closely together to ensure that they are meeting a common goal: providing the best education possible for each child in that school.

By all accounts, however, my daughters' school is an exception, and these days it is the exceptional parent who is able to express satisfaction with his or her child's public education. More and more parents are voicing complaints about the inadequacy of their children's schools; curriculum choices, teacher competency, discipline and behavior codes, and fiscal issues are becoming increasingly worrisome to parents who feel that they are paying too much — and getting too little — out of this country's public school system.

In 1988, the total U.S. public school enrollment stood at just over 42 million students, the first year in which enrollment increased since the early 1970s. Those students attended 94,000 schools with an overall budget of nearly $160 billion, which works out to a national average of about $3,500 per student per year. But of course that figure does not reflect the vast differences between a school in, say, Shelby County, Tennessee, which has an annual per capita expenditure of $1,875, and one in Montgomery County, Maryland, with an annual expenditure of $4,707. And it doesn't account for the greatly increased costs of urban education; the annual per capita expenditure in Boston, Massachusetts, is $5,768; in Alpine, Utah, it's $1,957.

Though school population has remained constant over the past twenty years, the number of employees has gone up three and a half times. We are spending, in inflation-adjusted dollars, nearly seven times more than we did back then — which, unfortunately, is still considerably less than we spend on defense, health care, and social security.

Where does all that money come from? From our own pockets, of course: 44.5 percent from local property taxes, 45.7 percent from state coffers, and 9.8 percent from federal funds, all of which are derived from our other taxes. But not all taxpayers are parents of school-age children — indeed, the number of nonparticipating taxpayers (parents with grown children, parents with children in private school, and adults without children) has more than tripled in the past twenty years.

Even though we're paying for them, control of our schools is difficult to maintain as the systems get larger and larger, and as more money is needed to fund special programs (the total number of children receiving special education services has grown from 8 to 12 percent in the past decade). Increasingly, parents and educators — once partners in a common effort — are finding themselves on opposing sides of the issues, or forced to fight among themselves over meager appropriations. What's more, the battle lines cannot be drawn around clearly defined social, economic, or political issues. The conservative religionist demands curriculum choice just as the liberal humanist does, and federal legislators support local control just as parents do.

What is clear, however, is that nonadvantaged families — the rural and urban poor, and minorities — have a proportionally smaller voice in what goes on in their schools, and in the way their children are educated. This has a negative effect on all of us, and the disenfranchisement of these groups means not only that public education is impoverished, but that the struggle for change will be that much more difficult.

THE FINGER-POINTING GAME

Why, then, doesn't someone do something? For one thing, there are too many issues, all of them complicated by local variables that make it impossible to centralize any efforts at reform. The system, for all its recent emphasis on decentralization, is simply too big to get a handle on. The problems in Minnesota are not the problems in New York, which are not the problems in Georgia. Besides, the track record of past accomplishments is not always impressive, and parents' perception of their impact on public schools is at an all-time low.

According to a recent Gallup poll, only one out of five parents said they would give public education a grade of A or B for recent performance. Are 80 percent of American parents right in saying that our public education system is, at best, average? Well, they're certainly not alone. From every sector come complaints and accusations over the sorry statistics on literacy and academic achievement — a 45 percent dropout rate among minorities, a 70 percent overall high school graduation rate nationwide, and a staggering 2.7 million adult illiterates, many of whom are among those graduates.

Politicians point to the specter of Japanese and Western European superiority as a threatening cloud on the country's horizon (neglecting to mention that those countries' public school systems are almost entirely underwritten by their national governments). Unfortunately, some of them spend a lot of time declaiming against the system, but not much effort legislating for reform. In fact, the United States (adjusting for population size) spends less on primary and secondary education than any other industrialized nation except Australia and Ireland.

Businesses warn of an illiterate and incompetent work force by the year 2000. They blame schools for not producing adequately educated workers and argue that lack of basic skills training and computer literacy programs will render the U.S. a distant loser in the competitive marketplaces of the world. Business leaders are calling for school districts to operate in a more businesslike manner in order to stem the tide of inefficiency that often threatens to drown even the most effective school programs.

Even educators are appalled by the current state of American education. According to Paul Cooperman, adviser to the Senate Subcommittee on Education and author of *The Literacy Hoax,* "This is the first generation whose basic skills will not exceed, not even approach, those of their parents." We are raising high school graduates whose skill levels in English, science, and math fall 25 percent behind those of a generation ago and 50 percent behind in terms of homework assigned and executed. Today's elementary school children have a written vocabulary two and a half times smaller than that of similar-aged children in 1950. Textbooks are becoming archaic at an alarmingly accelerated pace, and those new ones that are being written are composed at reading levels two grades lower than the grade for which they are intended because of fallen reading scores.

The finger pointing doesn't stop at the public school level. School administrators blame colleges for the lack of well-trained teachers, and colleges blame school systems for graduating students unprepared to attend institutes of higher education. Teacher unions blame school boards for their reluctance to upgrade teaching salaries and benefits, and chide school administrators for limiting teacher autonomy and effectiveness in the classroom. School boards, in turn, bemoan the lack of city and state funding that forces them to curtail programming, and the city and state legislators warn the schools that they must spend their limited dollars more effectively.

The federal government blames poor management at the local level; local governments blame a tightfisted federal government. Teachers blame unresponsive administrators, and parents blame inadequate teachers. And everybody blames the parents: We're not teaching our children basic skills necessary for learning; we're not letting the teachers do the teaching. We're not being tough enough on them; we expect too much of them. We're not there for them; we overschedule their lives. We're not providing positive role models; we're too pushy. In short, we're not doing enough, and we're not doing it right.

NO EASY ANSWERS

With all those voices raised in complaint, there is no consensus about the cause of the current turmoil in education. What *is* wrong with our schools? In 1989, a Dallas newspaper ran a survey asking that question and got 11,000 angry responses:

> "They're teaching a little of everything and not enough of anything. We need to bring back basic education or we'll lose the race."
> "Our curriculum is hopelessly out of date with the times."
> "We have to start respecting the child."
> "Bring back the cat-o'-nine-tails!"

"Concentrate on educating minorities, since they represent the future of our economic growth in a service economy."

"The average child is neglected."

"Teachers' salaries are too high for a nine-month job. No wonder they're lazy! Make 'em work for it!"

"Pay our teachers what they're worth and stop treating them like second-class citizens and baby-sitters."

"Our kids are brought up to demand instant gratification. No wonder they can't pay attention in class."

"Drugs. That's the whole problem in one word."

With so many opposing views in just one community, it's not surprising that no one can seem to agree on how to define the problem, let alone resolve it. There may be no easy answers, but there *are* answers. Taxpayers in Passaic, New Jersey, have turned down 84 percent of their local school budgets. Parents in Watertown, Massachusetts, have raised an extra $17,000 annually to meet the costs of a new computer program. Teachers in Rochester, New York, have been given a broad range of extra responsibilities over their students, and teachers in Boston have been trained in communicating more effectively with minority families.

Parents in Cambridge, Massachusetts, have acquired local university funds so that outdated books can be replaced with state-of-the-art materials. There is a highly successful "parochial-style" magnet school in Harlem, and a New Haven, Connecticut, ghetto school whose curriculum is aimed at increasing primary-grade students' self-image and self-expression. Carnegie grants are awarded to schools to promote school-based management, and "academic deregulation" programs strip management staffs down to the bare bones to direct more funds into the classrooms.

There *are* answers. They're not simple, and they don't work everywhere, for everybody. But there are basic issues that engage all of us. Quality curriculum and accountability, reasonable discipline and behavior codes, school personnel attitudes, and fiscal responsibility are just a few of the issues that concern all parents. And there is a commonality of intent among us — to get the best education possible for our own children, for the children of our community, and for those children who most need the benefits of such an education to overcome their disadvantages.

PARENTS: THE ONLY SOLUTION

As population patterns change and the nuclear family becomes more isolated and less common, it seems that it's harder and harder for parents to find shared interests, much less work together toward common goals. But it doesn't much matter whether we're single-parent families, extended families, or step-families, whether we come from white suburbia or minority ghettos. We all want the best for our children, and we all want to do something about it.

Despite the blame being cast in our direction, the truth is that we *have* been involved for years. We've joined the PTAs, sat in on parent conferences, made decisions about curriculum. We've voted for school committee members and approved school budgets. We've learned the new math, and we've done battle on busing. The charge that we are not minding the store at home is inaccurate — we are all doing the best we can given the circumstances under which we must live.

We've been involved and aware of the problems since the 1960s, when the educational reform movement first took off. It's clear, though, that the level of intervention we've engaged in so far has simply not been enough to turn the tide. After a brief improvement in the last decade, SAT scores and dropout rates have stagnated in the past few years, a sure sign that we have to increase our efforts if we are to make a difference.

Now that education reform is once again on everybody's lips, and no one's agenda, it is up to us as parents to act — to stop dwelling on the damage and pointing the finger, and to start coming up with some real solutions of our own. If we don't, who will?

How can we achieve real solutions? We need to direct our activities more powerfully and more efficiently toward achieving specific goals. We need to learn how to manage our childrens' schools the same way we manage the rest of our lives, in an organized fashion and for maximum effect. We need to go beyond the traditional image of the PTA, beyond the skills required to sit through a back-to-school night or meet with our child's teacher. We need to work effectively on our own and with others to initiate necessary reforms.

We must become activists, advocates, and innovators of a system in crisis. We must find ways to create *real* change in our children's schools, not provide Band-Aids for emergency situations. It's not enough to act after the fact, to protest poorly designed or inadequate budgets, to decry outdated or inappropriate textbooks, to complain about poor teachers and humdrum curriculum methods. We must look forward to the next issue and the next century, and provide viable solutions with far-ranging effects for both.

We can't afford to think or act only on a local level. The most important issues are ones that directly affect our own children, but those issues have wide-ranging implications, and we have to learn how to make changes that have a broader impact. We have to look beyond our own classrooms to the schools, the districts, the cities, state and federal governments. We have to make sure our voices are heard and our plans implemented on every level.

These are not pipe dreams. All over the country, parents are acting in an organized and powerful fashion to initiate, implement, and monitor major improvements in their schools, locally, regionally, and nationally. In Boston and Miami, in Harlem and Cincinnati, in Memphis and Indianapolis, in Little Rock and Chicago, parents are dramatically altering the face of education, making it more accountable, more relevant, and more effective.

How are they doing it? What steps can we take? On a local level, we can get involved in making decisions about curriculum, about hiring and firing teachers, about choosing schools and raising money to fund necessary programs. On a citywide level, we can get involved in school board elections, become active on education committees, and oversee the allocation of local taxes. We can involve our business communities and our other institutions in an active relationship with our districts. And we can see to it that our state and federal legislators are responsive to our agendas and that they keep our education issues on the front burner.

A SOURCEBOOK FOR TAKING CARE OF OUR SCHOOLS

It is my passionate belief that parents are the most effective instruments of change, and that we cannot afford to minimize our power. I am not alone in this conviction. In 1973, the United Nations Declaration of the Rights of the Child said, "The best interests of the child shall be the guilding principle of those responsible for his (or her) education and guidance, and that responsibility lies in the first place with his (or her) parents." The U.N. Human Rights Charter itself says "parents have a prior right to choose the kind of education that shall be given to their children," and the U.S. Supreme Court has backed up this right in numerous pivotal court cases going back as far as 1925, when the Court upheld parents' rights and obligations to guide the upbringing of their children over those of the states. Even that seminal report on the state of American education, *A Nation at Risk,* instructed parents, "You have the right to demand the best education possible . . . and the responsibility to be a living example to your children by participating actively in their education."

Parenting Our Schools was written to help parents achieve those goals. It provides in-depth information about the cause and effect of the current educational crisis, but it also offers the practical skills necesssary to initiate effective educational reform in response. It provides specific advice on acting effectively alone, on joining existing groups, on forming new groups and putting pressure on opposing interests. It examines those issues that are most important to all parents and offers both examples and advice on how best to address them.

This book is divided into three parts. In the first, "Where We Stand," we'll define advocacy as it applies to parents and schools. We'll look at our rights and responsibilities as parents, and at the legal system that provides us with those rights. Then we'll briefly examine the history, structure, and financial organization of our public schools and look at the hard facts about their current condition. Most important, we'll look at the tools needed for both formal and informal advocacy, and at the skills required to advocate for our own children and for other children, both from outside the school structure and from within.

Part II, "Issues," examines four basic areas of concern: teachers and administrators, curriculum and instructional materials, legal rights issues, and special cases. Then, in the final section, "Answers," we'll look at some of the major reform efforts under way today — school-based management, parental school choice, corporate involvement, and alternative systems — and how parents are integrally involved in each of them.

In addition to providing basic information and practical skills, each chapter is filled with examples of programs that are already working around the country, ranging from tiny ad hoc committees of parents who want to get their school's dress code changed, to huge nationwide consortiums like the National Committee for Citizens in Education, which provides parents with information and support. Sections offering hands-on advice on how to achieve a specific goal — anything from how to conduct a personnel inventory to how to read a school budget — appear at chapter ends.

Parent involvement — any kind of parent involvement — in education has consistently been proven to be the single most important ingredient in a child's school success. The focus of *Parenting Our Schools* is on programs that go beyond the basic types of participation in our children's school life, such as helping them with their homework, joining in fund-raising drives, and attending parent-teacher conferences. The book's purpose is to provide you with the support and skills necessary to enact *real* changes. It's not just about how to make the system work best for your child — although that's certainly important. It's about what to do when the system isn't working. It's about going beyond the programs mandated by the schools themselves, either by restructuring them to meet the real needs of an individual or a group, or by creating a new structure.

As parents, we have had to develop the skills necessary for raising our own chldren. We've had to learn to focus on their needs without ignoring our own, to offer them direction without taking over their decision-making powers, to provide them with guidance without laying down absolutes. It's been a hard job, but we've had no choice; they are our children, and it is our obligation to parent them, not just to be their parents.

Exactly the same mandates hold true for our schools. We must focus on the needs of the schools without ignoring our own needs, offer them direction without denigrating their expertise, and provide them with guidance without laying down absolutes. Our children's public schools belong to us, and it is clearly our obligation — more than that of the teachers who come to work in them, the administrators who run them, or the legislators who structure them — to see to it that they are the best schools possible. Like raising children, parenting our schools will not be a simple job. But it is ours.

PART I

Where We Stand

From Parent Involvement to Parent Advocacy: A Natural Progression

A LL of us want the best for our children. This is the primal parenting instinct. It's not unlike the fierce protectiveness of a mother tiger for her young, and is responsible for the basic urge we all feel to cuddle and hold very young children and animals, as well as the inclination to feed them and protect them from harm. The gentlest mother won't hesitate to attack if her children are being threatened.

For human beings, this urge extends to educating our young. Eavesdrop on any parent in the park with a two-year-old and you'll hear a lesson in progress, covering a wide curriculum, with discourses on physics, language arts, social skills, and math. Researchers have learned that adults automatically speak to small children in a higher-than-average voice, and arrange their features in such a way as to gain the attention of their infant students.

When it comes to public education, however, that primal instinct to protect and educate seems to have atrophied over the past few decades. In part it's because we feel that, once our children are older, we can leave their education to others more suited to the task. It's also because we understand they've evolved out of the stage where we parents can provide them with everything they need to know. Some of the reason for the decline seems to be our own misconception of our place in public education. We know that our schools need to make some dramatic changes in the way they educate our children, and we know that our children are suffering because these changes have not yet been made. But our ingrained perception of public education is that it is not our problem, or that we are not the appropriate source of the solution.

Thus, while we simultaneously trust in the authority of professional educators and look to them to come up with solutions, we complain that they are not dealing adequately with the problems facing our schools today. Naturally, this double standard creates a lot of animosity. Parents resent the fact that their children aren't getting the best education possible, but don't see what they can do about it beyond very basic home intervention (although home intervention — helping your child with homework and monitoring his or her academic progress — is most certainly an important way to improve your child's skills). Educators, for their part, gripe about the lack of interest of many parents in their children's schools, and wonder why parents do so much complaining if they're not willing to take on the burden of making improvements. Unfortunately, what parents perceive as necessary improvements may not jibe with what educators see as necessary improvements.

A HISTORY OF FRUSTRATION

It wasn't always so. Think about your own public education, which probably began twenty, thirty, or more years ago. Your parents supported the public schools in your community because they understood that those schools represented the same goals and values that they held. There was communication between parent and teacher and between parent and administrator, but there was also a distinct separation between home and school. Parents were considered experts at bringing up their children, and schools were considered experts at educating them. In the homogeneous communities of the forties and fifties, both parties had faith that the other would uphold his or her end of the bargain.

In the sixties, the distance between home and school evaporated as parents actively began to seek more individual identities for themselves and their children. The assumption that everyone had the same goals and values was no longer valid. Parents, radicalized by the political climate, began looking more critically at what was being taught in the schools. Was it relevant? Did it reflect their varying educational, social, and moral goals?

During the seventies, parent involvement in public schools became institutionalized. It was written into the provisions of many federally and state-funded programs, especially inner-city urban programs like Head Start and Title I. Not only had parents insisted on such inclusion, but educators were beginning to see the need for parent involvement. But the effect of those parents was somewhat blunted precisely because their presence had been mandated from above. Parent participation began to drop off as inner-city parents found their voices being drowned by the vast bureaucracy of the programs. In fact, formal federal support of parent involvement in Title I died entirely when the program was rewritten in 1981 as Chapter 1. Although provisions for parent input were reinstated in 1988, parental involvement in national entitlement programs has yet to be restored to its original levels.

The seventies was also the decade during which the Parent Teacher Association, that bastion of bake sales and paper drives, began to look for a stronger voice in the public school hierarchy. Until then, the PTA (which began in 1897 when Alice Birney and Phoebe Hearst organized the National Congress of Mothers) had, as one educator put it, "a long-standing identification with having their feet firmly planted on both sides of the fence." In other words, because it served as a joint organization for both parents and teachers (teachers were admitted in 1922), the PTA tended to act in a supportive, uncritical role. Although it became a major organization for the articulation of parent interests during the sixties, those interests were often dictated by the teachers and administrators of the schools. They, in turn, were most interested in keeping parents involved in nonirritating functions such as health care issues, safety, and fund-raising, all of which kept mothers (for it was mostly mothers) busy and out of the way of the more fundamental issues of education.

Increased teacher militancy and the closed doors of bargaining sessions all worked against parents' priorities in the PTA. Perhaps that was why membership in the PTA dropped from 12 million to 6 million in the decade before 1973, when the PTA finally caught up with the times and eliminated a bylaw preventing parents from "interfering" in school decision- and policy-making issues. Today PTA interests range across all areas of education policy and practice, and even into union contract negotiations, a traditionally hands-off area for parent involvement.

While PTAs are clearly getting more aggressive, their 1989–91 mandates still concentrate mainly on sex education and dropout prevention, areas unlikely to arouse the ire of school personnel. On the other hand, special interest advocacy groups, such as special education and bilingual PACs (parent advisory councils) have been able to make stronger gains for their members despite sometimes-unwilling educators. These groups work from a prototypical advocacy stance, moving from strong personal interest to the larger issue of all special needs or bilingual children. They use all the ingredients of sophisticated lobbyists — the coalition of similar interests, financial and legislative pressure, and the threat of lawsuits — to make impressive gains on both the state and federal levels.

In the eighties, parents became polarized. Those working- and middle-class parents who stayed in the public schools became active once more and were instrumental in supporting innovations such as parent choice, school-based management, and fiscal reform. Other parents reacted by pulling their children out of the public education system — into parochial or private schools — or by moving to suburban systems in an attempt to recreate the homogeneous communities of the fifties. But some parents, particularly those from poor, inner-city, or minority backgrounds, became more disenfranchised from the system and were therefore less likely to get involved. Working mothers contributed to a drop in parent involvement, especially since most educators were unwilling to expand their hours of availability. Of course, the parents who were least likely to get involved with their children's schools — the working poor, the non-English-speaking, welfare, or homeless families — were the parents of children who most needed assistance.

Decentralization and an increase in local school management made it possible for some groups of parents to become very involved, while others were stymied by a lack of effect on an overburdened and over-complicated system. A poorly balanced tax apportionment system made it possible for some schools to develop innovative programs while others languished for want of basic resources. A sense of laissez-faire gripped both government and private businesses, who felt that it was up to local communities to solve their own problems.

Today that stand-back attitude has given way to an increased sense of urgency. The current frustration with public education has affected everyone, and parents are in the front lines of those most concerned. Parent Teacher Organizations (PTOs), offshoots of PTAs but more dedicated to creating changes within the system, are multiplying, as are ad hoc parent groups devoted to instigating a specific change or promoting a specific issue. Parent involvement on all levels seems to be on the rise, although it is still an unfocused and largely grass-roots phenomenon.

Many more parents are getting involved with broader education issues, and many more educators are recognizing their value. But the fragmentation of parent groups is still a big problem. What mobilizes parents in one school district may be totally irrelevant to parents in another. Even more damaging may be the conflicts among parents themselves over the best solution to the problems facing their schools. Parents who want to get involved with a particular issue often feel isolated and ineffective because theirs is just one voice. Groups do form, but around limited or specialized issues; then, once the problem is resolved (whether in the group's favor or not), the organization tends to disappear, leaving parents feeling vaguely dissatisfied. Many of these parents, of course, go on to use their newly honed advocacy skills in other areas.

PARENT INVOLVEMENT — WHAT FOR?

There is no doubt that parent involvement works. The National Committee for Citizens in Education — a research and support organization dedicated to increasing parental input into public schools — has compiled two impressive reports (*The Evidence Grows*, in 1982, and *The Evidence Continues to Grow*, in 1987) to indicate just how successful it can be.

"Programs designed with strong parent involvement," writes NCCE staff member Anne Henderson in the introduction to the later volume, "produce students who perform dramatically better than students in otherwise identical programs that do not involve parents at all, or as well." Furthermore, she writes, "Schools that relate well to their communities have student bodies which outperform other schools. Children whose parents help them at home perform better than children of similar aptitude and family background whose parents do not. And schools where children are failing improve dramatically when parents are called in to help."

Specifically, parent involvement results in:

- higher test scores
- long-term academic achievement
- positive behavior and attitudes
- more successful programs
- more effective schools

Henderson backs up her strong statements with an impressive array of studies and statistics. Longitudinal studies in England have shown the dramatically positive effect of parental involvement, as have other international surveys of educational achievement. Researcher Ira Gordon, who pioneered the study of the effects of different kinds of parent involvement, conducted studies comparing preschool children in programs that had active parent participation as a core component with those whose programs had no parental involvement. The children in the parent-involved programs scored ten points higher on the Weschler scale measuring intelligence. The percentage of children in the first group requiring special education was significantly lower (6 percent, versus 30 percent in the control group). Perhaps most important of all, Gordon reported a significant improvement in the home environment of those children whose parents were actively involved in their preschool education.

Even for older children, where the results are perhaps not as dramatically measurable, the effects are clear; dropout rates are significantly lower in schools with strong parental input, and some researchers have cited lower juvenile crime rates as another benefit. The effects, moreover, don't end at the schoolroom door. Parents report feeling more in control of their children, just as the children, feeling better about themselves, are more positive in their family interactions.

These feelings of control and self-worth extend even beyond family dynamics; parents who are pleased at the positive results of their involvement with schools are more likely to get involved in other efforts to improve their standard of living. It doesn't matter what form parental involvement takes — any program will have a positive effect, as long as it involves a strong parent component. Parents, in fact, are the *one* ingredient essential to all the programs studied, and the greater the degree of parent involvement, the more successful the children and the program will be.

PARENTAL INVOLVEMENT: WHY US?

But what, exactly, can parents do? And why do *we* have to be the ones to do it? In an article titled "Why Johnny Can't Think" (*Harper's,* June 1985), William Karp says "Only ordinary citizens can rescue the schools from their stifling corruptions, for nobody else wants ordinary children to become questioning citizens."

Keep in mind, please, that we're not talking about armed revolution here — although some parents have gone into schools and closed them down, reopening them with new staff, new administrators, and new curriculum. We're talking about *sane and reasonable measures to make necessary changes in those areas that most affect our children. And we have to be the ones to do it, because we are the ones with the most to lose.*

We're also the ones who have the most immediate and dramatic effect on our children's education. When we talk about parent involvement in the public schools, we can mean anything from running a bake sale to dismantling the school board. The term has become a buzzword, and there is no doubt that it is being touted as the panacea for all the ills that have befallen our public schools — especially since it doesn't require a huge outlay of money. But what exactly is parent involvement, and why is everybody so excited about it?

Parents can play critical roles in the schools in a number of ways, ranging from basic *involvement* with their own child's education, through more active *participation* in school life, to true *advocacy* situations. While researchers have broken down the types of parent involvement in various ways, we can identify seven prototypes at three levels:

I. Involvement
   A. Parent as spectator — you monitor your child's progress, check homework, read school memos and report cards, and attend school-initiated meetings.
   B. Parent as teacher — you actively assist your child with homework, establish home instruction routines to augment or reinforce school curriculum, and periodically assess your child's progress.

II. Participation
   C. Parent as accessory volunteer — you help out with field trips, provide nonclassroom support services, disseminate school information via newsletters and phone chains, and conduct fund-raising activities.
   D. Parent as educational volunteer — you serve as an aide to the teacher in the classroom, check homework and other assignments, listen to children read, and provide remedial tutoring.
   E. Parent as employee — you work as a paid employee of the school in any of the above capacities.

III. Advocacy
   F. Parent as decision maker/policymaker — you function as an integral part of the administrative structure, participating as a voting member of school councils or steering committees, mobilizing other parents around specific issues, and serving as monitor of the changes that result.
   G. Parent as mover and shaker — you function as an independent force to initiate, implement, and monitor basic changes in the school structure, on a local, district, or statewide level.

While parent involvement and participation is crucial to a child's success at school, it is the parent-as-advocate functions that are most important to us — and potentially the most explosive to schools. Parents who act as advocates have a say in everything that goes on in the school (or the district), from planning and authorizing programs to implementing them and evaluating their effectiveness. And when their power is ignored or overridden, they can go even further, changing the institution's framework, its roles, and its power structure.

Teachers and staff can be trained to deal with the first five types of parent involvement — even to welcome it when it is productive and falls within the bounds of school authority. Programs all over the country have sprung up to include parents as home teachers and as more active school participants, and educators are quick to jump on the bandwagon for more active parent participation in the schools. Most popular, it seems, are those programs that provide basic skills to parents (most often inner-city, poor, minority, or non-English-speaking parents) to enable them to participate more effectively in their child's education, and those programs that foster closer communication between parents and teachers.

In Dade County, Florida, parents are given training to help them learn what their children are learning in their first school years. A cooperative preschool involves parents during the day as aides and asks them to return at night for training in parenting and education skills. Each spring letters are sent out — in Spanish and Haitian-Creole as well as English — welcoming parents of incoming kindergartners and giving them material to help them prepare their children for school. Parents of first-grade students attend workshops that offer information on first-grade curriculum and at-home projects to support it.

In addition, families with children of all ages receive free passes to zoos and concerts that parents can use to reinforce basic skills in their children, and the Miami Herald *cooperates with a ''Newspaper in Education'' project that provides basic skills reinforcement to children at all levels.*

*   *   *

Jerold Bauch, of the Betty Phillips Center for Parenthood Education at Vanderbilt University in Nashville, developed a model to increase the interaction between parents and school personnel. It's based on two technical systems. One is an electronic mailbox that allows teachers to leave prerecorded messages summarizing the day's activities and offering suggestions for homework help. (Parents can also leave messages for teachers.)

The other system is known as Compu-Call, a computerized phone system that automatically dials any or all parents with messages. Compu-Call can remind parents of meetings, conferences, or special interest events. It can also monitor attendance and automatically call the homes of absent students. The model is in use in Nashville, in Huntsville, Alabama, and in Gainesville, Florida, among other cities, and Bauch reports an improvement in parent involvement of 400 to 800 percent.

FROM INVOLVEMENT TO ADVOCACY

Everyone agrees, then, that parent involvement — at least on those first five activity levels — works beautifully. What people don't agree on is how far parents should go, and how deeply they should become involved in the actual power structure of the system. And of course, those with the most power to lose by inviting parents in to participate in a major decision-making role — the teachers unions, for example, and the administrators or school boards — are the least comfortable with the prospect of parent involvement.

We can understand their reluctance. How do educators deal with a parent or group of parents who say things have to change fundamentally in a school, especially if the changes they propose represent a possible threat to the authority of educators? Parents who seek to serve as advocates for their own children and/or other children often find themselves in a much more precarious position than parents who, for instance, volunteer to read in the classroom two mornings a week. Parent advocates are not necessarily welcomed by the school, or even by the parent group that is supposed to represent them in the school. Rather than being welcomed as a source of support or solutions, they are often seen as a problem to be overcome.

DEFINING AND REDEFINING ADVOCACY

What is advocacy all about? Most of us think about legal representation. Legal advocates plead a case on behalf of an individual who may not be willing or able to do so alone. Child advocacy is defined by the Children's Defense Fund as "standing up for your own children and for the children of other people." We've used the term *parent advocacy* in much the same way, but we've expanded it to mean standing up for our rights as parents to ensure that all children get the best education (or social program, or medical attention, or nutritional program) possible. For the purposes of this book, the term will be limited to educational intervention.

We should also make an important distinction between the kinds of advocacy parents can undertake. You can work as an individual, representing only your own child on a specific issue — talking with a teacher or principal about a behavior problem that is being improperly addressed, for instance, or convincing a teacher that a bright child needs extra work to keep him or her interested in class. Or you can work with a group on an issue that concerns all of you — the establishment of safety rules for bus-riding children, or the need to hire additional personnel for large classrooms. In addition, you can broaden your perspective even further and become an advocate for basic structural changes in an entire system.

In other words, you can act as a *case advocate* for one child's specific needs (he or she need not be your own if you are convinced of the child's right to intervention or if you have experience that might benefit his or her case). You can become a *class advocate*, representing all children who share similar needs. Finally, you can act as a *system advocate,* working to change an entire program or system that you feel is not in the best interests of the entire community of children.

The nature of the advocacy will depend on the receptiveness of the school to change. In a growing number of schools, administrators are clearly ready to entertain new ideas about education, and to hear those ideas from new sources — the parents themselves. The proliferation of parent membership on steering committees, leadership councils, and planning teams is evidence that much of our work as advocates can be done from *within* the system — that is, by working together with teachers and administrators to alter the existing structure.

But there are occasions when school personnel are less receptive to parental input, or when the school structure itself is a barrier to effective change. Then it becomes necessary to work as advocates *outside* the system, in order to alter the structure so that it becomes more accommodating to the needs of the school community as perceived by parents. While this type of advocacy presents the greatest challenge, it is not as dangerous as it sounds. In Chapter 4 we'll look at some of the tools needed for all types of advocacy work, but it's important to understand the distinctions between the types of advocacy available to parents.

Sarah Darwin (not her real name) of Cambridge, Massachusetts, began by advocating for her son, who was diagnosed as having special needs in the third grade. She convinced the Cambridge School Department to provide the special services she and other evaluators had determined would be necessary for her son's progress.

During the course of her personal quest, Darwin became involved with the Cambridge Special Needs Advisory Council, a school-department-sanctioned group of parents, teachers, and specialists whose mandate was to monitor and advise on pertinent issues. As an active member of SNAC, Darwin helped other parents navigate through the special needs service system, and worked with school department personnel on budget, personnel, and service-delivery problems.

"Working with SNAC was helpful in several ways," says Darwin. "The involvement of staff members gave me a different perspective on some issues, and allowed me to open fruitful dialogue on others. And it was wonderful to be able to tap in to the support of other parents when I needed it."

As a pediatrician, Darwin also gets involved in advocating for her special needs patients with their local schools. It's different from her personal involvement in her son's school career and in her SNAC work. "I don't have the personal involvement in my clients' cases that I had in my son's case or with SNAC. But those experiences certainly sensitized me to the issues that concern parents, and helped me to be a more effective caregiver and advocate. I see my advocacy career as a continuum, starting with my son, moving to a small group of children with similar needs, and ending up by advocating as a professional for all special needs children.''

HONING THE PRIMAL PARENTING INSTINCT: PARENTS AS EXPERTS

Of course, parent advocacy goes beyond the act of intervening when a child's best interests are not being served. It's an attitude about how one's children are raised, and how their education is conducted by those outside the home. To adopt this attitude, parents must see themselves as the ultimate authority on their own children. Why should we consider ourselves, and not our children's teachers or administrators, to be the experts? Because we have had the closest experience with them over time. Because we have been constant observers of their strengths and weaknesses, and are privy to all the mitigating circumstances of their lives out of school. Because we can apply our intimate knowledge of their genetic, physical, social, and emotional history to their progress in school and out.

This does not mean that educators are not experts in their fields, or that we should discount the information they give us about our children or the methods they use to teach them. On the contrary, it is our job as parents to seek out as much assistance in raising our children as we can muster. If we had no professionally trained advisers, we would be inadequate to the task. But we must remember to think critically about the services provided in our schools rather than accept them as immutable; we must learn to bounce all input off the sounding board of what we know to be true about our own children.

In any case, seeing ourselves as the ultimate authority on our children is only part of the picture. Parent advocacy is also a process by which we can use what we know about our children and ourselves to get involved with a community of parents who share our needs and goals. The process may involve us with our geographic neighbors in a community school, or it may involve us with parents all over the country whose children have similar special interests and needs. The community with which we ally ourselves may have to do with a shared perception that basic education is essential, or that all our children must be computer literate. It may involve our commitment to participation in the curriculum development process or in the evaluation of teachers and principals.

Why advocate for children? It seems unnecessary to answer such a question, but there are some surprisingly satisfying reasons for parents to get involved in advocacy issues. A Children's Defense Fund pamphlet defines both the simple rationale and the larger benefits of advocacy. We must stand up for children because:

- Children need their parents to be their advocates.
- Children need other adult citizens to be their advocates.
- It is in your self-interest to make sure that not only your own but all children grow up to be healthy, productive members of society.
- You gain power over your life and your family's lives at home as well as in school.
- You can begin to address larger social and economic problems affecting your life.

(from *It's Time to Stand Up for Your Child: A Parent's Guide to Advocacy*, 1979)

Despite the clear benefits of advocacy on behalf of schoolchildren, the concept is not entirely acceptable to many educators or even to a large number of parents. Part of this resistance to the idea of activism has to do with the image of the parent as hysterical and pushy, out only to promote a spoiled and unworthy child and heedless of who gets stepped on in the process.

In a wonderful book on advocacy for parents of special needs children, Suzanne Stevens talks about the power of the Hysterical Mother and the Big Daddy. The very names evoke images at once amusing and horrifying — the prototypical pushy parent steaming up the front steps of the schoolhouse with fire issuing from his or her ears, out for blood over the mistaken perception of a slight to precious Johnny or Jane. There are probably times when such images can be very useful. But they can also be destructive because they undermine the effectiveness of those parents who are neither hysterical in their approach nor self-serving in their intent.

Despite increasing evidence to the contrary, it is still most often the case that the hysterical mother, and not the big daddy, is the one who interacts with school authorities. "He who goes to school to advocate is probably a she," quips education psychology professor Frank Nardine, and this statistical truism can be turned to the advantage of the school system, which historically has tended to undervalue input from women.

Whoever is doing the talking, it must be done to achieve maximum results. Stevens talks about harnessing the power of aroused and aware mothers and fathers, and she shows parents of needy children ways in which they can channel and hone that primal protective instinct so that they can use their energy most efficiently. Parent-education expert Sadie Hofstein calls it "appropriate aggressiveness," and it is perhaps a more realistic, if less evocative, phrase than Stevens's.

Using appropriate levels of aggressiveness means learning to advocate without hostility, to use the friendliest and most cooperative measures possible under the circumstances. You have to begin with the assumption (very often correct) that teachers and school officials are willing to work with you on constructive measures for improving the system. Only if such measures fail should you move on to more confrontational methods and a broader use of power.

OVERCOMING THE FEAR OF ADVOCACY

Some parents are very resistant to the notion of using their power. Perhaps they are affected by the same negative imagery that pervades so many educators' views. Certainly parents report fear of reprisals as a major cause of their reluctance to approach their school with complaints. They're afraid that if they speak out on an issue that makes them unpopular with teachers or staff, their children may be forced to pay a price.

There is also the continuing perception that parents are not professional educators, and that the education of children is therefore better left to those who are. Most parents are unwilling to question a practice that has been followed in the schools for years, even if it does seem grossly ineffective. We've all grown up with the image of our schools as benevolent but absolute authorities when it comes to educational decisions. Even for those parents who believe that that authority is no longer so benevolent, it's hard to speak out against such a cultural monolith.

When parents do muster the courage to speak out, their fears are often exacerbated by experience, even with well-meaning school officials. The range of excuses handed to parents by educators who perceive parents as a threat is wide. Here are some excuses that parents have reported to advocates at the Children's Defense Fund offices in Washington:

"We're the experts on your child."
"There's no problem here — you're just imagining it."
"This is an exception — it's not usually like this."
"It's your fault."
"It's the child's fault."
"It's the fault of other parents."
"Be patient, it will change."
"We can't control it — it's the bureau's fault."
"No one else is complaining."
"We have no money to solve the problem."
"It's worse elsewhere."

There are other reasons for the perception of advocacy as a dangerous or ineffective tool for parents. The amount of time it takes to enact a real change can be so long that the children involved are no longer affected by the problem. Parents with advocacy skills and resources are often those who are most likely to leave the system for other reasons — better jobs, "better" community, et cetera. It may be so difficult to get a consensus among parents about what issues to fight for, or which side of those issues should be fought for, that nothing is ever done on an organized basis. The same parents speaking out over and over again may begin to feel that their voice is muted when they are not joined by other parents, even when those parents agree with their cause.

Unfortunately it is often parents whose children are most in need of advocacy who have the weakest advocacy skills, or who have no time, energy, or money to pursue their goals. Language or cultural barriers may undermine even the best efforts to impact the school system, and some parents have been so conditioned to the failure of their efforts to make a positive change in their family on *any* level that it never even occurs to them to continue trying, or that they have legal protection and support to do so.

But advocacy is *not* just for the disenfranchised. The parents of children who are doing perfectly well in school often have concerns that go beyond their own child's experience. A third-grade boy may be doing excellent work, and his teacher may have nothing but praise for his behavior and progress. His parents, however, may feel that their son is not adequately supervised on the playground, or that the peeling paint on the walls poses a health threat. Parents of high school children may feel that the school is evading the important issue of sex education and counseling, or they may feel it is overstepping its bounds in providing those services.

We have a voice in the process of our children's education, and we must make that voice heard. Just as educators receive training in how to do their job more effectively, we can learn to be more effective advocates for our children. Advocacy, as defined here, means taking charge of a situation that's not acceptable and assuming responsibility to create a change. It means working within the prescribed framework or going beyond it and making a new framework ourselves. It means carrying the idea of parent involvement to its logical conclusion and acting in the best interests of our own children and of others. After all, if we are the ultimate experts on our children, and if we can create a coalition of other parents, also experts on their children, then we will have tapped into the most basic needs of our particular community.

Karen Voci moved to her neighborhood because of the schools. She helped paint walls in the classrooms, taught a family history project to second graders, and was involved with the schools in a supportive way. "I was trying to be the best little girl I could be. But I just happened to go to a neighborhood meeting where someone from the school committee just happened to mention that the committee had voted to divide the community's four elementary schools, thus creating two K–3 schools and two schools for fourth through sixth graders.''

Almost before she knew it, Voci found herself a founding member of Tax-payers Against Pairing, a group of citizens who saw no educational value to the proposal and objected to the committee's lack of community input in implementing it. ''I started going to school committee meetings to see what was going on, and the more I went, the more outraged I got. So I just took one step after another — how could I not? It became a personal issue for me. I couldn't let my kid see me back down from a position I was so sure was right.''

It was not an easy task. The group distributed flyers, held meetings, and organized a phone-in campaign to school committee members. ''I was very much made to feel that I was violating the code of politeness by challenging the school committee on this issue. But it became clear to me that I no longer had the choice. I had to act, and I had to continue acting.'' Working with hundreds of other parents, Voci took her issue as far as the Rhode Island state education arbitration board, which found that the school committee had not acted arbitrarily and capriciously in making the pairing decision.

But the battle is not yet lost. Voci and three other members of TAP are now running for school committee themselves. ''I never thought it would go this far, but I can't imagine stepping back and letting nature take its course. Not knowing what I now know about how things could be and should be. Somehow, getting on school committee means losing sight of that.'' In order to ensure that they don't lose sight of what should be, Voci and her running mates are signing notes to themselves promising to resign if they do. ''It would make no sense to get up there just to become them. That's not where the road of advocacy should lead.''

All this is not as intimidating as it sounds. Remember, parent advocates like Sarah Darwin and Karen Voci are not fomenting armed insurrection, or advocating the overthrow of the entire school system. But what they are interested in may *seem* revolutionary to some parents, and certainly will to some educators. It's a matter of perspective. At its best, parent advocacy means working positively and integrally with the system on a broad variety of issues. If there is resistance to clearly mandated goals set by carefully constructed parent coalitions, then advocacy can mean gently, wisely, and competently leading the school officials and staff to see the need for those changes, and showing them constructive possibilities for implementation.

The most positive tool for change, then, is to break down the barriers between parents and educators so that they can work together to create whatever changes they see as important in the system they share.

Parents and educators need to see each other in a new light — as collaborators rather than enemies — and they must look to each other for active involvement in improving a system at risk. Parents have an expertise that they have the right to exercise, just as educators have an expertise that they have the obligation to execute. The two groups will most certainly have varying opinions about what is important, as well as about how things can be improved.

The Three R's:
Realities, Rights,
and Responsibilities

PAYING attention to our public schools seems to be a national obsession these days. The media provide daily reminders of the crisis in education, and everyone from the local principal's office all the way to the Oval Office is searching for solutions. In the past few decades a raft of reports by national commissions has provided a flood of information, accusations, and testimonials for public consumption. With their horrifying statistical evidence of failure, these reports have generated a firestorm of dissent.

It's important, however, to keep the gloom and doom in perspective. While the commissions and reports vary dramatically, they all share a fundamentally political nature. They are reflections of a state of mind, not a set of absolutes. This doesn't mean that the numbers have been manipulated, but that they have been used selectively to support a specific goal. Furthermore, those goals reflect the political climate of the time in which they were written. Just as the definition of "literacy" has changed over the decades to reflect a growing sophistication among the general population, so the definition of a successful educational system reflects an ever-changing perception of what that success should entail.

THE PARENTS SPEAK

While the many recent studies have galvanized public and political awareness of the conditions in our public schools, none of the major reports mentions parents in a leadership role. That's not surprising, since the nine major reports, written with the expertise of more than four hundred professional educators, businesspeople, college board committees, education researchers, and officials, had *not one parent* serving on any of the commissions in a position of leadership.

Because of this lack of representation, parents have felt that their childrens' needs were often ignored or misperceived, and that the results of all that attention had nothing to do with their personal experience of school, whether that experience was good or bad. But such disenfranchisement is dangerous, to the education establishment and, more important, to parents themselves. It is our voices that must be raised in discussion and dissension along with those of the legislators, the educators, and the business community, if any real progress is to be made.

It's not that we have been silent, but that our voices are too often muted or indistinct, or that our concerns are seen as too local to be of national importance. However, there are common denominators in parents' concerns, and they may be surprising to many of those who served on the education commissions. Perhaps the most comprehensive survey of American public opinion (which includes non–public school citizens) is the annual Phi Delta Kappa/Gallup poll, published every September in the *Phi Delta Kappan* magazine (PDK is an organization of professional educators). The 1990 poll examined the responses of thousands of adults (68 percent of them were public school parents, 26 percent were nonparents, and 6 percent were parents of private or parochial school kids) to a variety of questions that clearly gauge what's on the mind of many Americans. What follows is a sampling of the most important results:

- The public favored parental choice in deciding where to send children to school by a two-to-one margin.
- The public supported, by a substantial margin, the push for a uniform national curriculum with consistent standards and goals.
- Eighty-three percent think more should be done to improve schools in our communities and, by a two-to-one margin, say they'd be willing to pay more taxes to support such improvements. Seventy-four percent think it is very important to improve inner-city schools and would be willing to pay more taxes to expand Head Start programs, to screen young children for health problems, and to provide day care.
- Seventy-five percent favored limiting class size in early grades to as few as fifteen pupils per teacher, with the majority of respondents indicating that they would be willing to pay higher taxes to finance such reductions.
- Seventy-one percent of the respondents favored after-school and summer care for the students of working parents.

- Eighty-three percent favored more state and federal assistance to high school graduates who want to go on to college but cannot afford to do so.
- People were not willing to extend the current school year or to allow early graduation from high school, although there is some evidence that such options might increase academic achievement.

The poll also examined specific issues defined by the respondents themselves. When people were asked (as they have been every year since the polling began in 1968) what they thought the most pressing problems were in their own communities (numbers indicate the percentage of respondents who gave that particular answer as their number-one cause of concern), they answered:

drugs — 34 percent (the number-one response since 1986)
lack of discipline — 19 percent (number one before 1986)
lack of proper financial support — 13 percent
poor curriculum/poor standards — 8 percent
large/overcrowded schools — 8 percent
difficulty in getting good teachers — 7 percent
parents' lack of interest — 6 percent
integration/busing — 4 percent
drinking/alcoholism — 4 percent
low teacher pay — 4 percent
teachers' lack of interest — 4 percent
crime/vandalism — 4 percent
pupils' lack of interest — 3 percent
moral standards — 3 percent
lack of respect — 3 percent
problems with administration — 2 percent
mismanagement of funds — 1 percent
lack of proper facilities — 1 percent
lack of after-school programs — 1 percent
declining enrollment — 1 percent
school board politics — 1 percent
strikes — 1 percent
high taxes — 1 percent
lack of family structure — 1 percent

The poll also asked respondents for a report card on the progress of their local and national schools. From a low of 38 percent in 1983 (when the report *A Nation at Risk* was published), the percentage of parents who gave their local schools A's or B's has risen to 43 percent (although only 8 percent rated their schools with an A). Residents of large cities and nonwhite residents gave their schools the lowest grades. An interesting note about the report cards: parents tend to give their local public school higher ratings than they do the national public schools, and they rate them more highly than do non–public school parents or residents without children in school. Twenty-two percent of all respondents gave the national schools an A or B (only 2 percent gave an A), while 71 percent of all parents with children in school gave their oldest child's school an A or B. Clearly, say the authors of the poll, familiarity breeds respect.

Still, that means that the majority of those polled (including all respondents) *do not* think their local schools deserve better than a C grade for performance, and they think even less of American schools in general. Those are perhaps the most disturbing statistics of all, and they have as much to do with our dramatically changing society as they do with our schools.

CHANGING DEMOGRAPHICS

Part of the reason it's so hard to get a grip on the problems afflicting American public schools is that the population served by them has become so diverse. The families who send their children to public school today are very different from those who sent children to school a generation ago. Just how different they are is a strong measure of how our schools have changed, and of how much further they must go to make sense in a new world such as ours.

The total U.S. population increased by 59 percent between 1950 and 1986, with 45 million of today's 245 million population falling between the ages of 5 and 18. That means that nearly one quarter of the population — about 22 percent — is attending school. Right now those numbers are holding fairly steady, and there's even been a slight drop in high school populations. But the baby boomlet (the children of baby boomers born in the fifties) has already been felt in the elementary schools, and secondary school enrollment is certain to increase within the next decade.

Even more important than the numbers is the question of who those children are. They come from smaller, often more fractured families, where divorce is the norm and single parents must struggle to keep the family functional. More distressing — and more destructive to public school stability — are the rising number of families at risk because of poverty. A dramatic increase in the birthrates among teenage girls accounts for a large number of these at-risk families, but solid nuclear-family units are also slipping below the poverty line in alarming numbers, and the rise of immigrant children living in poverty is irrevocably changing the landscape of our schools. In the 1990s, an even more desperate group has emerged. There are now 750,000 homeless children in our schools, and the number of homeless and drug-addicted children who are themselves becoming parents is increasing at an alarming rate. Both the children of divorce and the children of poverty will grow up amid new — and not always adequate — support systems that will have an effect on their school careers.

The explosion of different races, religions, cultures, and ethnic groups has vastly altered the face of America's public schools and given rise to a whole new set of issues. How do we integrate the children of such families into our society without forcing them to give up their identities? How do we deal with children who are refugees as well as immigrants, and who are dealing with the trauma of political and social upheaval as they try to adjust to a new culture? How do we ensure that such children will not grow up to be second-class citizens in America, reinforcing an expanding cycle of racially determined poverty and despair?

CHANGING SCHOOLS

Any of the population shifts mentioned above would put a tremendous burden on any system; together they seem to represent insurmountable difficulties, making even the best-laid plans for reform seem futile. And in the midst of all this demographic upheaval, the public schools themselves have undergone wrenching changes. School population has exploded in the past two decades, not because of population growth but because the configuration of our school systems has been dramatically altered. Due to school consolidation, the number of school districts has dropped precipitously since 1966 — from 160,000 to 15,300 — even though the number of children being served has doubled.

Half of those new districts serve over 10,000 children, which means that the degree of centralization and bureaucratization has become alarmingly high. That means more people in middle management and administrative positions, more generalization of programs, and less individualization to meet the rising tide of variety in the student population. It also means less power for individual principals and almost none for the classroom teachers.

In addition, those burgeoning school populations are more likely to contain children for whom English is not a native language, children who are considered "at risk" for school failure, and children whose needs are simply not being met by the schools. The increasing fiscal problems of large cities and small towns alike adds to the possibility that school systems will become less able to satisfy the growing needs of their students. But parent-driven programs on both local and national levels can make the difference.

Chapter 1, the federally funded program that provides school reading and math assistance to children from low-income backgrounds, has a fairly strong parent-involvement component. Parents are given support in helping their children with their work as well as with education resources of their own.

According to researcher Diane A. D'Angelo, federal parent-involvement programs can be used as models to bring in other parents. In semirural McAllen, Texas, where the local Chapter 1 program has always involved the parents of Chapter 1 children, the problem was to provide similar involvement for parents of all other schoolchildren. School administrators felt it was important to broaden their federally funded support to include every family in the system. Superintendent Pablo Perez wanted to build a strong home-school connection for all families, while at the same time keeping Chapter 1 families involved according to the guidelines set by the federal government.

The first step was to increase the local budget for parent involvement so that parent-involvement programs no longer depended solely on restrictive federal funds. District-wide staffing was also increased. Informational handbooks were provided in English and Spanish. Each school in the system formed a partnership with a local community organization. Today, parent-involvement programs are integrated into the regular school program, and each principal is responsible for designing and directing a particular program for his or her school.

The objective is to ensure district-wide family involvement and to make sure that specially targeted families know they are part of a district-wide program and are not different in some negative way. The district's motto is ''All children can learn and together we can make a difference.'' District officials estimate that 99 percent of all parents have some direct and productive contact with their children's schools, and they are working to draw in the remaining 1 percent.

TOWARD LEGAL LITERACY

Now that we know a little more about the real and perceived problems facing our schools, we can begin to gather information about what we can do about them. Our first step is to understand our legal and ethical rights and responsibilities as they regard our children and our public schools.

The federal government does enact certain strong guarantees to the right of equitable education, and protects the constitutional rights of parents and students in public school settings. Thus, the federal and state constitutions are the first line of defense for education protection, if not for the specifics of how children are educated. These U.S. constitutional amendments most directly affect the rights of parents and students in public schools. Some famous examples follow a few of the applicable amendments:

Amendment I

"Congress shall make no law respecting the establishment of religion, or prohibiting the free exercise thereof; or abridging the freedom of speech, or of the press, or the right of the people peaceably to assemble, and to petition the government for a redress of grievances."

TINKER V. DES MOINES

The most famous example of an abridgment of First Amendment rights was in the 1969 Supreme Court case *Tinker v. Des Moines.* A group of Iowa high school students refused to honor a school's edict prohibiting them from wearing black arm bands to school to protest the country's involvement in the Vietnam War. The Supreme Court ruled that, while school officials must have authority to control student behavior and conduct, neither students nor teachers "shed their constitutional rights to freedom of speech at the schoolhouse gate."

In other words, as long as they weren't interfering with school activities or other people, students were free to express their religious or political beliefs. The "schoolhouse gate" ruling was expanded in 1975 to include due process rights for students facing expulsion or suspension.

Amendment IV

"The right of the people to be secure in their persons, houses, papers, and effects against unreasonable searches and seizures, shall not be violated, and no Warrants shall issue, but upon probable cause, supported by Oath or affirmation, and particularly describing the place to be searched, and the persons or things to be seized."

NEW JERSEY V. T.L.O.

In the case of *New Jersey v. T.L.O.* in 1985, the Supreme Court ruled that school officials *did* have the authority to search the pocketbook of a student who was caught smoking in the bathroom. When that search turned up drug paraphernalia and evidence of recent drug sales, the police were summoned.

The Court ruled that the search of the young woman's property was within legal boundaries because two important prerequisites had been fulfilled: the initial search was based on reasonable suspicion, and the scope of the search was appropriate, under the circumstances. Similar rulings have allowed officials much leeway in search-and-seizure matters, as long as these two conditions have been met.

Amendment V

"No person shall be held to answer for a capital or otherwise infamous crime, unless on a presentment or indictment of a Grand Jury . . . nor shall any person be compelled to witness against himself, nor be deprived of life, liberty or property without due process of law."

GOSS V. LOPEZ

When nine Columbus, Ohio, high school students were suspended without a hearing for various school-rule infractions, their parents claimed that the Ohio law allowing such suspensions was unconstitutional. In *Goss v. Lopez* (1975) the Supreme Court agreed. Once a state establishes public schools, said the Court, students have a property right to attend them (that is, a right that cannot be denied without a fair hearing of some sort). Suspension and expulsion are violations of students' rights and cannot be undertaken without due process.

Amendment X

"The powers not delegated to the United States by the Constitutions, nor prohibited by it to the States, are reserved to the states respectively, or to the people."

As applied to public education, this simply means that the states have the power to determine education policies not laid out by the Constitution, as long as those policies do not contradict what is in the Constitution.

Amendment XIV

"All persons born or naturalized in the United States, and subject to the jurisdiction thereof, are citizens of the United States and of the State wherein they reside. No State shall make or enforce any law which shall abridge the privileges or immunities of citizens of the United States; nor shall any State deprive any person of life, liberty or property without due process of law; nor deny to any person within its jurisdiction the equal protection of the laws."

The Fourteenth Amendment ensures that what the U.S. Constitution has granted, the states cannot deny to their citizens. It is also known as the equal protection clause, and as such has been the basis for most of the Supreme Court's desegregation decisions.

BROWN V. THE BOARD OF EDUCATION OF TOPEKA (I)

In 1954, the Supreme Court ruled that segregation by race in a Topeka, Kansas, elementary school was unconstitutional, even if equal facilities were provided for both blacks and whites. This landmark decision opened the way for a series of subsequent decisions enlarging on the rights protected by the Fourteenth Amendment. In fact, in 1955, the Supreme Court handed down a second ruling, "Brown II," because the justices felt that "Brown I" was too passive. In the latter decision, the Court ruled that desegregation cases should remain under the courts' jurisdiction until the situation was corrected. Means of correction, such as school-attendance-pattern restructuring, school building site decisions, busing, and teacher hiring were also mandated by the courts.

Constitutional law is based on rights laid out in the U.S. and state constitutions; statutory laws are those based on legislative actions. Excessive corporal punishment, for example, is illegal but not unconstitutional. State and/or federal statutes guarantee the following rights to all students who attend public school (and their parents), or whose schools receive some sort of federal funding (virtually all of these rules have conditions attached to them, some of which we'll examine in the following pages):

- the right to a free education
- the right to be protected from harm in the schools
- the right of parents to inspect their child's records and protect them from unauthorized inspection
- the right to special education for special needs
- the right to equal opportunity
- the right to freedom from unreasonable search and seizure
- the right to freedom of expression
- the right to freedom of religion and conscience

A few of these rights reflect the guarantees of constitutional law made more specific or exacting. Some of them reflect rights directly construed to the students themselves, while others reflect rights of the students' parents in regard to the students' education. For instance, in a 1924 decision that was reaffirmed in 1972, the Supreme Court said that parents have the right to direct the education of their children as they see fit. This law has been reinterpreted a number of times, particularly with regard to parents who believe that the public education their child is receiving does not reflect their religious, moral, or conscientious beliefs (see Chapter 6, on curriculum, for more on this subject).

Parents also have very specific rights regarding their children's school records. Federally mandated record keeping is relatively new; the use of standardized formats to store information about public school children throughout their school careers is only fifty years old. Even after such systems were in place, records were routinely handed out to prospective employers, recruiters, police officials, and others. In addition, information often went into records that had no basis in fact, and could affect a child's future. In *You Can Improve Your Child's School,* William Rioux and the National Committee for Citizens in Education staff compiled some examples of the kinds of mistreatment this could lead to:

- "A mother read in her son's records that her son had 'exhibitionist tendencies.' After some research, she learned that the anonymous note dated back to the second grade, when the child forgot to zip his pants after going to the bathroom."
- "A parent was informed by a guidance counselor, who was about to write a college recommendation for her son, that his psychological file labeled him a 'possible schizophrenic' back in elementary school. The mother had never known the file existed."
- "Student files [in several school districts] were routinely made available to health and police department personnel, juvenile court officials, and FBI and CIA agents, while only a small percentage of school systems gave parents the same access rights."

In 1974, Congress passed the Family Educational Rights and Privacy Act (FERPA), sometimes called the Buckley Amendment. FERPA applies to all schools receiving federal funds, including colleges and private schools (if they get any state or federal money). Under FERPA:

1. School districts are required to establish a written policy regarding students' records and to inform parents of those policies every year.
2. Parents can examine all their child's records.
3. Schools have to establish procedures for challenging the accuracy of all records and for having erroneous or unfavorable information removed.
4. Parents can include their own comments or disagreement if they cannot get the unfavorable material removed.
5. Parents can refuse access to unauthorized persons. (No one gets to see those records without parents' written consent. This includes other school applications, employment or financial aid applications, other school officials, and other community groups.)
6. Parents are entitled to file complaints with the FERPA office of the U.S. Department of Education (Room 3017, 400 Maryland Avenue, Washington, DC 20202; 202/472–6032).

FERPA and other information-protection legislation went a long way toward establishing parents' rights over the education of their child. The rights of school-age students over their own education was harder won, and still excites more controversy than FERPA.

In 1984, Congress passed the Pupil Rights Amendment, known as the Hatch Amendment, to an earlier Education Amendment. The Hatch Amendment (full name: Student Rights in Research, Experimental Programs and Testing Act), states that students have the right to refuse psychological testing that might reveal private information about themselves or their families. Furthermore, they — and their parents — have the right to examine any instructional material that might be used in conjunction with any research or experimental program.

(Other important federal and state statutes affecting public education — the Education for Handicapped Children Act of 1973, the Bilingual Education Act of 1974, and the Education Consolidation and Improvement Act of 1978, are discussed in Chapter 7.)

The legal tradition known as common law is reflected in the written decisions of courts that interpret the Constitution and statutes and regulations and apply them to specific factual situations. These decisions concern, for example, segregation issues, student injuries and right to protection, accountability for teachers and curriculum, and the education policies of the state departments of education as well as the local authorities.

PARENTS' RIGHTS

Obviously, parents have broad legal powers to oversee the general state of their child's school career. Those rights diminish only as the student becomes old enough to protect him- or herself, and, even then, parents still have enormous control over the education of their minor children in public school. The National Committee for Citizens in Education publishes and distributes a small but potent Parents' Rights Card that, in several languages, provides invaluable basic information on legal rights to parents and schools. The NCCE card divides twenty-four topics of parental concern into four subject areas.

NCCE Parents' Rights Card

A. Student Discipline: You have the right as a parent in any of the states listed
   • to take legal action against a school official if your child has been disciplined with "excessive or unreasonable" physical force (all states);

- to appeal the suspension of your child (all states except KS, UT, WI);
- to appeal an administrator's decision to place your child in a class for students labeled "disruptive." (all states except GA, KY, MI, MO, ND, SC, UT, VT, WA, WI);
- to protest the physical punishment of your child because it is prohibited by law (AK, CA, CT, DC, HI, IO, KY, MA, ME, MI, MN, MT, ND, NE, NH, NJ, NY, OR, RI, VA, VT, WI).

B. Student Instruction: You have the right as a parent in any of the states listed
- to see instructional materials used in research programs funded by the Department of Education and National Science Foundation (all states);
- to have your handicapped child placed in an "appropriate" public school program. Parents must give written consent for such placement (all states);
- to appeal an administrator's decision prohibiting your daughter from trying out and playing in male-dominated sports (all states except AR, CO, IL, IN, KS, KY, MN, MO, ND, TN, WI, WY);
- to visit your child's classroom at any time during the day providing you first notify the school office (AL, AK, AZ, DC, FL, IN, IA, LA, MD, ME, NC, ND, NH, NM, NV, NY, OH, OK, SC, TX, UT, VA; local policies may prevail in some states);
- to attend a minimum number of conferences with your teacher(s) (AK, AL, AZ, DC, FL, LA, MD, MS, MT, NC, NH, NV, OH, OK, TN);
- to educate your child at home, providing you meet conditions and standards set by your state (all states);
- to request that your child be excused from studying subjects you object to on religious, moral, or other reasonable grounds (AK, AZ, CA, CT, DC, FL, IA, ID, IL, IN, LA, MD, ME, MI, NC, NV, OH, PA, SC, UT, VA, WA, WV);
- to request that your child be excused from reading assigned books you object to on religious, moral, or other reasonable grounds (AL, AK, AZ, CA, CT, DC, FL, IA, ID, IL, IN, LA, MD, ME, NC, NH, NV, NY, OH, SD, UT, VA, WA, WV);
- to request that your child be excused from school activities that you object to on religious, moral, or other reasonable grounds (AL, AK, CA, CT, DC, FL, ID, IL, IN, KS, LA, MD, ME, MI, MS, NC, ND, NH, NV, NY, OH, OK, PA, RI, SD, UT, VA, WA, WV);

C. Student and Other Records: You have the right as a parent in any of the states listed
- to look at all your child's school records. You may challenge any

record you believe is untrue or unfair. School officials must respond to your challenges within a "reasonable time." If you are still dissatisfied, you may request a hearing (all states);

- to look at all official school policies (all states);
- to look at other official school records, such as research and planning reports — but not personnel records (AL, AK, AR, CA, CO, CT, FL, HI, ID, IN, KS, KY, LA, MD, MO, ND, NH, NM, NV, NY, OR, SC, SD, TX, UT, VA, VT, WI).

D. Other Rights: You have the right as a parent in any of the states listed

- to appeal a school policy or decision that prevents your child from expressing controversial views, so long as they are not obscene, slanderous, libelous, and do not cause serious disruption (all states except AR, CO, KY, MI, MN, MO, TN, VT, WI);
- to speak at all public meetings of the local school board (CA, HI, MI, MT, ND, UT, VT, WV; in other states, many local school boards make provisions for parents to speak at public meetings);
- to attend all meetings of the school board (except for executive sessions on personnel and property issues) and to be present at the voting on all school board decisions affecting the school district (all states);
- to appeal some local school board decisions to a higher state authority, other than a court (AL, AZ, CO, CT, DE, FL, GA, IL, IN, IA, LA, MA, MD, ME, MS, MT, NE, NH, NJ, NM, NV, OH, OK, RI, SC, TX, VT, WA, WI, WV);
- to appeal a policy or decision that prevents your child from joining a club or activity that is controversial but otherwise lawful (AL, CA, CT, DC, DE, FL, GA, HI, IA, ID, LA, MD, ME, MO, MS, MT, NC, NE, NH, NJ, NV, NY, OH, OK, OR, RI, SC, SD, TX, WA, WV, WY);
- to be a member of any parent/citizen group and have your group recognized and heard by school officials (AL, AK, AZ, CA, CT, DC, FL, HI, ID, IN, KY, LA, ME, MN, MS, MT, NC, NE, NH, NV, NY, OH, RI, SC, VT, WA, WY);
- to appeal an action, policy, or decision permitting an unreasonable search of your child or his/her property by school employees (all states);
- to challenge the removal of books from a school library based on school officials' personal dislike of ideas they contain (all states).

All these rights are granted by federal or state laws, regulations, or court decisions as of October 1, 1991. Some of them, you will notice, are also governed by constitutional protections — in many cases, a Supreme Court decision was responsible for the enactment of the legislation at the state and federal level. In addition, local education authorities may offer legal entitlements that go beyond these statutes. They cannot, however, be more restrictive.

PARENTS' RESPONSIBILITIES

Of course, as parents, we may believe that our rights go far beyond those legally entitled to us. We may believe, for instance, that we have the right to decide the kinds of textbooks our children read in school, or how the budget is structured, or who runs our schools and who teaches in them. But parents' rights — both legal and ideal — are useless if we don't assume the responsibilities that go with them. We have responsibilities not just to our own public school children, but also as overseers of our public education systems.

As parents, we have the responsibility to ensure that our children's physical needs are met to the best of our ability. We must see to it that they get enough love and attention as infants, enough guidance and affection as youngsters, enough continued support as adults. We must socialize our children so that they are receptive and responsible to our community and our society. And we must ensure that they maintain their cultural heritage as well as the ethical, moral, and/or religious constructs that are important to us.

When we send our children to school, we have the additional responsibility to see that they adhere to the school's rules and values (insofar as they don't directly contradict our own). We must encourage proper work and study habits, and demonstrate our interest and support of school curriculum, activities, and programs. Then, as parents, we have the additional job to see that the school is meeting our children's needs, and to act accordingly if it is not.

The school also has responsibilities toward its families that go beyond the strict legal requirements of the law. The school must inform parents about its goals, rules, programs, and grievance procedures, and keep them regularly informed of school activities. It must make itself open and available to parent involvement and parent input, both formally and informally, allowing parents to establish real relationships with school personnel.

How do these responsibilities — parents' and schools' — translate into practical action? The National Committee for Citizens in Education provides us with an excellent checklist that can help us do our job and help us make sure that the schools are doing theirs as well:

Annual Education Checkup

Review of Material at Home:

- Do I have a school file at home for each child?
- Do I have all previously issued report cards?
- Does any correspondence with teachers or the principal remain unanswered?
- If our school produces a handbook, do I have a copy? Does it clearly answer any questions I may have about school policies?
- If our school does not have a handbook, do I know who to go to for answers to questions?
- Are my child's immunizations up to date, and have I made an appointment for an annual medical checkup in the fall?
- Have I made a list of questions I want to ask my child's teacher, and have I set aside materials from my home file that I plan to take with me?

Questions for the Parent-Teacher Conference:

- Is my child performing at grade level in:
  math?
  reading?
  writing?
  other courses?
- Has my child taken achievement, intelligence, or aptitude tests in the past year?
- Do I understand what the scores mean?
- Does my child have strengths and weaknesses in major subject areas that I don't know about?
- Does my child need special help in any subject?
- Does my child need help in social adjustment?
- Does my child need help in learning skills?
- Would you recommend referral to school specialists?
- Has my child regularly completed classwork?
- Has my child regularly completed assigned homework?
- Has my child regularly attended classes?
- Does my child get along well with teachers/students?
- Have you observed any changes in learning processes during the year?
- Has learning improved or declined dramatically?
- Have you observed any changed behavior that might be a sign of medical or emotional problems?

Annual Review of School Records:

- Has my child's entire school record been gathered in the school office?
- If not, where are the other parts of the records?
- How are the other parts of the record stored (microfiche, microfilm, or computer)?
- In looking through the records, are there any unexplained labels used to describe my child?
- Have I seen the following parts of the records and had them explained to me?
  - grades, year by year
  - attendance records
  - health records
  - test scores
  - psychologist and school social worker report to school staff (if applicable)
  - reports from welfare and social service agencies (if applicable)
  - transcripts from other schools
  - guidance counselor's career or college recommendations
  - disciplinary actions
  - honors, awards

Our children have responsibilities too (which we must see to it that they follow): to behave appropriately, to make an honest effort to complete assigned work, and to ask for help if it is needed. But the school must be a safe place where children are respected and encouraged by every means possible to achieve their full potential. And we would be remiss in our responsibility as parents if we did not see to it that the school meets its obligations.

Cambridge, Massachusetts, Public Schools Rights/ Responsibilities Bookmark (distributed to all students every September)

A student has the right

- to be treated with dignity and respect
- to a meaningful education
- to fair treatment under reasonable rules and regulations
- to a school atmosphere free from intimidation, harassment, or threats
- to free access to inspect his or her records
- to freedom of expression
- to due process of law

A student has the responsibility

- to respect fellow students, teachers, and school personnel
- to take full advantage of educational opportunity by regular, punctual attendance of all classes
- to uphold school rules and maintain a positive classroom environment
- to participate in school government activities
- to give reasonable notice of intent to inspect records
- to be orderly, fair, and accurate when exercising rights of free expression

GETTING READY TO ACT

Now that we know where the schools stand, and where we stand in terms of our legal and ethical rights and responsibilities, we can begin to get practical. We can find out how our local schools are structured, how they are funded, and we can acquire some basic advocacy skills to enable us to act in the best interests of our children and our schools. We can begin by working on a local level to create what educator Sarah Lawrence Lightfoot calls "a continuity of values between home and school."

In spite of — or perhaps because of — the greater variety of cultural and social backgrounds parents bring to the public school forum, we must develop common standards to share with our public school community. We must create caring bonds with school personnel that enhance the bonds we are struggling to create and maintain at home. We must acquire the information and skills necessary to make us effective advocates and valuable assets to our schools. We must clarify our concerns and solidify our position of active involvement in the school improvement process. We must establish ourselves as necessary decision makers and essential components to the success of our schools. Only then can we go ahead and work on enlarging our concerns to join with those in the larger community.

HOW TO: Assess Key Characteristics of the Families in Your School

You already have a pretty good idea of what your child's individual needs are — after all, you are the expert. You've probably already done some informal advocating on his or her behalf — talking to the teacher about your child's learning style, checking with the school nurse about a health issue or with the transportation department about a bus problem.

But what do you know about the interests and needs of other families in your school community. Do they share similar backgrounds, or are they a diverse group? Do other families share your concerns about the local school, or are they confronted with issues that you have not experienced?

The first step in becoming a successful advocate lies in knowing who your potential allies are, and in defining common interests and diverse needs. The following checklist, adapted from *Beyond the Bake Sale* by Anne Henderson, Carl Marburger, and Theodora Ooms, is a good place to start. The information should be gleaned from anonymous questionnaires or city statistics. (More information on surveying techniques is offered in Chapter 4.)

1. What proportion of the students come from
   _____ single-parent households
   _____ two-parent households
   _____ nonparent households
   _____ foster homes or institutions

2. What is the economic status of these families (estimate proportion at each level)?
   _____ below poverty level
   _____ 10–18K per year
   _____ 18–25K per year
   _____ over 25K per year

3. What is the educational status of the families (estimate)?
   _____ no high school graduates in family
   _____ high school graduates without college
   _____ some college
   _____ completed college/graduate school

4. What is the racial/cultural background of the families?
   _____ Estimate proportion of racial minorities (and identify).
   _____ Number of different languages spoken by parents (and identify).
   _____ Number of cultural or religious minorities to which school should be sensitive in terms of diet, holidays, medical issues, et cetera (and identify).

5. What proportion of children live in families where both parents, or the custodial parent, are employed outside the home for most of the day?
   _____ less than 25 percent
   _____ about half
   _____ the great majority

6. How many children are left unsupervised for long periods before or after school?
   _____ less than 25 percent
   _____ about half
   _____ the great majority

7. How many children participate in organized before-school and/or after-school programs (identify types of programs)?
   _____ less than 25 percent
   _____ about half
   _____ the great majority

8. What proportion of families are new to the community this year?
   _____ less than 25 percent
   _____ about half
   _____ the great majority

9. What proportion of children live in multigenerational or extended-family households (i.e., with step-siblings and/or -parents)?
   _____ less than 25 percent
   _____ about half
   _____ the great majority

10. What proportion of children are handicapped or in need of special services at school?
    _____ less than 25 percent
    _____ about half
    _____ the great majority

11. What proportion of children are working at grade level in school?
    _____ less than 25 percent
    _____ about half
    _____ the great majority

12. What proportion of children are enrolled in bilingual classes?
    _____ less than 25 percent
    _____ about half
    _____ the great majority

13. What proportion of parents/guardians regularly turn up for school-related activities such as open houses?
    _____ less than 25 percent
    _____ about half
    _____ the great majority

14. What proportion of parents/guardians participate in classroom activities or attend parent-teacher conferences?
    _____ less than 25 percent
    _____ about half
    _____ the great majority

15. What proportion of families have more than one child in school?
    _____ less than 25 percent
    _____ about half
    _____ the great majority

16. What proportion of parents/guardians are homeowners or pay local property taxes?
    _____ less than 25 percent
    _____ about half
    _____ the great majority

17. How do children get to and from school (estimate proportions)?
    _____ school bus
    _____ car/car pool
    _____ walk
    _____ public transportation

HOW TO: Find Out How Your Community Feels About Your Schools

Every time you hear a new report on the state of American education, your natural inclination is to compare what you hear with what you know about your own school. But the first step in being able to advocate for change is to gather information on your own community's attitudes about its schools. Do other people feel that there is something wrong with your schools? Do their concerns mirror yours, or are they experiencing problems dramatically different from yours? If so, why?

It's important to remember, when you begin to assess how your community feels about your schools, that parents of schoolchildren are not the only people to ask. Parents of older children, or non–public school children, adults without children, and local businesspeople are an important part of your community. Not only do they vote and pay taxes, but they might be valuable resources for your school. Don't forget to include them when you are trying to get a feel for the state of the schools on a local level.

The following are suggestions for questions you might want to ask when trying to determine your community's attitudes about your local schools, and about education in general.* They can be answered via interviews, questionnaires, or discussion groups; as always, tact and discretion in collecting data are advised in order to be sure of the most honest answers. (More information on surveying techniques is offered in Chapter 4.)

1. Are the methods of instruction used in our schools today equal to or better than those used during your school career?
2. Have schools gone overboard along progressive lines to the neglect of the three R's?
3. Are schools responding strongly enough to the realities of the modern technological world and the competitive demands they place on our society?
4. Are class sizes too large for effective learning to take place?
5. Is the discipline in school too lax or too permissive?
6. Are we penalizing bright children by failing to see that they get an education equal to their ability to advance?
7. Are we providing enough support for children who are at risk?
8. Should there be a uniform standard of excellence that all our children must meet before they can progress to a higher grade?
9. Are the schools operated by the school board in an efficient and businesslike manner with an appropriate balance between a concern for quality and a concern for fiscal responsibility?
10. Are the so-called frills such as art and music instruction, which increase the operating budget, worth their cost?
11. Do you think the state's share of financing the schools is high enough?
12. Do you think there should be more federal support for school programs?
13. Do you think the population and the curriculum in the schools accurately reflect the social, ethnic, and economic makeup of the community?
14. Do you think parents should be able to choose the school that is most appropriate for their children?
15. Do you think parents should be more involved in the basic decision-making processes such as hiring personnel, developing a budget, and creating a curriculum?

*Some of these questions were taken from *Finding Out How People Feel About Local Schools* (NCCE, 1984)

How Schools Work

*N*OW that we have some background on the state of the schools and our legal rights and responsibilities to them, let's examine the schools themselves more closely. Our success as advocates depends on our ability to navigate through the existing system, to use its structure to our own advantage, and to make sure that our position in that structure is not ignored. How did public education evolve in the United States, and how do schools run today? What is the structure of a typical school system and how is it paid for? What role do parents play in the organization of that system and in the disbursement of money?

We can use this basic information to evaluate our own schools, and to see if they measure up in terms of organization, efficiency, and quality. Then we can begin to acquire the skills necessary to make those changes we — as individuals and as a community of concerned parents — deem appropriate and necessary for our schools.

HISTORY

First, a little history. U.S. public education got its start in the Massachusetts Bay Colony in the 1600s because the Puritans needed to train ministers. Other colonies had private, independent training schools, but it was in Boston that the first legally mandated elementary school opened in 1647. The school taught the basics from a strictly religious point of view, and a secondary "Latin" school taught the classics to older boys. The initial student body was over a hundred strong — females, of course, were excluded, as were slaves and most impoverished gentlemen, since the schools were neither free nor compulsory. Many tuition fees were paid with livestock, grains, or grants of land.

Even among those who could afford the fees, many chose to enter family trades and saw no purpose to years spent languishing in an unprofitable classroom.

In other states, most of which had more diverse populations than Massachusetts, education was less available. By the middle of the eighteenth century, however, the country had grown well beyond its rural agrarian roots and out of its minimal educational needs. By the late 1700s, the concept of secular public education grew along with the size and variety of the population. A better-rounded employee was needed to meet the growing demands of American commerce and industry. So private academies began to appear, offering practical skill training as well as the classics and Bible study.

Then came the Land Ordinance of 1785, which annexed the Northwest Territories and established the use of public lands for the purposes of public education. It was important for all white settlers to have a basic education if the West was to be rescued from the "heathens," so even girls were allowed to attend. By the nineteenth century, the idea of free education for all citizens had gained national support. In Massachusetts, Horace Mann lobbied for the establishment of public schools and was even successful at getting a school for black residents opened in Boston in 1820. But the first statewide public school system was established by Pennsylvania in 1834.

Other states soon followed suit, and a series of federal laws were enacted, beginning with the 1876 Department of Education Act, establishing that federal office. Most of the federal effort went into establishing vocational and military academies, but by the 1890s public elementary schools were common. In 1918 compulsory attendance for children between the ages of six and twelve became required for all states.

What kind of education did those children receive? The structure of turn-of-the-century public schools did not differ drastically from that which exists in many schools today. All but gone was the one-room schoolhouse where everyone proceeded at his or her own pace, and where older students tutored younger children. In accordance with the tenets of the Industrial Revolution, instruction was conducted on a rote basis, with mass absorption of the required material as the goal. Such assembly-line tactics, with the teacher serving as both source and supervisor, was also necessary for discipline. Samuel King, a superintendent in Portland, Oregon, boasted in 1874 that he could tell, at any given moment in any school day, exactly which pages in which textbook the students in his schools were reading. To avoid undue influence from external special interest groups, who ranged from religious conservatives to urban "bosses" who sought patronage jobs and control, a centralized administration system was developed that officials expected would streamline and unify schools within larger districts.

As the administration grew more and more cumbersome, there was less and less input from the clients of the system — the students and their parents. It was difficult to change so unwieldy a system, and there was little opportunity to have a voice in the decision-making process. There were some early efforts at reform. Angry parents in New York City stormed a school board meeting in 1894 because their children had been turned away from an overcrowded school. Then, in 1917, faced with an unstanchable flow of European immigrants whose children required education, New York enacted the Gary Plan. It offered educational opportunities for immigrant children that were much more limited than those available for others, and stressed vocational training over academic skills. The Anti-Gary League, a coalition of immigrant, suffragist, and progressive groups, banded together and succeeded, after much angry lobbying, in getting the plan defeated, despite solid political support.

On the whole, though, parental power, like local school power, was severely limited. The forties and fifties saw an increase in centralization and consolidation in a country that revered efficiency and melting-pot homogeneity in all things. It wasn't until the late sixties and early seventies that fissures began to appear in the wholesome fabric of American education. Functional illiteracy, especially among inner-city minorities, became a growing problem, and test scores in general began to drop precipitously. Costs were rising and strong teacher contracts were pressing already overburdened budgets.

Yet an increasingly distant central administration could — or would — do little to effect changes in the system. Public approval rates dropped and citizens began rejecting school bond issues. Those who could afford to transferred their children to private schools or moved to suburban neighborhoods where the threat to public education was not perceived as so imminent. Enrollment in U.S. elementary and secondary public schools plummeted from a high of nearly 46 million in 1969 to 39 million in 1985. During that same time, total expenditures nearly quadrupled.

Since the mid-1980s, the emphasis on decentralization and school reform has led to some changes. But for the most part, American public education is based on the same principles as those Industrial Revolution–era schools: an assembly-line approach to teaching, an unwieldy central administrative system, and an inequitable local tax base.

THE SCHOOL STRUCTURE

The nineteenth-century factory system also accounts for the structure of our present-day school systems. Let's look a little more closely at how that structure operates. Most public schools are consolidated into districts or systems. There are currently 15,300 districts, with a total of nearly 85,000 schools. Some states have only two or three districts, and some districts have only two or three schools, while other, more populous states have hundreds of districts with nearly a hundred schools in some of them. Hawaii and Puerto Rico, for instance, have only one district, while the state of Illinois has nearly a thousand. The great majority of school districts enroll fewer than 2,500 students, but over a quarter of our students attend school districts of more than 25,000 students.

Naturally, not all school districts are set up in the same way. There are different kinds of districts — urban, suburban, rural, community, and county-wide. Some states have regional education agencies that supervise a number of districts, and some have, in addition to their geographically defined districts, state- and federally operated agencies that also operate in a supervisory capacity to administer education to children in state- or federally funded programs.

Given the great variety of systems, however, there is still a typical structure we can look at. The organizational chart on page 56, provided by Terry Frith in her book *Secrets Parents Should Know About Public Schools,* will give you a good idea of how a typical good-sized school district of about 10,000 students might be organized.

Frith's chart is revealing because it lets us see how complex most school district systems can be, and also how well-intentioned. Nearly every aspect of our children's education has been considered and a department developed to meet its particular demands. That hierarchical structure is true of virtually every school district in the country.

Of course, the names of the various offices vary from district to district, and those in charge may have varying degrees of authority. There may be no migrant child services coordinator in your district, but rather an assistant superintendent for bilingual curriculum. And smaller school districts have neither the personnel nor the budget to fill all Frith's positions, just as larger ones are broken down into many more departments. The average school district has a support staff or noninstructional staff that accounts for nearly half of its payroll, and the administrative support staff alone of a large school district could run over 2,000 people, excluding school principals.

What goes on at the school level? Most schools are run by a principal,

A TYPICAL ORGANIZATIONAL CHART

SCHOOL BOARD OF ANONYMOUS DISTRICT

SUPERINTENDENT OF SCHOOLS

ASSISTANT SUPERINTENDENT FOR INSTRUCTION

ASSISTANT SUPERINTENDENT FOR NONINSTRUCTIONAL SERVICES

- DIRECTOR Curr. & Staff Dev.
  - SUPERVISOR Reading
  - SUPERVISOR Science
  - SUPERVISOR Language Arts
  - SUPERVISOR Social Studies
  - SUPERVISOR Mathematics
  - SUPERVISOR Music
  - SUPERVISOR Phys. Ed.
  - SUPERVISOR Ed. Media
  - SUPERVISOR Health Ed. & Services
  - COORDINATOR Measurement & Research
  - COORDINATOR Volunteer Serv. & Public Info.

- DIRECTOR Secondary Ed.
  - Principals Middle & High Schools

- DIRECTOR Elementary Ed.
  - Principals Elementary
  - COORDINATOR Student Accounting

- DIRECTOR Student Services & Excep. Studt. Ed.
  - School Psychologist
  - School Social Worker I & II
  - Placement & Follow-Up Spec.
  - COORDINATORS Excep. Studt. Ed.
  - COORDINATOR Guid. Couns.

- DIRECTOR Vocational Tech. & Adult Ed.
  - DIRECTOR Voc. & Tech. Center
  - SUPERVISOR Voc. Home Ec.
  - COORDINATOR Adult Ed. & SUPERVISOR Business Education
  - SUPERVISOR Voc. Agriculture & Ind. Arts

- DIRECTOR Personnel Relations
- DIRECTOR Personnel Services
- DIRECTOR Planning, Reports, Fed. Prog.
  - COORDINATOR E.C.I.A.
  - COORDINATOR Child Migrant

- DIRECTOR Food Service
  - Assistant Director Food Service
  - Cafeteria Managers

- DIRECTOR Operations, Maint. & Trans.
  - SUPERVISOR Operations & Energy
  - SUPERVISOR Buildings & Grounds
  - SUPERVISOR Veh. & Equip. Maint.
  - SUPERVISOR School Bus Operations

- DIRECTOR Budget & Finance
  - Manager Payroll
  - Manager Spec. Rev. Accting.
  - SUPERVISOR Accounting

- DIRECTOR Materials & Serv.
  - Buyers
  - Manager Stores

- Manager Projects
- DIRECTOR Data Processing

or headmaster, and larger schools often have a vice principal as well. In addition to the classroom teaching staff, a school has specialists, some of whom work only in that school and some of whom are committed to more than one school in a district. There's also a support staff, including clerical, custodial, health, and food-service employees. Then, of course, there are the students and their parents.

Still, we can't get a good picture of the structure of a school district unless we can also take into account the various agencies outside the district that are involved in public school education in some way. That includes the state and federal courts, the legislatures, the unions, and anyone else who wields power over the decision-making process in the schools.

Power. It's the key concept in understanding the hierarchical structure of American public school systems. There are various types of power; superintendents have nearly absolute power over the day-to-day operations of the schools, while school boards have a higher power to decide the nature and purpose of those operations, and legislators and courts can determine if those operations are legally viable. The district structure, the individual school structure, and the external structure have their own spheres of influence, and have been set up as a system of checks and balances so that no one institution — the state department of education, or the teachers unions, for example — can exert too much influence over the education of the students.

In fact, the three systems are set up more like interlocking circles than like a linear chain of command. But since getting a handle on the levels of power in a school district is important to effective parent advocacy, it might help to adapt the pyramidal model that Michael Berger uses in his book *The Public Education System* in order to get a simpler picture of the levels of power we might encounter.

What is immediately clear about the pyramid model is that there are an alarming number of levels of power to go through before you get to the top. Even more alarming is the position of parents and other community residents at the bottom of the pyramid. Students, too, are at the bottom of the pile, and there are many advocates who say it is the students, not their parents, who are the most disenfranchised group of all, since most students cannot vote.

But parents aren't really in the least powerful position in the structure. In fact, they form the base of the entire structure, which can be a very powerful position indeed. In addition, there can be parent and community representation at higher levels, particularly in school boards and courts.

The following glossary offers brief descriptions of all the players in the education game, and examines the influence they have on the entire

Apex
of Power

Federal
Courts

Federal Department
of Education

Unions

State Courts

State Officials
(Departments, Superintendents,
Boards)

Local School Board/Superintendent

Assistant Superintendents

Other Admininistrators

District Staff*

Principals

Assistant Principals

Teachers and Specialists

Support Staff*

Parents and Community Residents

Students*

(Base on which system stands)

*largely disenfranchised

structure. Each level is listed in compact form for easy reference, and we will discuss each in more detail in other chapters. Though the list may look daunting, you need not master every detail. The system, though sprawling, is *not* impossibly complex, and you *can* have an impact at every level. Let's start at the top:

- **Federal Courts:** The U.S. district courts and courts of appeal and the Supreme Court are the highest bastions of power regarding all legal issues involving education. As we've seen, landmark education lawsuits have altered the face of American education forever. Traditionally, the courts do not set education policy, but rule on the legality — or illegality — of existing policies that concern the constitutional and civil rights of children, parents, or school personnel. They have, however, broad authority to specify exactly how unconstitutional situations, involving school prayer, desegregation, or special education, must be remedied. The famous busing crisis in the Boston public schools, which led to the schools being placed under the receivership of a federal judge until the law was upheld, is a prime example of the federal courts' commitment to overseeing the implementation of its own decisions. The federal courts are the courts of last resort for unresolved education issues involving any U.S. constitutional or federal statute protecting the rights of individuals.
- **State Courts:** Since most of the power to enact broad school policy was left by the federal government to the states, all states have constitutional and statutory mandates concerning public education. State courts are likely to get involved in the nuts-and-bolts issues of how their schools are run, and any violations of or challenges to state policies are dealt with at this level. Like the federal courts, some state judiciaries have recently handed down decisions that not only interpret the state laws, but get actively involved in determining and even overseeing specific solutions.
- **Congress:** Representatives and senators are supposed to be sensitive to the issues of their constituencies, and when those constituencies demand action on education, federal legislators are usually responsive. Unfortunately, at the federal level it is nearly impossible to get consensus on school-quality issues, although the legislature can — and certainly has — enacted powerful laws to enlarge the constitutional rights that the courts protect. The Education for Handicapped Children Act of 1973 and the Family Educational Rights and Privacy Act of 1974 are prime examples of congressional action on the part of public education. But recent federal legislatures have been unwilling to commit to expanded funding even to

meet their own mandated programs and, because they have so many constituencies to answer to, their power is somewhat diluted.

- **State Legislatures:** The problems of accountability plague state legislatures as well. But, charged with the constitutional power to define, direct, and monitor education, the state legislatures have had to get much more involved in mandating the specifics of public education policy. If the state courts have to uphold the state's constitutional definition of appropriate education (and those definitions vary wildly from state to state, as we'll see in Chapter 8), then it is the state house's job to put those laws into effect, and to enact laws that enable the schools to run.

  That means everything from certifying teachers to developing graduation requirements and providing for the funds to keep all students in school, regardless of their academic, economic, or physical status. So state laws can cover a lot of ground. In New Jersey, for example, a law was passed permitting qualified professionals without formal teaching certification to teach in the public schools. And in Rhode Island, a state statute gives parents the right to add courses to the school curriculum if enough students want to take them.

- **U.S. Department of Education:** The department's primary responsibility is to guarantee the right of all children to equal educational opportunities and to provide programs designed to enforce those guarantees. The best-known federal program of this sort is Head Start. The department can also redress funding inequities, especially by withholding federal funds — or making it illegal for states to disburse their funds — to programs that do not meet federal equity guidelines.

  The department has three subsidiaries: the Office of Educational Research and Improvement, which conducts educational research; the National Center for Education Statistics, which maintains exhaustive figures on U.S. education trends; and the Office of Information Services, which provides information on federal programs to citizens. Although the department disburses federal funds for federally mandated programs and often recommends broad changes in state and local systems, less than 6 percent of a school's budget comes from the federal government through the Department of Education.

- **State Department of Education (SEA):** Also called the State Bureau of Public Instruction or Public Education, this state education agency is the policy-making body for the state. The legislature will usually consult with this body when it is preparing education legislation, since most members of the SEA are professional educators. Aside from setting policy, the SEA conducts the day-to-day business of education for the entire state, serving mostly as an administrative and managerial organization. Various offices may handle operations such as budgets and accounting, personnel and labor relations, equal education services, curriculum instruction and technologies, and nutrition services. Regional centers may divide up such operations in larger states.

In most states, the SEA turns around and reallocates some of its decision-making power to the local education agency (LEA), meaning the district school board and school administration. However, all states mandate curriculum guidelines (what must be taught in each grade), but vary in the flexibility they give to LEAs to fulfill those guidelines — the choice of textbooks or teaching methods, for example. The SEAs also certify teachers, define the age parameters for compulsory school attendance, set high school graduation requirements, and decide the length of the school year.

- **Unions:** There are approximately 2,300,000 teachers in this country and most of them — more than 85 percent — belong to the National Education Association, making it the second-largest union in the country after the Teamsters. Another 500,000 belong to the American Federation of Teachers, and several hundred thousand belong to the National Association of Professional Educators, which, unlike its larger competitors, does not believe in the right to strike or support collective bargaining. In addition, school principals, clerical workers, food-service and transportation workers, even superintendents, have their own unions.

  The NEA is extremely active at the state level, while the AFT has a heavy concentration in large cities; together they have a powerful impact on our schools, because they control the salaries and working conditions of our teachers. Traditionally these unions concerned themselves with employment matters, but recently both have begun to get involved in school policy and curriculum issues as they affect member teachers. Unions are powerful for a number of reasons, not the least of which is their voting power due to sheer numbers. (More on unions in Chapter 5.)

- **Local School Board (or Committee):** School boards are a uniquely American institution. They are almost always made up of elected citizens (3 percent are appointed by other elected officials) whose job it is to oversee the operations of the school administrators. The National School Board Association has 100,000 members on over 15,000 boards with 3 to 14 members sitting on each board (some states call them school trustees). Most members are unpaid, or receive a nominal fee for their work, and terms of office are usually two or four years long.

Aside from its role as overseer, the school board serves as the policy-setting and goal-setting arm of the LEA. Of course, school boards have to work within the guidelines set by their state, but as representatives of their community they must also reflect local concerns. Board members are, after all, elected officials, and they must be attuned to their respective constituencies. As a result, many boards maintain a delicate balance between opposing factions within a community, which can make for interesting meetings and many compromises.

The school board also serves an important function as the go-between for the administrators who request funding for programs and the city officials who allocate such funds. The board can decide how much money is spent on schools, how it should be raised and distributed. It makes decisions on whether new schools are needed or whether old ones should be closed. However, since they are not professional educators, members must often rely on their superintendent for information about a particular program, making it possible for the superintendent to wield more than his or her share of the power.

- **School Superintendent:** The school superintendent is the plant manager for the school system. He or she is charged with the daily operations of the entire system and is the figure to whom all personnel are answerable. Most school superintendents are appointed by other elected officials, although some are elected and some (particularly in rural school districts) are provided by the larger county system. The superintendent is charged with seeing to it that the system meets the goals set by the state and by the school board, and must also answer to those agencies on behalf of the district. The superintendent is responsible not only for curriculum development, program operations, and personnel management, but for the business end of running the schools. Most superintendents have risen up among the ranks of teachers and principals, but their non-instructional assistants may not have had direct classroom experience.

The superintendent is also a city official, submitting an annual budget to the school board, and recommending construction and/or bond issues when new schools are needed. Superintendents are also political animals, since they must court the cooperation of the school board, the city and state government, and local businesses in order to gain the most good for their system. Big-city superintendents can command high salaries (sometimes the highest in the city government), and many move from city to city rather than remain within one system.

- **School Principals:** Despite their relatively low position on our pyramid, school principals are probably the most important people in the system. They are certainly the administrators with whom parents have the closest contact. And they are in charge of their own schools, defining those schools through their own personality and educational philosophy. Particularly today, when school-based management is becoming more and more prevalent (see Chapter 9), principals are pivotal figures in our children's education.

  Although they have broad latitude to operate within their own schools, principals do not act alone. They are answerable to the central administration and to the school board, and may be guided by the individual policies of their school and supported by their own administrative staff. Since they were once teachers themselves, principals often have a good understanding of the needs of their own teachers, but may have a hard time reconciling those needs with the disparate demands from students, parents, and administrators. If principals are the first line of defense in maintaining a functioning school system, they are also often the first to be attacked.

- **Specialists:** The number and variety of school specialists differs from school to school. But most mid- to large-sized school systems have the following positions filled in all their schools, even if some positions are shared by a number of schools:

  librarian/media specialist
  art instructor
  music instructor
  physical education instructor
  special needs coordinator/tutor
  guidance/adjustment counselor
  curriculum developer/staff support
  speech and language specialist
  occupational or physical therapist
  bilingual specialist
  parent liaison
  school psychologist
  school nurse
  nutritionist (cafeteria director)

- **Teachers:** Individual teachers, as a separate entity from their unions, tend to have a lot less power in the school hierarchy. They can, in most cases, run their classrooms with relative autonomy, but they must obey the curriculum guidelines of their district as well as the classroom control systems set up by their principals. They are subject to intense and sometimes arbitrary scrutiny from above and below — from administrators and parents — and must fulfill countless bureaucratic obligations. The hours spent planning lessons, correcting schoolwork, and recording students' progress are often overlooked when teachers' "easy" hours are considered.

Perhaps the most damaging issue for teachers is that of professional status. Teaching has never been considered a status career in the U.S., and the image of the single woman who teaches because she has nothing more fulfilling to do persists even today. Salaries reflect the low status accorded teachers — after similar amounts of training, graduates of technical and professional schools can go on to make two, three, and four times the average teacher's salary.

Yet teachers are responsible for the real nuts and bolts — the ongoing education of our children on a daily basis — whereas parents may have passing or special interests in the classroom, and administrators or unions sometimes have conflicting interests to those of educating the child. It is the teacher who spends hours a day actually teaching the child to read or write, or to understand American history or calculus. Teachers are, in effect, the foot soldiers of the immense bureaucracy created just for that purpose.

- **Support Staff:** Seldom consulted and always there, the support staff is the backbone of any school. The staff include classroom aides, janitors, secretaries, cafeteria workers, and transportation workers, many of whom are hired from the local communities to perform these jobs on a part-time basis. Some — particularly janitorial and transportation workers — have their own unions and negotiate their own contracts with the school board. While these workers are not always directly involved in educating our children, they certainly affect the quality of life in school, and can make the difference between a positive school environment and a stressful one.
- **Parents and Community Members:** It's important to remember that educators — everyone from the state superintendent to the classroom teacher — are the servants of the public interest, and that parents are the primary (adult) consumers of those services. We are also the primary funding source for those services. The entire pyramid is designed to provide us (via our children) with an effective and efficient education. That's why, even though we sit at its base, we are a powerful force in public education.
- **Students:** While there has been a recent upsurge in the students' rights movement, especially at the high school level, students remain largely at the mercy of the adults who are legally responsible for their care until they reach age eighteen. Nevertheless, many

young adults are becoming increasingly outspoken on topics such as dress codes, health education, and the right to speak their minds on political issues. Many school systems are beginning to listen to what their students have to say, and many parents are beginning to see the wisdom of incorporating student power into their advocacy efforts.

In March of 1989, the Rindge and Latin High School of Cambridge, Massachusetts, became one of the first schools in the nation to offer condoms to students in the school clinic. The idea grew out of an AIDS awareness program offered to the school by the Cambridge AIDS task force. The program involved lectures, classroom discussion, videotapes, and discussions with teenage AIDS victims. Naturally, prevention was an important topic, and many students, formerly unaware of the reality of the AIDS threat, began to see the need to provide protection as well as education for themselves.

The initiative for adopting the policy came entirely from the students, several of whom had already been involved in distributing condoms as part of the AIDS awareness program. Three hundred fifty signatures were collected on a petition calling for wider availability of condoms through the school's on-campus teen health center. On the basis of that petition, the students were able to go to the school committee, where they lobbied enough support to put the petition up for a vote.

Several meetings were held to discuss the delicate issue, including one large public hearing at which strong support for the students' proposal was voiced by parents and community members. At every meeting, students came forward to speak eloquently in support of the program, which was finally passed by the committee by a four-to-three margin.

There were objections from parents and school committee members, and some from the students themselves, mostly arguing that it would be embarrassing to get condoms there, or that the people who truly needed them would be those least likely to take advantage of their availability. But student advocate Emily Case felt that the vote was both an affirmation of a real need and a message of confidence in the students' ability to make their own decisions. ''I'm very glad the school committee took this step to say that AIDS is really a major threat to students, and that they supported our efforts.''

The condoms were made available for a nominal fee, but no one who cannot afford the price will be turned away.

THE MONEY PIT

The school structure wouldn't exist without the money to make it run. Where does that money come from, and what input do parents have in how it is spent? What is the relationship between the nature of the budget and the quality of the education our children are receiving? How can we become informed and involved with the annual budget process, and how are we likely to make the most impact on the design of that budget?

Budgets can be formidable documents, and they do require some time and energy to understand, but they are probably the single most important tool for effective advocacy. The ability to understand a school budget can give you a clear insight into what is really happening in the classrooms, and the opportunity to come up with realistic alternatives if need be.

Most individual school system budgets must follow a format provided by the state, which requires uniformity for its own bookkeeping services. Unfortunately, the state's budget-system format, or chart of accounts, is usually incompatible with individual schools' budget needs. It has the additional drawback of being incomprehensible to everyone but state accountants, rendering it difficult for school officials and parents to decode.

However, there are some common elements. Most budgets use a system known as the "function/object" method, which breaks down expenditures in terms of their general function, and then further in terms of the object of the function. Money spent on teachers, for instance, would go under the function of "instruction," and would then be further broken down into salaries, benefits, et cetera.

But this method has serious limitations for school budget purposes. It leaves little room for flexibility, makes many expenditures incomprehensible, and offers no way to gauge the effectiveness of money spent in one area. Let's say a school budget has allocated $400,000 to its special needs department for direct instruction. The money is clearly divided into amounts spent on salaries, benefits, and the like, but the budget does not make clear how many teachers are allocated to the special education classroom, and how many are working with students in the regular classrooms. It doesn't tell us what percentage of students are being serviced by what types of programs, and it gives us no way to assess whether more restrictive placement is as efficient as mainstreaming.

A more effective budget system, according to Oliver Brown, senior consultant for The Co/Op (a nonprofit educational management organization), would be a budget based around specific programs, known as a "program budget." With the program method, each expenditure is described in terms of where the money is going to be spent. Each program devises its own budget, and then the budgets are submitted centrally to the school committee. In some municipalities, each school is invited to submit a budget; in others, the programs might be broken up into grade levels system-wide.

Not only is the program budget format much easier for parents and teachers to understand, but it can be expanded or contracted as areas of concern arise. Let's say a school system is concerned about its art budget. The budget director would ask the art director to submit a detailed budget describing how much money was spent on how many children for paper, paints, markers, et cetera. If there was an area where too much money was being spent, it would emerge clearly. Once the issue was resolved, the program could go back to submitting a more generalized budget, reducing the amount of paperwork necessary.

Program budgeting's greatest asset is its accountability. By looking at the money spent on an individual program, school administrators and parents can easily see if it is worth the expenditure. The number of children served and the breakdown of expenses within the program can be examined as well as its results. Unfortunately, since states do require uniform budget systems, many program budgets being developed by local schools have to be translated back into the function/object system, and arduous and expensive task.

READING INTO THE BUDGET: MORE THAN MONEY

Explicitly or not, every budget will reflect the short- and long-term goals of the superintendent who proposes it and of the school board who approves it. But a budget is not just a series of numbers on a balance sheet. In addition to offering information on where the money is coming from and where it is being spent, a good budget should offer a detailed picture of the kind of education the system plans to deliver. A budget is not just about the acquisition and allocation of resources. It's also about planning, prioritizing school goals, about dovetailing with the state education system, and about meeting federal requirements. In fact, a good budget should have four components, as described in Rhoda Dersh's *The School Budget: It's Your Money, It's Your Business:*

1. *A revenue plan* detailing all moneys the district expects to receive and where it expects them to come from (also listing the previous year's revenue figures and an explanation of where the difference, if any, is to come from).

2. *An expenditure plan* detailing all moneys that are being spent and where, on a line-item basis, including per-pupil or unit-cost figures (also

listing the previous year's expenditures and an explanation of why the difference, if any, is called for). No matter how they are organized, most expenditure plans include:
- a breakdown of teacher-salary schedule
- an employee-benefit schedule
- student-enrollment projections
- teacher/student ratios

3. *An educational plan* including the goals and objectives of the school superintendent and school board by describing each line item according to its proposed function in fulfilling those goals and objectives;

4. *A priority plan* ranking each existing and proposed program and its relative value in relation to the goals and objectives.

It is these last two aspects of the budget that are of most concern to parents. Parents may not be able to affect how much money is coming in or how much is spent on each pupil, but they can influence the goals and objectives of the school board and help determine which programs receive top priority. The educational plan should describe each program or line item in terms of its function in fulfilling the educational goals, and should describe the criteria by which the program should be judged. The objectives are the short-range plans for meeting the longer-range — and more general — educational goals. Educational plans are often included as addendum or appendixes to the expenditure plan.

The priority plan should rank both existing and proposed programs and their objectives in relation to other expenditures. In this way, decisions can be made about which programs most effectively meet the goals and objectives of the school district. In order to do this, it is necessary for the school to conduct a needs-assessment evaluation. This is usually done by the school department early on in the budget process, and there should be room in any needs-assessment evaluation for parental input.

A good needs-assessment evaluation will identify the educational needs of the community, and a good budget will prioritize its programs to meet those needs. Some needs assessments are done on a school-by-school or program-by-program basis. Some are done district-wide. A sample of the citizen's participation form for the early-childhood-education needs-assessment evaluation from the Dallas Independent School District follows:

DISD NEEDS ASSESSMENT: 1991–92 Budget Development

Name of Group: _____

In the following areas, please give your opinions on improvements, proposed program enhancements, possible program reduction/consolidation, et cetera. If additional space is needed, please attach an additional sheet(s).

Instructional Program: (Reading/language arts, math, science, social studies, et cetera).

Instructional Program Support: (Staff development, testing, staff services, research/evaluation, data processing, et cetera):

Staffing: (Pupil/teacher ratios, pupil/adult ratios, paraprofessionals, clerical support, et cetera):

Supplies/Equipment:

Maintenance:

Parents/Staff Communications:

Facilities: (School buildings, structures, plants, et cetera)

Summarize Priority Needs:
1.
2.
3.
4.
5.

Other:

When should all this work be done? Very early in the school year, since so many phases are involved. Here's a time line for the typical budget preparation process:

September/October/November — needs-assessment phase
December/January/February — program planning phase
March — superintendent submits proposed budget
April — school board examines tentative budget
May — real budget is developed
June — real budget is finalized

Community members have the greatest opportunities for input during the needs assessment and tentative budget phases, although concerned parents can certainly get involved with every phase of the budget process. But exactly how does the process work, and how would you fit into the schedule? A hypothetical situation will make this clearer. Let's say your school system does its planning in January. That would mean that in November you and a group of other parents who were concerned about the lack of higher level foreign-language classes would want to meet to assess the needs of the students in that area. You would want to gather statistics on what was being offered in which schools system-wide, and on which students were taking the classes that were available.

At the same time, you would be working on a proposal for five new classes to be taught at the schools where your research has shown there is the greatest demand. You would be careful not to propose taking money from existing programs and to make the source of program funding (usually the reallocation of existing funds) very clear. To determine possible sources you should examine the existing budget to see if there are any allocations not yet spent or spoken for that could be applied to your proposed program. Make sure that your budget is not extravagant, and that the short- and long-term gains from your proposed program (from money, time, or personnel more efficiently used to a higher percentage of college admissions) is also clear. Any documentation of the positive effects of advanced foreign-language training, and of the exclusion of minorities or special education students from the existing classes, would also be presented here.

In January you would take your proposal to the school committee's open meetings (a call to the school department will give you the exact dates, which must, by law, also be published in the local papers). Many other special interest groups will be presenting their proposals, and you may feel defeated or disappointed. But while the budget is being deliberated, you can help by making yourself available to answer questions, and by making it very clear to the superintendent that many community members are backing your proposal. Follow every meeting with a letter to the officials with whom you have met, reiterating your plan and its benefits. Keep up interest with a phone campaign or a meeting, and invite school officials to participate.

When the proposed budget is submitted in March, your program may be on it, but at a reduced expenditure. Be prepared to bargain, and also to compromise when it is clear that there is no other way to fund the program to your proposed level. The school board now gets to look at the budget, and you can again go into lobbying mode, making phone calls and attending meetings to attest to the value of your proposed program. Follow up every appearance with a letter.

In some localities, the school budget is voted on by the entire population; in others, by those citizens attending a town meeting, or by elected representatives. In many cities, the school budget is voted on as part of an entire city budget package and cannot be considered separately. In any case, gaining popular support for your program is the best way to get it approved. Once the budget is approved and finalized, you must keep close track of what happens to the money, and how the program is administered, to make sure that your original goals are being met.

It sounds like a lot of work — it is a lot of work. But concerned parents can act as watchdogs over the budget process without taking on a specific program proposal. You can carefully examine every item in the budget and ask for clarification or even changes. You should certainly examine other budgets in nearby school districts, and even look at school or program budgets within the system itself to make sure there is an equity in funding. *Budgets are a matter of public record.* Any school department will release copies of finalized budgets to concerned citizens, although you may have to go to the administration building and make a copy yourself. The burden of making the budget comprehensible to the taxpayers lies with the school department, not with the taxpayers. Studying the school budget requires patience, but not as much financial acumen as many parents think. And the lessons to be learned from examining it are well worth the effort.

WHERE DOES THE MONEY COME FROM?

In 1920, the total budget for all U.S. public schools (elementary and secondary) was under a million dollars. In 1990, the total was $200 billion. The latter figure represents 6.9 percent of our gross national product, nearly a full percentage point down from the 7.6 percent of the GNP spent on education in 1970. Less than 5 percent of that money comes from the federal government. States pay an average of 40 percent, while local cities and towns pay the lion's share — 56 percent.

These figures vary dramatically from state to state. In New Mexico, for instance, the federal income for public schools amounts to 12.2 percent of the total revenues, while in Wyoming it's only 3.7 percent. Washington-state schools get 72.4 percent of their income from the state, while the state of Oregon provides only 28 percent of the public school revenues. In Hawaii, where the entire state is run as a single unified school district, only 0.01 percent comes from local taxes, while in New Hampshire local communities must raise a full 90.7 percent of their own school income.

Clearly, the burden of paying for public education falls on the state and even more on the local taxpayer. And if we are going to pay for it as well as "consume" the services we finance, it seems natural that we be integrally involved in developing the priorities of the budget. The bulk of the local money comes from our property taxes, both residential and commercial. Income is also received from out-of-district fees, earnings from investments, and rental fees for nonschool building use.

But there's a problem with using local property and/or income taxes to fund district schools. Since neighboring towns can have widely vary-ing tax bases, there can be a dramatic discrepancy in the amount of money available to the schools. The discrepancy is tied in to property values, since that is what the tax rate is based upon. In wealthy Weston, Massachusetts, the town spends 87 percent of its municipal taxes on its schools. In nearby blue-collar Chelsea, the town allocates only 17 percent to its schools. If the property values in a prosperous community are high, there will be a lot of money available, even though the tax rate may actually be lower. In a suburban community that taxes a $200,000 house at $14.00 per thousand, the annual property tax paid by the homeowner will be around $2,800. In an urban community, however, a $100,000 apartment building may be taxed at $26.00 per thousand, meaning that the owner would be paying about the same amount of money for a much less valuable property. And if the apartment house is home to ten children of public school age, all of those children must be served with those tax dollars.

In towns like Weston and Chelsea, the basic inequity in school funding is exacerbated by the fact that the state pays each municipality a flat rate for education, based on the number of students in school. For cities or towns that have an ample tax base, state aid provides them with additional moneys that can only enhance their education budget. But for those cities and towns struggling to pay for the bare essentials through their local tax levies, the state aid is crucial to their survival.

Most states have established systems to parcel out other money more fairly. Most take into account the numbers of poor, minority, or special needs students, since those children are more expensive to educate. But the state formulas are often archaic and overly complex, and they account for only a small proportion of the total amount of money given to the schools. Schools are forced to plan minutely detailed programs to get small amounts of money that can only be used for specific purposes.

Within any community, there can be a schism between those who think that more money should be spent on schools and those who think that no more money should be spent, or that it should be spent elsewhere.

Increasingly, non–public school citizens (parents with grown children, parents with children in private or parochial schools, and citizens without children) are working to regain some control over what they see as runaway spending on the public schools. These groups are the most frequently cited "no-new-taxers." But even parents with public school children often feel that their burden, as evidenced in their local and state taxes, is too high. They blame the high price on poor management, both at the government level and at the school administration level. The idea that good schools produce higher property taxes, more productive citizens, and a reduction in social service costs in the future falls on deaf ears for many Americans who simply feel that they are being taxed to death.

Statewide, 38 percent of New Jersey's 1990–91 school budgets were defeated. The antitax wave that hit the state did not discriminate; aging industrial centers like Passaic and Hudson counties turned down respectively 84 and 71 percent of their school budgets, rapidly growing counties like Middlesex and Ocean had respective rejection rates of 64 and 57 percent. Even upper-class communities like Saddle River, Englewood Cliffs, and Alpine defeated their budgets.

And it's not just non–public school parents who are doing the voting. "I love the education, and all the programs are wonderful," says one Somerville, New Jersey, mother. "But my taxes have gone up quite a few hundred dollars. This budget has just pushed everyone over the edge."

Until the mid-seventies, property taxes underwrote most of the local school budgets. The New Jersey Supreme Court ruled that system unconstitutional and a state income tax is supposed to have ended the overreliance on local property taxes. But local education authorities don't always receive all the money to which they are entitled by the state's new income distribution formula, and so they still have to rely on local revenues.

"I don't think it's anti-education," says Bergen County Superintendent Dr. Ray M. Kelly. "I think it's directed at every aspect of municipal government. The taxpayers are saying to all, 'be as frugal and as responsible as you can without destroying the services we're getting.'"

The idea of using taxes other than local property taxes to fund schools usually has to come from the state, and several are considering alternatives to the traditional methods of apportionment. Gasoline taxes, sales taxes, and even a gambling tax are among some of the alternatives being used or examined in Arkansas, South Carolina, and New Jersey. But there is a problem with moving the burden of paying for local public schools even further onto the shoulders of the state. The greater the percentage of revenue provided, the greater the amount of control demanded. Federal funding, which accounts for a small percentage of the school budget — and most of it is targeted for federal programs to benefit the disadvantaged and the handicapped — is clearly not a viable solution. As with many state programs, there are far too many restrictions and limitations, rendering the programs inflexible and of little use to many systems that might need them.

OTHER FUNDING OPTIONS

The dilemma of having to pay more money for local control or having to rely on a sometimes undependable state revenue source has parents all over the country looking for alternatives. Additional tax levies, construction bonds, deficit spending, private corporate intervention, user fees, and legislative action are all remedies that parents around the country have tried, with varying degrees of success. In Hackensack, New Jersey, for instance, the city overcame an inadequate new construction budget by acquiring a cheap parcel of land on both sides of a highway and using free airspace above the road to bridge the building. Schools are renting space in commercial buildings and apartment complexes all over the country, a practice that has a double advantage because the city does not lose the tax value of the property.

Another budgetary possibility open to parental input is community fund-raising. For many years parents have participated in bake sales and premium sales to boost their local school's coffers. Today such efforts are likely to be far more efficiently run and financially effective. They are organized around specific goals, are highly structured and well executed, and take advantage of all the legal and tax allowances available to charitable organizations.

In the winter of 1990, the National Committee for Citizens in Education conducted a survey of parent fund-raising groups. Most groups work with revenues of between $3,000 and $5,000, although some raise as little as $75 and others as much as $4 million. But many parent groups say fund-raising is a waste of their valuable efforts, which could be put to more important advocacy use. "The history of parent groups as fund-raisers creates a comfort level for many parents who are fearful or don't understand the need for moving beyond this limited role," says a member of one PTA. Even the national PTA now discourages fund-raising, which it says encourages schools to rely on PTAs to buy them needed equipment and services.

But parent groups still need money to operate. So do schools, and sometimes fund-raising is the only way to get it. If you do engage in a fund-raising activity, it must be done carefully. Gaining tax-exempt status for your fund-raising group means that donors will be able to deduct the donation from their taxes and your organization will not have to pay taxes itself. It's important that tax-exempt status be applied for before funds are solicited. A parent who is also a lawyer or tax accountant should be able to help your group file the appropriate 1023 forms. Do be aware, though, that nonprofit organizations cannot engage in lobbying activities.

Parents have also found that investing their fund-raising money means there is more of it, and that it is better protected than straight fund-raising accounts. Several school districts have established private foundations to invest and disburse their fund-raising moneys. The moneys themselves are raised in the time-honored ways — through raffles, benefits, door-to-door sales, premiums, and auctions. Some fund-raising efforts have focused on a "parent tax" — essentially asking parents of local schoolchildren to ante up for their children's schooling. But problems have arisen when neighboring communities unable to muster additional funds from among their residents charge that such elitism makes poor schools suffer. When local fund-raising efforts *are* successful they can enrich the schools through special programs.

The Weston Education Enrichment Fund Committee in suburban Weston, Massachusetts, was created by town meeting as a permanent subcommittee of the school committee. It's aim is to solicit, invest, and distribute funds for the public schools. WEEFC solicits modest donations as well as substantial ones, and in-kind donations such as the gift of lights for the high school theater. Funds are invested by the town manager, and then distributed by the committee.

WEEFC funds projects that are not part of the regular school budget. They are distributed in the form of mini-grants available to teachers for use in and supplying materials for enrichment projects. In recent years, WEEFC has funded an annual Word Fest, which invites actors, poets, authors, and illustrators into the elementary school classrooms for short-term residencies. Science field trips and desktop publishing projects were also funded.

Grant writing is another source of funds to which parents have access. You don't need to be a professional grant writer in order to write a successful grant. Many books are available to help you choose grant targets and handle the technical details of the process. Philip and Susan Jones, in their book *Parents Unite!*, offer suggestions for effective grant writing:

- Check local sources first (they may be eager to help out in their own community, and may have funds earmarked for local services).
- Check into government grants at the local, state, and federal level. (Write for information on available grant programs — the U.S. government, for instance, publishes an annual catalog of federal funding sources.)
- Do your homework. (Spend time in the library reading books like *The Foundation Director's Information Quarterly* and learn the exact requirements of each grant. Foundations will not even read grant proposals tendered by organizations that do not meet their guidelines, or that do not match their specifications.)
- Join a grant-writing information group to network about available grants (other groups may have heard of a grant possibility that would fit your organization and not theirs).
- Write an effective proposal:
  Cite specific uses for the money you want and demonstrate clearly the positive effect those funds would have.
  Explain why your group got together by citing statistics on your

constituency, how long you've been together, how many people would be serviced, et cetera.

Cite the problem clearly by detailing specific issues involved, with supporting evidence of each.

Cite your objectives (how to solve the problem and how to measure results).

Cite your proposed methods for achieving those objectives (be very specific).

Detail your proposed budget for achieving objectives and provide information about where future funding might come from. (Will it be self-supporting or eligible for public funding once the program has reached a certain level?)

If parents can get school committee members to vote wisely on budget issues, they can get them to vote wisely on general policy issues as well. And they can get the entire city council to commit itself to improving the educational goals and methods of the local school system. As with budget improvement, getting involved in challenging local education policies and priorities requires a good deal of time and effort. But parents have been able to create major changes in the way local education authorities operate.

When the crippling cuts of the 1980 budget left Washington's already beleaguered schools in chaos, parents reacted. They organized a massive rally to protest the cuts, and prepared detailed studies comparing the District of Columbia schools with those of neighboring districts.

After the crisis was resolved (many budget cuts were restored), the group formally organized into Parents United for the DC Public Schools. For the past decade the group has continued applying the potent combination of close scrutiny and legislative pressure to school issues. In addition to increasing the school budget by $10 million, Parents United has lobbied successfully to increase the length of the school day, link teacher ratings to pay scales, increase capital-improvements funding for buildings, and define budget terms more clearly.

Parents United issues a yearly report card for the District of Columbia schools and conducts studies on educational effectiveness. The group worked for passage of the DC Public Schools Initiative, which legally defined public school funding as "a matter of highest priority." As a result of the group's efforts, prekindergarten programs were expanded to full-day schedules, class sizes were reduced, spending for textbooks and supplies increased, and teachers received additional professional support.

The group is directed by a board of parent representatives from 110 participating schools. Representatives from each of the city's political wards keep the parent network active, and an additional thousand people volunteer for specific projects. A newsletter keeps parents informed and an executive director handles daily operations and fund-raising. Parents United receives donated legal and financial support from the local community and passes many of these gifts on in the form of enrichment programs developed by parents at low-income area schools.

WHERE DOES THE MONEY GO?

Perhaps the only issue that generates more bitter controversy than that of school revenues is that of school expenditures. How is the money spent? Who decides that the foreign-language programs get two teachers and the physical education program gets six? Who decides that the library must go without a new video system while the math department gets four computers? Those are the most important decisions that the budget process entails, and the decisions where parents can have the greatest effect.

The Department of Education's Office of Educational Research and Improvement publishes a thick book of education-related statistics every year (most of the figures in this book come from the twenty-fifth edition of that volume). A table depicting the distribution of expenditures for public schools over the course of the past sixty years is worth reproducing here:

% in 1920	Type of Expenditure	% in 1980
3.5	administration	4.4
61.0	instruction	55.5
11.2	plant operation	10.2
2.9	plant maintenance	(incl)
0.09	fixed charges	12.3
3.5	other school services*	8.3
14.8	capital outlay	6.8
1.8	interest on school debt	2.0

* adult education, summer school, and community services

We still spend most of our money on our teachers, which is as it should be. That 55.5 percent, however, does not just account for teachers' salaries. It also includes employee benefits such as health care and pension funds, as well as instructional materials. Many of those costs are fixed by union contract and not negotiable (see Chapter 5). Others, such as the cost of textbooks and other instructional materials, cannot be controlled locally, since they must be purchased from the companies that make and sell them (see Chapter 6).

Through clever manipulation of available funds and careful monitoring of staff ratios, new purchases, and contracted expenses (such as transportation and lunchroom costs), we can control some costs. But we have an equal responsibility to see to it that the money we do have goes to the right programs. We can demand explanations for the overstaffing of custodial positions, which are often tied into local school committee elections. We can insist on a downsizing of the school bureaucracy, and see to it that poorly managed programs do not get to make up their deficits out of the much-tapped general funds. We can monitor energy expenses and make sure our schools don't use outdated equipment that ends up costing more in the long run.

One little-known approach to increasing quality through the budgetary process is getting the local school board to attach conditions to funds. Any voter can approach the school committee with a suggestion for attaching conditions to existing program budgets or to proposed budget items. If, for instance, your group feels that traditional bilingual education programs should offer the opportunity for two-way bilingual education, then perhaps the condition attached to the bilingual program budget would call for an experimental two-way program to be incorporated into the larger program.

Attaching conditions is a powerful voter's bargaining chip. It allows citizens to say to school committee members, ''If program A is funded, then improvement B must be made.'' Of course, there is no guarantee that the school committee will agree to your request. A well-organized and broad-based coalition has a greater chance of being heeded than one or two parents with a peripheral request. But most school board members will entertain the attachment of reasonable conditions to budget items — after all, the local taxpayers are responsible for their reelection.

Clearly, we have a pivotal voice in determining where the money comes from and where it goes. We must look for accountability in the budget system, for power in choosing which programs will get funded, and we must try to find additional sources of income, as well as alternative ways to spend available income.

In St. Paul, Minnesota, Citizens for Better Public Education looked for ways to keep schools open despite declining enrollment. They convinced local officials that it wasn't worth it to close the ''empty'' schools because

- *salaries would remain, since the mostly tenured staff would have to be transferred to other schools;*

- *there would be the loss of a tax advantage; in fact, the taxpayers' share of burden could actually go up because the state only pays the mortgage for public school buildings;*
- *energy savings tactics could reduce the cost of the school while still keeping it open;*
- *volunteer citizens were willing to help fix up buildings, increasing their value to the school district.*

PARENT POWER: WIELDING THE CHECKBOOK

How can parents decide if the money is going to the right place? Says Rhoda Dersh in *The School Budget,* "Don't count on the administration to reveal all the possible ways in which the budget can be reduced without sacrificing quality, especially if administrative salaries, school board travel expenses, and high maintenance costs are involved." This is a good opportunity for parents to come together, to assess their common needs, to join forces, and to come up with viable alternatives to the system's budget.

Parents can resolve even the most pressing budget issues by looking at them through a microscope and answering the following questions:

- What programs present the greatest rate of educational return for the most students?
- What is the local consensus on existing programs? What new programs do parents want? What programs are nonnegotiable?
- What are the relative long-term benefits of those programs?
- Does the budget pit parents against one another, forcing them to vie for the same dollars to fund their "pet" programs? If so, are there alternative solutions that the proposed budget does not address?
- What effect does the teacher contract have on parents' voice in teacher accountability? How can improved teacher performance be tied into the budget?
- Does the local rate of inflation match the rate of inflation of the school budget? If not, why not?
- Where have budget costs risen most? Administration? Property costs? Salaries?
- Where can costs best be trimmed without sacrificing quality?
- In what areas (such as special needs, bilingual, elementary, or secondary) has enrollment declined or increased, and what does the change mean for the budget?
- What will new construction, if desired, really mean in terms of increased educational quality? Smaller classes? Safer buildings? Increased handicap access?

- Are administrators advising on teachers' salaries even though their own salaries are tied into the teachers' salary levels?
- Is there an effective competitive bidding process for outside services? Can parents monitor it?

We must judge our programs by a broad range of factors:

- activity involvement
- low dropout rates
- low teacher turnover
- low grade-retention rate
- low violence level
- high attendance level
- high test scores
- high college admissions

Addressing issues like these may be time-consuming, but the process will provide us with the real answers we need to make sure that our school budgets live up to their obligations. The only way we can do that is to keep a close watch on the process and make sure that it doesn't get out of our hands. Review, propose, ask questions, demand answers. Make sure your school superintendent and school committee know that you are involved and aware. As Rhoda Dersh says, "The most powerful weapon public school parents have is the fact that they write the checks."

Unfortunately, our concepts of what is in the best interests of our children can often conflict not just with those of the providers of that education but with those of one another. Consumers of television sets, for example, are united in their desire for high-quality pictures at a decent price. Consumers of public education have no such common interests. Until we can come to some understanding of the common denominators that bind us all, our formidable power base will remain unexploited.

HOW TO: Ask Real Questions of School Budget Officials

The following questions, culled from the U.S. Department of Education's pamphlet *Making Sense of School Budgets,* can provide you with a sample of the kinds of questions you might want to ask your local school officials in order to help them design a more effective budget. The questions are divided under specific headings for each stage of the budget process. Your local budget may be designed differently, but these questions will give you an idea about how to approach budget advocacy — clearly, politely, and with relentless attention to detail.

Budget Timetable

1. Has the school board voted on this budget. When?
2. Is their decision final? If not, what are the steps taken before it is finalized?
3. If the budget is finalized, when will the proposed budget for next year be made available to the public?

Types of Accounting Funds

1. Are there restrictions on the uses of some dollars included in the general fund? What are the amounts subject to each restriction?
2. What are the restrictions on the other funds shown in the budget statement?
3. Who imposes the restrictions on each fund? Which are liable to change by the board or other local officials?
4. Are all funds maintained by the district shown in this budget statement? If not, where can such information be obtained?

Beginning Balances

1. How confident is the district of this estimated beginning balance? Are there major expenditures that may still change between now and the start of the fiscal year? Are major revenue changes still a possibility?
2. How much of this balance was planned? Why was it thought necessary?
3. How much of this balance was unanticipated and what unexpected factors led to its creation?
4. What basis of accounting was used to determine the beginning balance? Was the same basis used for all revenues and expenditures?
5. Does the district intend to encumber dollars available during the current year to cover needs for next year? If so, how much money, and how will it be used? Are those sums included in the beginning balance shown in the proposed budget?

Expected Revenues

1. How confident is the district of its revenue estimates?
2. Have the state and federal governments made final decisions on their contributions?
3. In past years, has the state rescinded aid after it was originally offered? Might that happen this year?
4. Are there reasons to suspect that the local tax base may change significantly?
5. What local tax rates will be needed to fund this budget? Who has the authority to approve those rates?

6. What will the district do if the requested taxes are not approved?
7. What will the district do if other elements of revenue do not come in as expected?

Planned Expenditures

1. What items are included under the "instruction" function? Under any other function or object?
2. Which expenditure items are subject to being altered by current collective bargaining negotiations?
3. How did the district determine the proposed spending on instructional salaries (or any other item) for the coming fiscal year?
4. What is the legal level of control entailed in this budget? That is, can alterations be made in this plan without the enactment of a budget amendment by the school board?

Planned Ending Balance

1. Is the district legally required to plan its budget to reach a zero balance for all its funds? For particular funds only?
2. How did the district determine the desirable ending balance?
3. If an ending surplus is expected, how will those dollars be used?

Data from Previous Years

1. What is the basis for projecting that outside revenue will be higher next fiscal year than it was this year?
2. How did the district decide to spend more next year on instructional personnel salaries (or any other item) than it did this year? How will the additional dollars be used?
3. Will next year's utility bills (or any other item) really be higher than this year's, or could this cost be reduced?
4. Has the district's total pupil enrollment been declining? If so, why have costs been increasing?

HOW TO: Find Out What Your Community Thinks about the School Budget (*adapted from the Howard County, Maryland, Community Opinion Survey, 1984*)

1. On the whole, how would you rate the public schools in your system?
   _____excellent
   _____good
   _____fair
   _____poor

2. What was the last level of school that you completed?

_____elementary

_____high School

_____college

_____graduate

3. If the public schools in your system need more money to *maintain* the current level of student achievement, would you support increased taxes for this purpose?

_____yes

_____no

4. If the public schools in your system need more money to *increase* the current level of student achievement, would you support increasing taxes for this purpose?

_____yes

_____no

5. It has been suggested that state taxes (income and sales) be increased for everybody to permit the state to pay a greater share of school expenses and thereby reduce local property taxes. Do you favor such an increase so that property taxes could be lowered?

_____yes

_____no

6. Do you think that spending more money makes a great deal of difference in the achievement or progress of students?

_____yes

_____no

7. Is it your impression that enough funds are now being provided to the public schools in this system to provide adequate programs?

_____yes

_____no

8. Below are listed many items that affect the school system budget. Indicate for each item whether you feel that it should be increased, maintained, or decreased, whether in monetary terms or in terms of emphasis placed on the item.

Item	Increase	Maintain	Decrease
class size	_____	_____	_____
after-school activities	_____	_____	_____
custodial services	_____	_____	_____
instructional aides	_____	_____	_____
number of teachers	_____	_____	_____
interscholastic sports and teams	_____	_____	_____
textbooks	_____	_____	_____

Item	Increase	Maintain	Decrease
instructional equipment	_____	_____	_____
classroom supplies	_____	_____	_____
counselors — middle/high school levels	_____	_____	_____
special services such as reading, speech, and hearing therapy	_____	_____	_____
music, physical education, art, home economics, industrial arts courses	_____	_____	_____
vocational training programs	_____	_____	_____
programs for the gifted and talented	_____	_____	_____
computer literacy programs	_____	_____	_____
programs for the physically, emotionally, or mentally handicapped	_____	_____	_____
library books	_____	_____	_____
salaries	_____	_____	_____
maintenance services	_____	_____	_____
extracurricular activities	_____	_____	_____
elective courses in high school	_____	_____	_____
length of kindergarten day	_____	_____	_____
age of kindergarten entrance	_____	_____	_____
use of school facilities by community groups	_____	_____	_____

9. In 1983, the National Commission on Excellence in Education released a report calling for major changes in schools. Many of these recommendations have financial implications. Indicate whether you favor or oppose the following:

Recommendation	Favor	Oppose
A seven-hour school day	_____	_____
An extension of the school year to 200 days	_____	_____
A requirement of three years of science for all high school students	_____	_____
A requirement of three years of math for all high school students	_____	_____
A requirement of three years of social studies for all high school students	_____	_____
A requirement of one half year of computer instruction for all students	_____	_____
A requirement of two years of a foreign language for college-bound students	_____	_____

HOW TO: Avoid Traps in Evaluating Your School (*adapted from* Your School: How Well Is It Working?, *NCCE, 1982*)

Trap #1: Believing that the popular will is demanding an elimination of all courses except reading, writing, and arithmetic.

In recent years, some people have said that schools should just "return to basics" or just teach academic survival skills. A danger is that those who evaluate schools will misjudge what is meant by a basic education.

Most people do not really want to eliminate music, special programs for the gifted, services to handicapped children, or vocational education. What they do want, however, is for schools to teach more effectively in all areas, especially the basic areas of literacy. A return to the basics is more a demand for standards and clearly stated expectations than for a massive reduction of the curriculum.

A return to standards may mean better-prepared teachers, more homework, tougher grading, better discipline, and the requirement of more solid subjects before graduation. People are more concerned about the quality of education than they are about the quantity of courses available.

Trap #2: Believing that all schools have abandoned the teaching of basic skills.

Parents and citizens must not fall into the trap of believing that all schools have given up on the teaching of basics. What is happening on the national average may not be happening in your school. Often people read newspaper reports or national assessment stories and believe that such information describes their local schools. Before coming to that conclusion, you should find out what is really happening in your school.

Trap #3: Believing that the schools must take over what the home should do.

Schools cannot replace families. In many cases, the heavy demands already placed on public schools have weakened their ability to do anything well. When parents have expected schools to do their jobs, schools have responded with mediocrity at best.

Schools should certainly support the home. But they cannot be all things to all people. They cannot teach all cultures, every language, all skills required by the young. Education must be a joint responsibility of the school and the home.

Trap #4: Believing that evaluating schools is a simple task, or that it can be done in a relatively short period of time.

Evaluating schools is a difficult job. It requires frequent school visits, close observation of what is happening, and the careful collection of information.

It is a complex process of examining that information to find out if the schools are doing what the community really wants them to do. Test scores reveal patterns of student achievement. Surveys tell us about people's attitudes. Reports from state and federal agencies assess the success of special programs. Accreditation information discloses whether schools meet certain standards.

In addition, we must take into account attendance rates, graduation rates, college attendance rates, dropout rates, grade retention rates, teacher turnover rates, frequency of behavior and discipline violations and how they are handled, the number of extracurricular activities and their attendance rates, as well as the general atmosphere in the school.

Trap #5: Believing that a poorly done evaluation is better than no evaluation.

Some people assume that having something is better than having nothing. A poorly done evaluation creates conflict, reduces parents' credibility, and leads to confusion. It can fracture the community, lead to unfair or injurious recommendations, and pit school employees against other citizens. When such conditions exist, students are forgotten and education quality decreases.

Trap #6: Believing that teaching can be evaluated easily.

For a good teacher, teaching is an art form, appreciated but not fully understood. Good teachers organize, motivate, control, and monitor, all at the same time, and may not know themselves exactly how they do it.

What works well for one teacher may not work for another. Good teaching involves a highly personalized set of values, skills, attitudes, and strategies. It is difficult, therefore, to study in bits and pieces. To evaluate teachers, you must observe them, talk with them, and think with them. As a practical consideration, citizens should make themselves acquainted with the teachers' contract before attempting an evaluation. The contract is a public document and should be made available to you.

Trap #7: Believing that what was effective teaching "back then" is effective teaching today.

All of us have gone to school and remember a favorite teacher. But we don't all remember the same favorite teacher, teaching in the same way.

And our nostalgia may not include the things that that teacher did wrong, or the limitations of our old grade school.

Times and society have changed. The way we raise our children has changed more than anything else. As a result, schools and teaching methods have also changed. Just as we cannot compare our families with those of a generation ago, we cannot compare schools.

Trap #8: Believing that the results of the evaluation must support values and priorities set before the process began.

An evaluation whose main purpose is to confirm preconceived ideas is not objective. It is not open to facts or to the most persuasive evidence of contrary findings. You don't always find what you expect to find when you undertake a school evaluation. It can be used to make a case for changing course offerings, the amount of the budget, or school personnel, but only if those are legitimate conclusions drawn from an objective examination of all the facts. Avoid the tendency to evaluate selectively to produce the results you want, or your study will lose credibility and all you will earn is ill will.

Trap #9: Believing that all schools are essentially the same.

Schools differ from one another in both the methods used and the values supported. Some schools are highly disciplined, some are not. Some require set courses, some do not. Some stress art and music skills while others concentrate on diversity of culture. Each community must decide what kind of school it wants to have, and then evaluate those schools on the basis of the values it wants expressed.

Trap #10: Believing that there is only one best way to teach a subject.

Learning is a complex human art. We know that children learn in many ways, and there is no one best method. There are, however, commonly used strategies that are better than others. The only way to tell if your school's strategies are working is to look at a variety of outcomes — test scores, skill levels, and your child's satisfaction. The key question to ask in an evaluation is not "How are they learning?" but "Are they learning?"

Getting Started: Tools and Rules for Advocacy

WE know our legal rights and responsibilities, and we know what we have to work with in terms of the general state of the schools. By applying what we've learned about the school structure and the fiscal structure, we can assess our own school's specific needs. Now it's time to begin amassing the tools we'll need in order to translate our concerns into viable goals, and to reach those goals by taking appropriate action.

First of all, we can't assume that our legal rights as parents or advocates will automatically come to us. Most of us did not enjoy those rights when we were in public school, and we have to remember that many of today's educators may not be aware of them either. It's our own ignorance as well as theirs that often stands in the way of progress, so education about our rights and responsibilities is a primary job for all parent advocates.

In order to make the system work to its maximum possible potential, we need to know how far we can go and what we can expect. And, of course, we need to push the limits of those expectations when we feel they do not go far enough to ensure that our children are getting the most effective education possible. And we need to act in a manner that is clearly in the best interests of our own children without detriment (and hopefully with great benefit) to other children.

What do we do when we perceive a problem in our child's school? What do we do when we know something is not right, but we're not even sure what it is? The issue can be as finite as one child's problem with a specific subject in the classroom, or it can be as broad as persistently low scores on statewide reading assessment tests. It can involve a clear violation of a child's right to an appropriate special education program or the school principal's vagueness on the subject of playground safety.

It can concern an ineffective teacher in one classroom or an unacceptable school placement policy enacted by the school board and affecting the entire district. Regardless of the scope of the problem, parent intervention is the key to discovering a solution.

Designs for Change, the Chicago-based education research and improvement organization instrumental in initiating the Chicago education reform experiment, published a report on effective advocacy groups around the country. Titled Standing Up for Children, *the report looked at the advocacy efforts of fifty-two groups of varying sizes and determined the most successful methods used by those groups.*

The report provided examples of successful intervention activities at various levels, from the individual school-building level to the federal level. Their list (slightly expanded) follows.

School-level activities:
- *negotiation with a classroom teacher*
- *negotiation with school principal*
- *conducting individual case advocacy*
- *filing a complaint against building personnel*
- *filing litigation against building personnel*

School district–level activities:
- *negotiating with school district administrators*
- *influencing school board decisions*
- *filing a complaint with government agencies against a school district*
- *filing litigation against a school district*

State-level activities:
- *lobbying for state legislation*
- *pressing for specific state regulations to interpret legislation*
- *pressing for state enforcement*
- *filing litigation against a state*

Federal-level activities:
- *lobbying for federal legislation*
- *pressing for specific federal regulations to interpret legislation*
- *pressing for federal enforcement*
- *filing litigation against the federal government*

In whatever arena of reform we decide to operate, we have to start at the same place and proceed through the same series of steps. The advocacy framework that follows was culled from several sources, and includes strategies and skills you'll need as well as some suggestions on how to handle yourself and deal with any problems that may arise.

It's particularly important for parents to know what to expect emotionally when they embark on an advocacy endeavor. While advocacy can be effective and rewarding, it can be stressful, too, especially for a parent who is undertaking it for the first time. Parents often report that they are "treated like trouble" when they come to the school with a problem, regardless of their willingness to be positive and compromising. They report being made to feel that they are "violating a sacred trust" or "breaking the rules of politeness" by requesting changes.

However, almost without exception, parents are not dissuaded by this attitude. They understand that the resistance comes from a fear of change as well as from a lack of understanding of parents' legitimate role as agents of change. It is reasonable to expect that a mutual education process needs to occur before the "powers that be" can accept us more equitably. Besides, parents insist that the temporary discomfort is more than assuaged by the fact that they are doing what they firmly believe to be essential for their child's education, and for the improvement of their community's schools.

SEVEN STEPS TOWARD EFFECTIVE ADVOCACY

1. Pick a problem with finite limits.
2. Get all the information, and gather it carefully.
3. Decide on the most appropriate course of action.
4. Create a coalition involving the broadest possible base.
5. Put everything in writing.
6. Develop effective advocacy strategies geared toward desired goals.
7. Monitor the results carefully.

1. Pick a problem with finite limits.

It does no good to rush into a principal's office and complain about everything that's wrong with your child's school. First of all, there's no way to fix everything that's wrong with any institution, public or private. Besides, what appears wrong to you may be just fine with other parents. And any complaint is diluted when it is accompanied by an entire litany of wrongs. In fact, the broader your base of complaints, the less likely you are to be taken seriously at all.

A better way to begin your advocacy program is to focus in on a single problem or a group of closely related problems. Often that one issue will be obvious to you — in fact, it will be the only real problem you perceive. As we have seen from our examination of the annual Gallup polls, parents don't perceive their own schools as being in total disarray. In fact, the majority of parents are satisfied with their child's school until one problem comes up that is serious enough to force them into action. Those problems fall into several broad categories (which we'll discuss in detail in later chapters):

- constitutional and statutory issues such as due process, the right to privacy, et cetera
- teacher and administrator issues such as teacher availability, competency, staff development and compensation, personnel evaluation procedures, and union contract negotiations
- curriculum issues such as subject matter and format, quality of teaching methods, relevance, effectiveness, and standards of measurement
- money issues such as revenue sources, equity of distribution, and program funding
- building and material issues such as new construction and school closings, textbooks and supplies, computer materials, and other instructional supplies
- safety issues such as school safety, bus safety, and behavior codes

Parents in the Philadelphia suburb of Bethlehem are suing their school system over the forced student volunteer work that has become part of the high school curriculum. Parents who have never acted as advocates before suddenly find themselves acting as plaintiffs in the suit filed in federal district court against the Bethlehem Area School District school board.

"I don't want my son being told what to do," says Thomas Moralis, one of the plaintiffs. "I went to school in a free America and I want the same for my children." Mr. Moralis and his wife, Barbara, are joining Thomas and Barbara Steirer in the suit being sponsored by Citizens Against Mandatory Service, the ad hoc advocacy group that formed around the issue of the forced volunteer program.

The program requires students to work for any one of a list of approved community organizations as part of a curriculum that seeks to instill practical skills and public service. All students must work for a total of sixty hours during their four years of high school. According to school administrators, the program is both healthy and legal, "something our kids ought to be working on," according to one school board member. It was modeled after a similar public service program in Atlanta.

But the CAMS parents argue that the program is not consistent with certain values and standards held by them, and that it is not safe. They argue that some of the sites are inappropriate, such as a religious-group meeting place and a hospital operating room. "We're not opposed to community service per se," says Mr. Moralis. "It's the way this has been set up that we oppose. The school administration said they don't care if the kids never perform community service again once they've graduated. That kind of attitude destroys whatever goodwill existed in the community.''

Mrs. Moralis says it did not take her long to agree to participate in the suit. ''I've never had an issue which I feel this strongly about, but someone has to represent those parents who feel this is unacceptable, and the way the school board went about setting it up was unacceptable.'' She says the narrow focus of the group has added to its strength and commitment, and that the decision to use legal action reflects ''everyone's confidence that a strong statement had to be made about the way we feel.''

Most of the time, parents are quite clear on the problems they or their children are having in school. Parents with common interests can easily come together to resolve issues such as an incompetent teacher, an inappropriate curriculum, or peeling paint. But there are times when parents feel they have to act but don't know where to begin. That's when it is most effective to rely on information from other parents, gathering informally or — even better — through a well-designed survey. You can design your own survey or use a general survey such as the one illustrated in Chapter 2 to determine what your school community perceives as the most pressing needs. Once the main issues become clear, you can choose the one that is most pressing or most important to you as your point of departure.

The National Committee for Citizens in Education, in another excellent pamphlet, *Finding Out How People Feel About Local Schools,* offers these basic steps to design a survey that asks the questions you want to ask:

- Decide what you want to know.
- Ask yourself why you want to know this.
- Decide whom you are going to survey.
- Outline the content.
- Determine the type of survey you want to conduct.
- Draw up the questions carefully so as not to build in a bias.
- Develop a timetable for the project.
- Determine the costs, if any.
- Train your interviewers.
- Conduct the survey and tabulate the results.
- Analyze the results honestly.
- Report and interpret the findings as widely as possible.

2. Get all the information, and gather it carefully.

This is the step requiring the most time and energy, because it involves the most extensive research. Once you have determined the issue, you need to gather as much information as possible about it. That means anything from keeping a log of all conversations you have with your child's teacher to collecting information on what other groups around the country with similar problems are doing in their school systems. It might help to use the following list of questions to make sure your information gathering is as complete as possible.

A. How harmful is the problem?
   Is it a serious issue that requires immediate attention?
   Is it a long-term problem that requires a carefully planned solution?
B. How widespread is it?
   How does it affect your child?
   How does it affect other children?
   How many children are affected by it?
   Is it limited to one school? One neighborhood? One district?
C. Who else is doing something about it?
   Are other parents concerned about the same problem?
   Are school personnel concerned about it?
   Is there an organization devoted to similar problems?
D. Who is in a position to do anything about it?
   Who are the important players on the issue, and where do they stand (system-wide)?
   What external support can you bring in for assistance?
E. What, if anything, is being done about the problem so far?
   What is your school's position on the issue?
   What is the school department's position on the issue?
   Where does the community stand on the issue?
F. What are the chances for resolution?
   Is there a sizable contingent of parents/personnel who agree (or disagree) with your assessment of the issue (see "How To: Organize for Effective Group Action," at the end of this chapter)?
   Are there any legal constraints (such as union provisions) that must be considered?
   What do the local, state, and federal authorities have to say about the issue?
   What information or assistance is available from outside organizations on the issue?

How do you get this information? The three types of surveys described by the NCCE are listed here, along with the advantages and disadvantages of each. But you may want to use a more informal method such as simply talking to other concerned parents.

Personal Interview:

Advantages — higher percent of return; more detailed information; information apt to be more correct; misunderstandings can be cleared up by more in-depth explanation; use of visuals possible; personal contact.

Disadvantages — personal and transportation costs; possibility interviewer can bias the response or record answer incorrectly; strict supervision of data collection required; time-consuming; training of interviewers required; lack of standard approach by multiple interviewers; volunteers needed.

Telephone Interview:

Advantages — inexpensive and fast; minimal interviewer training required; wide geographic reach in a short time; small response bias because of fixed response questions; easy to call back if line is busy.

Disadvantages — limited to listed telephone numbers and people with telephones; easy for respondent to hang up; difficult to get detailed information; volunteers needed.

Mailed Questionnaires:

Advantages — wide distribution at low cost; can reach remote areas; respondents may be more honest; shorter time getting survey to all respondents; fewer volunteers needed.

Disadvantages — time-consuming; lower possible number of returns; returns may not represent the entire group being surveyed; inability to clarify questions; possibility of "stacked" results by special interest respondents; may need to send reminders.

The Washington-based advocacy group Parents United for the DC Public Schools, has designed a school survey that it distributes to all parents on both the elementary and secondary school levels. The elementary school version is included here because it is an excellent example of an information-gathering project that is both simple and comprehensive.

SURVEY OF SCHOOL RESOURCES: Elementary Schools

Name of School _____ **Date** _____

I. School staff:

Category	How many people?	Do any of these people work only part-time _at your school?_	
		_No_	_Yes—how many and how much time per week?_
Principal	_____	_____	_____
Assistant principal	_____	_____	_____
Secretaries and attendance aides	_____	_____	_____
Teachers:	_____	_____	_____
• Prekindergarten	_____	_____	_____
• Kindergarten	_____	_____	_____
• 1st grade through 6th grade	_____	_____	_____
• Resource teacher	_____	_____	_____
• Chapter 1 teacher	_____	_____	_____
• Special education teachers who stay with the same class	_____	_____	_____
• Other special ed teachers	_____	_____	_____
Librarians	_____	_____	_____
Counselors	_____	_____	_____
Special education aides	_____	_____	_____
Other education aides (don't count aides paid by parents)	_____	_____	_____
Security aides	_____	_____	_____

Are there any staff jobs at your school that are empty now?
Yes _____ No _____
If _yes,_ what jobs? _____

How many times each week does each child have PE, art, and music from a special teacher? Phys. ed _____ Art _____
Music _____

How much time do other special teachers spend in the school each week? Reading _____ Math _____ Science _____

How many classes in the school have: 26–29 pupils? _____
30–34 pupils? _____ More than 35 pupils? _____

How often do nurses, school psychologists, and social workers come?
Nurse _____ School psychologist _____
School social worker _____

Do the last two work only on special education? Yes _____ No _____

II. Texts, supplies, equipment, libraries

During the current school year, have children had to share textbooks in any classes because there weren't enough for each student to have his or her own? No _____ Yes _____ If yes, name a few of these books as examples:

During the current school year, has the school had significant shortages of paper or workbooks or other supplies and materials?
No _____ Yes _____ Please give a few examples:

About how many hardcover books are there in the library? _____

How many of the following does the school have now?	Working	Not working	Bought by parents or corporate donations
Copying machines	_____	_____	_____
Computers	_____	_____	_____
16mm projectors	_____	_____	_____
Overhead projectors	_____	_____	_____
VCRs	_____	_____	_____
Video cameras	_____	_____	_____
Televisions (not counting VCR monitors)	_____	_____	_____

III. Building

Does the roof leak anywhere? No _____ Yes _____ If yes, where and for how long has it done so?

Is there plaster falling or threatening to fall anywhere in the building? No _____ Yes _____ If yes, where?

How long has it been since Buildings & Grounds painted most or all of the inside of your building? _____

Do any school floors need repairs? No _____ Yes _____ If yes, please describe (e.g., cracked or broken tiles, uneven spots, warped places, etc.)

Do window frames in the building need any work? No _____ Yes _____ If yes, what's wrong with them? (e.g., partly rotted, need paint, etc.)

Does the school have cracked or broken window panes? No _____ Yes _____ If yes, about how many? _____

Do all the outside doors open and shut properly? Yes _____ No _____ If no, what's wrong with them? (e.g., don't fit, frames rotted, etc.)

About how many square feet of floor space does your library have, counting librarians' offices? _____

Does the boiler need repair or replacement? No _____ Yes _____

Does your playground have adequate equipment in good repair?
No _____ Yes _____ Briefly describe specific problems.

Does your school have a *separate* gym or only a multipurpose room/
cafeteria? No _____ Yes _____

Are there any other problems with lack of staff, lack of supplies or
equipment, or need for repairs that you want people to know about?

Student _____   Principal _____

Student phone number _____   School phone number _____

Once the necessary information has been collected, you will have
compiled a comprehensive record of the problem as well as pointed out
for yourself some possible avenues for seeking solutions. Perhaps the
most important aspect of advocacy is this step, the documentation of all
aspects of your case. This is true whether the case involves a problem
with an individual teacher or a problem with an entire system. The need
to keep records cannot be overstressed.

Aside from collecting as much information as possible, it's important
to keep records of phone conversations and meetings, to verify all
information from school personnel in writing, and, if possible, to have a
third party present during negotiations to ensure accuracy. By working
with one another, parent advocates can provide essential backup, information, and encouragement.

*In Providence, Rhode Island, a group known as Direct Action for Rights and
Equality has developed a powerful model for helping parents cope with advocacy issues. DARE trains parents who have some advocacy skills or experiences
so that they can accompany less-experienced parents to school conferences,
meetings with principals, or complaint hearings.*

*According to Mark Toney, director of the program, DARE serves a largely
minority population, many of whom are not proficient in English or not well-*

versed in the culture and behavior expected of parents in American public schools. Such parents are often intimidated by the mere thought of facing a teacher, and are liable not to act in their child's behalf because of their own misperceptions.

By training other parents to act as supporters for case advocacy issues, DARE enables parents to act in their own behalf with the guidance of another parent who has similar interests but better skills. They can use the parent-supporters as translators to steer them through the official language and procedures, or simply for reinforcement. Not only are parents more successful in advocating for their children with such support, but they are also more likely to stay involved with their child's school and to have continuing positive impact on the child's education and on the direction that the school takes.

3. Decide on the most appropriate course of action.

Now comes the moment of truth. You've found the important issue, documented its existence and the position of the school on it. What are your choices now? You have several, each with its advantages and disadvantages, and each determined by your personality, your level of commitment, the commitment of other parents, and the issue itself. For instance, you can work

- alone;
- with a support person (a friend or a professional advocate);
- with an existing group;
- with a group you form;
- to make a specific change at a very local level;
- to initiate a system-wide change based on your concerns;
- informally, using meetings, telephone calls, et cetera;
- through public meetings and school-held meetings;
- formally, using system-mandated advocacy channels;
- from the bottom up, going to the least-powerful person involved first;
- directly, going right to a higher source of power;
- to publicize the issue as broadly as possible, thereby putting pressure on the administration;
- to take action without broad public support.

Effective advocacy would naturally involve making several of the above choices, and perhaps trying every avenue of advocacy in succession until your goal is achieved. You must decide, first of all, if you want to handle the problem on your own. If the problem has been a relatively contained one, such as a communication breakdown between you and your child's teacher, there is certainly no reason to bring in the big guns. A meeting with the teacher or with the principal will probably suffice —

either alone or with someone to accompany you for support, advice, and corroboration. If, however, the problem is more pervasive or sustained, such as the continued lack of an appropriate basic skills curriculum or lack of money to hire needed classroom aides, then a broader plan is necessary.

And what if that meeting with the principal over that reluctant teacher brought no improvement? What if other classroom parents feel they, too, are being shut out of their children's educational process, or being given inappropriate information? It may be more effective to work together with other parents, forming a group to discuss common concerns and decide on a unified plan of action.

The question isn't only one of deciding whether to work alone or in concert. Some issues simply do not call for joint action; others will probably not be resolved without it. Often it's not an either/or situation, but a matter of deciding when to join with others. Some parents who have resolved their own advocacy issues choose to help others with similar — though not necessarily identical — issues. Parents may begin by resolving their own small problem and then see a larger related issue that remains unresolved; they may use the impetus of their own case advocacy to stir other parents to action, or they may join forces with an existing group of parents who are concerned with that larger issue, moving from case advocacy to class advocacy. Finally, parents who have not been satisfied with the results of their own case advocacy may join in a class action of some sort. Or they may be invited to join in a class advocacy suit being brought against a school (or a district) by the state itself.

Cathy Hilton started her advocacy career as the mother of a youngster in a small school system in Ellington, Connecticut. She worked on funding issues, spoke up to resolve a battle between the school board and the town manager, and supported the formation of the Ellington Foundation for the Support of Education.

Hilton also formed an advocacy group, Citizens for Better Education, and published a newsletter aptly named The Squeaky Wheel. *She continued her advocacy work until her family moved to El Cajon, California, a suburb of San Diego. It was there, in a much larger venue, that Hilton says she became really politicized.*

''I realized that there was so little I could do that made any real difference in the quality of children's education. It made me feel angry and helpless to think that we could go to all those meetings and do all that talking and nothing much would come of it.''

But Hilton was not deterred by the size of the problems facing California schools. In addition to persisting in her local efforts as a member — and soon president — of the Cajon Valley PTA, Hilton became an expert in statewide education legislation. She travels regularly to Sacramento to participate in state legislative sessions and lobby for effective education legislation. "I am still trying to turn the PTA around and focus on real goals and objectives rather than fund-raising. There is a growing grass-roots movement of people like myself who are dedicated to making changes even though it sometimes feels as if we aren't making much of a difference. At the same time, I feel parents can make a real difference at the state level, and that the issues relevant to children are growing by leaps and bounds."

Most legal advocates will advise you to exhaust all other methods before you consider formal, legal advocacy — that is, pressing charges against an individual, school, or district. They point out that the vast majority of all advocacy issues are settled informally, and that it may be far more effective and efficient to stand up in front of your school board or city council and state your case than it would be to initiate formal proceedings. But even if you decide that your concerns are best addressed privately, or through nonlegal channels, it's a good idea to have a basic working knowledge of the court systems:

The *federal court system* is divided into three categories:

- U.S. district courts — One or more courts are located in each state. Both civil and criminal cases involving federal laws, the United States Constitution, or diversity of citizenship (residents of different states) are heard in these courts.
- Circuit courts of appeal — When a party chooses to appeal a U.S. district court decision, he or she must go to one of the eleven circuit courts of appeal.
- U.S. Supreme Court — The highest court of appeal, its decisions binding on all lower courts, the Supreme Court decides to hear particular cases in each session because the cases present significant or new issues of broad national importance or because there is a split of authority in the lower courts.

The *state court systems* are different in every state, but they follow a basic pattern that is analogous to the federal system. Though most states do not have two separate trial courts, the following description allows for the different levels *possible* in an individual state.

- District courts — Also known as petty courts or county courts, these are the courts that most of us are familiar with. They deal with nonlitigious matters such as traffic violations, and do not normally seat a jury.

- Superior courts — Also known as trial courts, these courts handle criminal or civil actions.
- Courts of appeal — These courts will handle appeals from both district and superior courts.
- Supreme judicial courts — The highest state courts, analagous to the federal Supreme Court.

Although it does not have federal jurisdiction, the District of Columbia has a court system that often hears government cases that have a bearing on all the states. All court cases are assigned to their geographic home courts, but the decision to go through the federal or state system depends on the legal issues involved. Usually the choice will be very clear. If only a state law has been violated and the litigants are citizens of the same state, then the case should be heard in state court. If both federal and state laws have been violated, it is often up to the advocates to decide which court to use. Most legal experts advise going with the federal system, since federal decisions are binding on the states.

So advocates who are looking for a court decision must decide on the viability of the legal issue as well as its appropriate jurisdiction. Then there are practical considerations like costs, in both money and time, that must be expended. Advocates must consider whether the possible outcome is worth the potential high price. A finding in favor of a parent or child can have several outcomes:

- the law being challenged is changed
- the school (or district or state) violating the law is forced to comply
- a fine is paid to the government
- government funds are withheld until the school (or district or state) complies
- the school (or district or state) is put into receivership by the court until it complies (the courts run the school)
- a monetary award is paid to the individual

Don't forget that individuals do get to carry their cases to the top. In other words, single-case advocacy does not necessarily equate with informal advocacy; in fact, most Supreme Court rulings have been based on individual or small-group cases. But remember, too, that the problem you may choose to address, whether as an individual or in a group, may not call for a Supreme Court ruling. If it does not, you still have substantial opportunity to advocate successfully in a number of other ways.

In 1982, the U.S. Supreme Court ruled on the case involving Amy Rowley, a hearing-impaired Massachusetts child. In elementary school, Amy was given an IEP — an individual education plan, under the federal Education for Handicapped Children Act of 1973. Under the provisions of Amy's IEP she was entitled to the use of a hearing aid, to speech therapy, and to a special tutor every day.

But Amy's parents decided that wasn't enough, and that their daughter also needed a sign-language interpreter in the classroom in order to help her understand what was going on. According to the provision of the EHA, which states that the handicapped child is entitled to the "most appropriate education" possible given his or her situation, the Rowleys argued that Amy was entitled to more intervention than her IEP allowed. The school district, pointing out that Amy was already performing above average in class, disagreed.

The Supreme Court held that the EHA had not been violated, since Amy was already receiving "appropriate" services under her existing IEP. The court further argued that the EHA did not intend to require the "best" education possible, only the "most appropriate." The Rowleys lost their case, although the state of Massachusetts later enacted legislation that enforced a higher standard than those used to judge Amy Rowley's IEP.

There are also criminal court possibilities, especially when corporal offenses by a teacher or administrator are involved. However, most states have placed limitations on the kinds of action that can be taken against public servants such as school personnel. In general, civil and criminal court proceedings are most effectively used as a scare tactic to force schools to comply with advocates' demands. Again, it may be more effective to put pressure on your local officials than to go immediately for a court procedure.

Several states have defined alternative solutions to the court systems, such as the alternative mediation program in Massachusetts, and out-of-court negotiation processes in New York and New Jersey.

4. Create a coalition involving the broadest possible base.

Regardless of whether your issue takes you to court, once you've decided to become an advocate, you may want to join with other like-minded community members. There's no denying the power of numbers when it comes to making a point to a principal or a school board. As a group, parents have more clout — they cast more votes, pay more taxes, have more powerful contacts, and attract more public attention. But how can we find others (parents and/or staff) who agree with our point of view about an issue? Hooking up with other parents who share common interests and concerns is not difficult — in fact, most parents do it often, although not with an eye to forming a formal group.

We can find other interested parents in our children's classrooms, in our neighborhoods, on our playgrounds. We can find them through other organized groups or in social situations. We begin to talk casually about what's going on with our children and discover we share similar concerns. Many special interest advocacy groups seem to form naturally — parents are unhappy with the special education programs their children are receiving, for instance, or parents feel the school board isn't giving their school enough money for computers. They come together over the issue, and then decide to work together toward a solution.

Schools will often cooperate in giving parents the names of other parents, particularly if the issue is one that the school supports, such as organizing parents to lobby for a school crossing guard or a safer playground. In that case, recruitment is easy. You can use school notices, classroom phone lists (which by law will reach only those parents who have agreed to have their names published on such a list), and community bulletin boards to publicize your intention of forming a group. Public service announcements in local newspapers and on the radio are often free. The school cannot give you special interest mailing lists, however, such as the names of parents of special needs students or students who are under disciplinary proceedings, for the obvious reason that it is an invasion of their privacy under the Family Educational Rights and Privacy Act.

Sometimes the potential members of an advocacy group are not known to one another, and it may be in the best interests of the school to keep it that way. If the issue is one with which the school doesn't necessarily agree, or if the principal doesn't want parents involved, parents will have to come up with other ways to find each other; the schools will naturally resist having their own resources used "against" them. Private phone chains and word of mouth can be very effective until a group is organized and can attract members more actively. Public announcements via mail, cable, or local media are still effective ways of attracting interested parents without making use of school facilities.

Don't forget that other public school parents may not be the only interested citizens in the community. Local businesspeople may be very interested in building a coalition to force the establishment of a high school internship curriculum, just as the elderly community may be very supportive of a drive to include intergenerational programs in the schools. Look for the broadest base of support, not the narrowest.

Why form a group? We've already looked at some of the reasons why parents may choose to broaden their concerns beyond those of their child alone — more power, more resources, and more public support. But there are other reasons for forming an advocacy group. The most important has to do with the parents themselves. Creating an advocacy group also means creating a support group. Parents whose children are having problems in school are parents who are under an additional stress, and it always helps to share those stresses with other like-minded adults. Other parents may have come up with some workable solutions that you haven't thought of. Group work also promotes nonlinear thinking — thinking in new ways about a problem that may have been obsessing you until you were unable to think about it at all, let alone creatively — and can certainly lead to the development of a greater number of possible solutions and tactics.

Cambridge's Special Needs Advisory Council is made up of parents of special needs children and school personnel involved in delivering services to those children. The group was formed in the early 1980s as a response to the need for better occupational therapy services in the system. Parents and staff worked together to find a solution to that problem, and then found that they had other issues in common that bore closer attention.

Attendance at the group's monthly meetings waxed and waned depending on the issues at hand. When the state threatened to remove the "maximum feasible benefit" clause from its special education legislation, SNAC members turned out in force to object. On the local level, discrepancies in staffing, transportation to other schools to receive services, and communication with parents have been rallying points for parents and staff alike.

Parents and staff don't always find themselves on the same side of the equation. There was a period when parents felt they needed to meet separately so they could vent complaints about the Bureau of Pupil Services (which provides special education services) without feeling constrained by the presence of staff. But it was soon decided that the group was more effective when it operated as a coalition; parents decided to meet at another time to discuss advocacy issues and support one another's case advocacy efforts.

Support of parents, both for school issues and at home, has always been a priority of SNAC. But it has served as a catalyst for change as well as a support network for its members. The group got the school department to authorize a paid parent liaison position especially for the families of special needs children. The parent liaison works independently of the bureau to provide advocacy, support, and information to all families in the system.

Your school district may have provisions that entitle you to meeting space and time in the school itself, even if it is not thrilled about your existence. You may even be eligible for certain support services such as mailings and newsletter production, as are the parents of special needs children in some states. If your issue is a sensitive one, however, it may be more comfortable for you to work out of a parent's home without feeling constrained by the school environment.

5. Put everything in writing.

Once you've formed your group, you'll want to codify some rules to govern it efficiently. This may not seem worth the effort if your group consists of only two or three parents who want to set up a new math curriculum for gifted students, but it makes things easier, and is certainly a must for groups who are undertaking a major reform effort such as demanding a more up-to-date math curriculum system-wide. Parents will have to divide themselves into subcommittees — one to deal with publicity, one to deal with school committee meetings, one to gather materials, et cetera. Large advocacy groups will have to find some way to raise money, and may find themselves wanting to incorporate formally and establish a separate lobbying arm in order to avoid tax problems. A spokesperson will need to be chosen — hopefully a member of the group with excellent communication skills and no particular ax to grind.

And the group will, at the very least, have to agree on written "by-laws" covering everything from a declaration of the group's focus and intent to a fair means of collecting coffee money. Written clarification of its goals is the best way for the group to define itself, and will prove invaluable once advocacy activities get underway.

6. Develop effective advocacy strategies.

It may be that, once we've joined with other parents, our point of view will need some modification if we are to work with a unified purpose and goal. This represents a watershed for some parents. Many choose not to consider other possible solutions than the one they've chosen, preferring to take the course of action they feel is most appropriate. Any discussion, these parents feel, will dilute their effectiveness. These parents are understandably reluctant to find themselves "co-opted" by a group of people who may be more willing to compromise with authorities — or even co-opted by those authorities themselves.

Still, it's always a good idea to listen to some possible solutions offered by other parents who share the same problem before deciding how to act. It may be that other parents have thought of constructive solutions, or have information that will help you solve your own problem more easily. Certainly other parents will be able to fuel your enthusiasm for your project and offer perspectives that may not have occurred to you.

At the very least, the coalition-building process will put you in touch with other parents or groups who have advocated on behalf of their children in the past, regardless of whether the issue was the same. It may also enable the group to get in touch with professional support, such as an advocacy agency or lawyer, education consultant, or legislator, who is sympathetic and knowledgeable.

Getting other parents to join with you in your advocacy efforts is only part of the publicity job facing you. You'll want to let other members of your community know about your issues so that you can get adjunct support from people who are not members of your advocacy group but agree with your goals. This sort of endorsement can carry a lot of weight if you're going up against an elected school board, for example, or if you're contending with a public safety issue that affects non-school parents, such as that of school bus routes and schedules.

The most potent tool at your disposal is your local media, and you'll want them to know about your scheduled meetings with public officials as well as your goals. You can also use public meetings at which you are not scheduled to speak as a forum for letting people know about your ideas. The most important goal of community education is to bring more people to see that your advocacy efforts are worthwhile, and to let the opposition know that you have a lot of public support behind you.

In 1979, a group of Atlanta individuals and organizations concerned with desegregation, white flight, and quality education for all students formed Atlanta Parents and Public Linked for Education — APPLE Corps. The group now has a thirty-member board, a staff of four (including a paid director), and an extremely high visibility quotient in Atlanta. The group does a lot of publishing: a citizen's guide to Atlanta public schools, a science guide, and a monthly newsletter. They hand out awards and arts grants, sponsor workshops and public forums, and staff a parent resource center.

APPLE Corps gets a great deal of publicity for itself through active fund-raising by members. An Atlanta television station, WAGA-TV, provided them with their brochure, which the city's public schools disseminate by the thousands. But perhaps the single greatest reason for APPLE Corps' familiarity is the organization's logo — a red apple formed from the word apple *dangling from a bright green stem formed by the word* corps. *The design was contributed by a member of the Junior League of Atlanta, the group's founding organization. The eye-catching logo is ubiquitous around Atlanta, and staff member Nancy Hamilton is certain that it is partly responsible for APPLE Corps' effectiveness and popularity among parents, educators, and community members. ''When the logo was designed,'' she says, ''the Junior League insisted that it always be done in red and green, so that people would always notice it. As far as it has been financially possible, that's what we've done.''*

Whatever the level of public awareness of your cause, it should go without saying that you should try to change things pleasantly first. The path of most cooperation and least upheaval should be the first choice of every advocate, whether an individual or a group. That means that abusive, threatening, or hostile behavior is out of the question. Such activity serves no purpose except to polarize the issue further and make any chance of constructive change less likely. Parents need to remember that when they present a problem to a teacher, a principal, or an administrator, they are automatically putting that person on the defensive. Impulsive behavior is the enemy in that sort of situation, and parents, who may have the element of surprise, numbers, and right on their side, must go out of their way to present their case in the most palatable way possible.

Think about how you feel when you go in for a teacher conference: If the teacher immediately attacks your child's performance on every level and, without offering any advice on how to improve it, demands that you do something about it, chances are you'll stalk out of that classroom. At the very least you'll be upset and disappointed and not prepared to do your best thinking. You'll respond defensively, angrily, and your child's problems will not be addressed. If, on the other hand, the teacher starts out by telling you about your child's strong points before going on to the areas in which he or she needs improvement (and asks for your input in finding ways for that improvement to be achieved), you'll be much more likely to leave the conference determined to do your part to help both the teacher and your child.

Parents, like education professionals, need to understand the basics of interpersonal communication:

- Start with something positive.
- Present the weaknesses without being accusatory.
- Offer constructive possibilities for solving them.

When meeting with school officials to advocate on behalf of a child or a group of children, then, it's important to remember the following steps:

- Maintain your narrow focus, and stick to whatever plan of action you or your group has adopted.
- Maintain cordiality as much as possible.
- Attack the issue, not the people behind it.
- Enlist the assistance and expertise of objective professionals wherever possible.
- Be flexible in considering workable solutions.
- Be vigilant in pursuing your goal.

When meetings in good faith fail to bring about the desired changes, or an acceptable compromise, it's time to take the gloves off. That doesn't mean you can get nasty, just that you have to begin to throw a little more weight behind your cause. It may be time to go over the head of the local principal or superintendent. Here, too, there are predictable steps you can take on the path to resolving the differences between the two sides. While federal laws of due process and free speech provide important protection for advocates, state and local laws vary widely. It's imperative to know your local grievance and complaint procedures, starting with those enabling you to file a complaint against your own school authorities, assistant superintendents, superintendents, the school board, and beyond. A clearly written description of your local district's grievance policies should be made available to all families attending school. If not, you can get one by calling your school department and asking for a copy in your native language.

Most school systems have carefully delineated procedures for such grievances, including allowances for the presentation of both sides of the issue, "witnesses" supporting each side, and, in some cases, public input to determine a fair conclusion. Remember, of course, that these "legal" opportunities are often balanced out by legal constraints against the kinds of changes that can be made as a result of advocacy. There are laws in every state limiting the kinds of action that can be taken by a private group toward a public institution such as a school system, and school personnel are similarly protected from private suit in many cases (this does not include criminal proceedings). If you come up against a legal wall, grievance procedures will do you no good, and you may have to set about changing the local, state, or even federal law that prohibits such changes.

Kathleen Boundy is a lawyer with the Cambridge-based Center for Law and Education, a watchdog agency that monitors and advises individuals and schools around the country on issues of education law. Boundy says there are very clear instances when formal legal strategies are not productive, and when, as she says, ''it's probably more effective to go and scream to your local school committee.''

She points to stipulations in the federal school records protection legislation (FERPA) that make it virtually impossible for a single individual to make a private complaint against a system for violating education rights. Complaints must be made on a class or group basis. But federal special education legislation does allow formal complaints to be registered by individuals. It all depends on the way the legislation has been written.

Tracking — the practice of determining a child's academic ability early on and placing him or her in classes with other children of similar ability — is another example of a legal limbo. Despite copious research proving that tracking is detrimental to both low- and high-achieving students, and that mixed-ability grouping is far more effective for all groups, there is no state or federal legislation barring its use in public schools — and it is widespread. ''There's nothing in the way of formal advocacy that can be done in a case like that,'' says Boundy. ''The only legal recourse would be to work to get such legislation on the books.''

The vast majority of case and class advocacy suits never get beyond the grievance procedure. A workable compromise is usually achieved at the school level, or the school board, recognizing the power of potentially damaging publicity, will go out of its way to resolve the problem. School board members, after all, are usually elected officials, or else they are appointed by elected officials; and they have a vested interest in protecting their constituency.

It certainly helps to have someone on your team who has good negotiating skills; a lawyer or professional advocate would be an excellent choice, even though you may not need official representation yet. If a member of your group seems to have natural bargaining and diplomacy skills, he or she would be a good representative, but most advocates say it's always a good idea to have a professional along, if only on an advisory basis.

If you are representing yourself, or if your group does not have the services of an advocate or lawyer, you'll need to learn the jargon of the officials. Often misunderstandings over terms can be at the root of serious disputes between parents and school personnel. In fact, most states now have laws demanding that all pertinent information (testing procedures, special needs evaluations, school regulations) be provided in a manner that is clear and comprehensible to parents; you have the right to ask for clarification of any term you don't understand.

Parents who are representing themselves must also learn the most effective way to deal with school personnel, and select the most effective person to do it. Will a forceful, knowledgeable person be more valuable than an even-headed, persuasive diplomat? The phrase ''know thy enemy'' does little justice to the integrity of school personnel, but it makes a lot of sense when you have to go up against an institutionalized policy and an entrenched mind-set.

Funding is a big issue for advocacy groups. Where are you going to get the money for all this work? You can raise it within the group or solicit money from other parents. There may be existing groups that can help you out financially — businesses that want to see student apprenticeship programs go through, or local colleges that want to help with a textbook drive. Tax exemption status, so that persons may make charitable donations, is a possibility for those groups that choose to incorporate as a nonprofit corporation, and it may be attractive to do so just to get those extra donation dollars. However, nonprofit corporations may not engage in lobbying activities. And don't forget the extra paperwork involved.

Advocacy groups must remember that their most powerful tool is their voice. Lobbying — actively presenting one's point of view in order to persuade others to adopt it — can keep even the thorniest advocacy issue out of the courts by convincing those in charge that it is in the best interests of all concerned to make changes. Part public education, part advocacy, and part pure entertainment, effective lobbying cannot be underestimated at any point in the advocacy process. You can lobby local officials on your own, in person or by phone, stating your views clearly and concisely and using your particular situation to support your points. In addition, you or your advocacy group can attend public hearings or rallys to let your views be known. Singly or in groups, advocates can lobby local, state, and federal lawmakers. Perhaps even more important, you can lobby your own community and the public at large to raise awareness about important issues. (More on lobbying later in this chapter.)

7. Monitor the results carefully.

It is of paramount importance to stay on top of whatever changes your advocacy program has achieved. If you have been successful in bringing about changes in your child's school, or in the entire school district, you and your group will need to make sure those changes are being implemented. If you have reached a compromise of some sort with the schools, you'll need to monitor the changes that do get made to make sure they fulfill your requirements as laid out by that compromise. And, if you have been unsuccessful, you'll need to remain even more vigilant, collecting more material that might help you reinstate your advocacy claims. Let's say you felt that your child's school building was unsafe, and you had been unsuccessful in getting the city to agree. You would need to continue collecting data on safety issues, organizing a phone chain to report broken windows or crumbling stairs and a committee to verify those faults. You would also have to lobby for more community support, and work on getting local officials to change their minds by presenting the mounting evidence along with evidence of mounting community support for the renovation or reconstruction of the building.

Whatever the outcome, advocates cannot assume that a given situation, having gotten out of control in the first place, will be set to rights without constant vigilance. Once advocates have been successful, their very presence is regarded more seriously by school personnel. Even if their initial efforts have failed, advocates who have gone about their task in a constructive way usually find that they carry a lot of weight around their local school district. It's gratifying to find that not only is the initial subject of the advocacy effort resolved, but other issues are given more immediate attention because parents are so clearly a presence in the successful operation of the school.

WHAT PARENTS CAN DO

Once the basics of advocacy are understood and established, parents and parents' groups can effectively address everything from a problem with one student-teacher relationship to the implementation of new legislation for entire systems.

New legislation can mandate institutional changes, offer funding to support that change, or provide a combination of both authority and assistance to local education agencies. While the lion's share of the responsibilities for educating our children lies with our school districts, it is important to understand that the states and the federal government do have some powers to help us improve our local schools. It is within the legal powers of the states to

- increase choice across districts;
- equalize funding between districts;
- coordinate fragmented programs;
- decentralize management of local schools;
- mandate parent involvement in decision making.

The U.S. Department of Education can:

- guarantee the right of equal opportunity to all children;
- authorize and subsidize school improvement programs;
- administrate all federal education laws;
- dispense federal moneys to all local education agencies eligible for compensatory and other federally funded education programs;
- establish policies and standards that must be met in order for those local agencies to qualify for funding;
- invite parents to participate in all education legislation;
- develop a nationally coordinated effort to get parental involvement on all school agendas;
- develop and disseminate publications on promising school programs;
- support research and demonstration projects to improve schools;
- promote teacher and administrator training;
- support the clearinghouse and networking efforts of parent groups.

How can you get your state and federal authorities to act on their powers? You can make a big difference even at this "macro" level. You can lobby for state or federal legislation. You can present legislation or propose specific regulations that clarify or interpret existing legislation. You can press for enforcement and monitor implementation. You can also, in extreme circumstances, file litigation against the state or federal government to force them to comply with existing or newly established laws.

Let's be more specific and itemize the options for legislative advocacy in the order in which they might be undertaken.

1. You can form a coalition based geographically or on special interests. Spread the net as wide as you can to attract the attention of groups who may share your concerns. Communicate via letters, telephone, computers — any way to get the word out and to open lines of communication. Congressional leaders love the phrase "grass roots." Keep your coalition low-key but broad based, whether you're working on a statewide redistricting plan or on a nationwide curriculum standards bill.

2. You can contact elected officials early on to let them know who you are and what you're doing. Try to gain their interest and support before you need to win their vote. Their support will enable you to broaden your base and win clout among other legislators.

3. You can make your votes count. Let legislators know how many people are concerned with the same issue as you — and how many of them vote. Get non–public school parents involved in your cause. Counteract the influence peddling of powerful lobbyists by reminding legislators that your votes keep them in office.

4. You can create a lobby of your own. Lobbying has earned an almost mythic status in state and federal governments, but what makes great lobbyists a success is really just a matter of organization and persistence. It's not necessary to establish luxurious offices and million-dollar budgets to attract the attention and respect of lawmakers. They will be willing to listen to anyone who represents a well-defined population with specific interests to pursue.

The ethics of lobbying, however, require some thought. It's one thing to persuade your legislator to support your project on its own merits. It's another to wheel and deal votes as if they were monopoly properties, and yet another to offer your legislator some form of persuasion in return for his or her vote. It is for this reason that there are laws prohibiting lobbies from tax-exempt status. If your group is tax-exempt, you will have to form a separate group to do your lobbying or risk the loss of public funding.

Learn lobbying skills. Identify who to talk to and how to talk to them. Start with a list of your local state senators and representatives. Get to know aides and staff directors who may be able to help your cause from within. Target the appropriate subcommittees for special attention. Determine how legislation is enacted or amended. Use your success with one branch of government (judicial, legislative, executive) to influence the others, and your success with one legislator to influence others.

All a good lobbyist needs is a sound working knowledge of the legislative body he or she plans to work with, a complete grasp of the details and options of the group's programs and goals, and a pleasant, persuasive manner of speaking. Good bookkeeping and careful record keeping are also imperative. An accessible office near the legislature is important as a center of operations and to lend legitimacy to your efforts, but it is not a prerequisite. A large network of parents willing to make phone calls, write letters, and show up at hearings makes any lobbyist's argument much more persuasive. You can also work to counteract other lobbies with interests other than yours. This may mean the teachers unions or religious groups, the computer industry, or the National Rifle Association.

5. You can make maximum use of the media to publicize your cause and make legislators aware of the fruits of those efforts. Have group members write letters to legislators. Employ the most effective spokespersons you have. Get advice from people who have legislative experience, and make sure you understand the language of legislation.

6. You can work with other groups who have interests complementary to your own. Many possibilities exist for piggybacking and coalition building to increase your power. Be flexible and be willing to broaden the range of your group's efforts if it means you can connect with a larger, more powerful group.

7. You can propose solutions. Write legislation! Work with legislators to draft bills in appropriate language. Choose the most auspicious time and place to introduce your bill — and the most effective legislator to sponsor it. Make sure the bill carefully targets the problem and leaves no loopholes. Work any possible opposition into the legislation itself to diffuse criticism. Make sure the bill allows for plenty of parental involvement at every stage. Make sure an appropriations figure goes along with the bill — legislation often authorizes expenditures without appropriating money to underwrite them, effectively destroying the bill. Keep your bill afloat with plenty of public exposure and constant lobbying.

8. You can make it work. Monitor implementation by working with the agency assigned to carry out the regulations authorized by the bill. The "regs" govern the conditions under which funding can be disbursed. Although government agencies are responsible for the regs, public input is invited. Make sure that an education component accompanies the bill that allows for education of the professionals who will be responsible for providing the new programs as well as for the families who will be affected by it. Set up a continuing coalition to help affected families make the most of the new bill, offering information, advice, and advocacy services. Act as a watchdog agency and initiate class action lawsuits to enforce rights that have been abused.

9. You can keep working. Along with working for your share of the pie, work to increase the size of the pie itself. Join a coalition of groups dedicated to a systematic and successful redirection of the flow of government funding to state and local education agencies.

WHEN THE DOORS WON'T OPEN

The prospect of successful advocacy sounds great, but what about parents who can't get beyond the front door? There are some parents who feel that the schools won't listen to them, or that other parents don't seem to be interested or willing to commit to their interest. All too often these are minority or low-income parents — parents who by virtue of their ethnic, racial, or economic background feel disenfranchised from the system. While all parents report some difficulties in working with the system in order to change it, minority parents have special problems; they may have cultural biases against intervening, a lack of time/money to do so, a lack of broad support, or a fear that voicing their concerns will exacerbate their alienation. But their goals are just as legitimate and worthy of attention as those of parents who are more adept at speaking out and are more likely to be heard.

If other parents don't include the nonadvantaged in their dialogues, it's clear that the schools will not either. But when parents do band together to address these important issues, the results can be far-reaching.

In 1988, citizens of Muskegon, Michigan, a small multiracial city on the western shores of Lake Michigan, went before their local school board. Over the course of several intense meetings, the group, which called itself the Citizens Alliance for Racial Equity in Education (CARE), had determined a well-defined agenda that they felt the Muskegon public schools needed to address. Their issues included:

- *increasing hiring of minority teachers*
- *creating minority scholarships*
- *establishing a multicultural curriculum committee*
- *bringing racial balance to the elementary schools*
- *commemorating Dr. Martin Luther King's birthday*

After months of meetings between CARE and the Schools and Teachers Committee of the board of education, some progress in each of those areas was achieved. Nine out of thirty-five professional positions were filled by minorities, who also comprised one quarter of all newly hired staff. A multicultural curriculum committee was established and recommendations were made for the observance of Dr. King's birthday.

No visible efforts were made, however, to redress the racial balance of the schools. CARE took the school board to task for blaming the segregated schools on segregated neighborhoods, and publicized their views in school meetings, newspaper articles, and CARE-published status reports. They also threatened legal action to force the schools to integrate if other measures were not taken.

By 1990, CARE had reorganized and rebroadcast its agenda. The new agenda called for measures to

- *promote minority professionals to administrative positions in majority (i.e., mostly white) schools*
- *defuse tracking programs that promote bigotry and disrupt the function of education*
- *hire a minority male counselor at the high school to address the needs of young minority males*
- *provide more support services to elementary schools with large at-risk populations*

CARE also demanded that the school board, since it persisted in organizing its elementary schools along racial and socioeconomic lines, provide additional resources to minority schools so that they would have an equitable opportunity for quality education. And in publicizing their agenda, CARE called on the entire community to play a vital role in promoting equality and quality in Muskegon's public schools.

Betty Harris James, of the Appalachia Educational Laboratory in Charleston, West Virginia, has compiled a powerful set of questions that address some of the real barriers to effective nonadvantaged parent involvement in the public schools. They are questions parents should ask themselves when considering their options for advocacy in their community. James's answers, paraphrased in parentheses following the questions, are based on extensive research on the subject, but she urges parents to come up with their own as well.

1. Is there a perception in the community that school personnel do not understand or respect the minority or nonadvantaged community? (Parents feel their basic attitudes are not considered, so the programs devised to "help" them are not valued.)
2. Why are minorities unwilling to accept the statements that teachers and researchers issue as explanations of why nonadvantaged students are not successful in academic settings? (These answers often presume a basic inequality or genetic deficiency that invalidates the conclusions.)
3. Are there specific examples of why minority and/or nonadvantaged parents do not participate in school activities? (School personnel tend to refute such arguments by defending their individual nonracist attitudes, ignoring the larger problem.)
4. How problematic are the cultural differences in language styles between minorities or nonadvantaged communities and school personnel? (Differences in style of communication and in cross-cultural communication rules result in minorities feeling powerless and condescended to.)
5. Is there a difference between parent involvement and parent/community involvement? (The focus is narrower in the former; it is more easily managed by school personnel; it is focused around the school building and school day; parents become adjuncts to school personnel.)

If you determine that nonadvantaged and/or minority parents are being excluded from the reform process in your area, you can begin to bridge the gap by having representatives of such groups on all councils, calling individuals in to discuss particular concerns, organizing "focus groups" to establish the relevant issues, and involving members of each group in activities. It is crucial to the children we hope to serve that all voices be heard.

MOVING INTO THE LARGER ARENA

Parent advocates who have been successful may make themselves available to parent groups with other interests who may need basic advocacy-skill instruction or need to learn their way around the local power structure. Skilled former advocates can explain the workings of a school committee meeting or reveal which members of the city council can be approached in person and which need to be addressed in formal meetings. They can even serve as expert assistants or provide testimony in negotiation procedures.

Advocacy groups may become resource centers for alternative services or for individuals with case advocacy needs. They may provide the single mother of four with help to complete the paperwork needed to get reduced-price meals for her children in school. They may offer parents of special needs students a list of independent evaluators if those parents are unsatisfied with the results of a school diagnostic workup. If they have been effective fund-raisers, they may provide a clearinghouse for money needed to pursue other advocacy goals. They may work to include non–public school citizens in broader education issues, bringing them in on income-distribution debates or new school bond issues. In fact, community members who do not have a direct stake in the daily functioning of the schools may prove to be the most effective voices in any advocacy group, and every effort should be made to include them.

Once an advocate, always an advocate. Parents who have gone beyond the bake-sale or parent-conference level of involvement in their children's education find it hard to go back to the hands-off policy they may have previously followed. It *is* important to know when to stop advocating and let the system work effectively on its own. But when the system breaks down not even apparent failure can stand in the way of an effective parent advocacy program.

In the fall of 1972, a group of parents from all parts of Philadelphia banded together in a response to a three-month-long teachers strike. They formed the Parents Union for Public Schools and brought suit against the teachers union, charging that their action was illegal because it prevented children from obtaining their legally mandated public education.

They lost the suit, but have been going strong ever since, providing Philadelphia-area parents with information, technical assistance, and support around school issues. The Parents Union has been involved in the negotiations for all subsequent strikes or near-strikes. They got the school district to adopt a Parents' Bill of Rights and Responsibilities as well as a district-wide school handbook. They have been responsible for the replacement of a district superintendent and several school board members, with whom they meet on a regular basis.

The union is also involved on the state level, joining with other groups to examine and advise on district budgets and state education legislation. They have received a federal grant for special education parent training. Parent organizers present workshops to parents on local and district-wide issues such as standardized curriculum and new promotion policies, and to individual parents on a case advocacy basis.

Members are elected from local school areas to serve on the executive committee and the union's board of directors, and all parents of Philadelphia public school children are eligible to become members.

We can use the concept of a unified parent lobbying group, whose concerns go beyond the individual school and even the local school district, as a model for new parent activism in the nineties. But while broad-based advocacy is important, don't underestimate the power of one "hysterical" or "appropriately aggressive" parent. A single advocate, working on behalf of a single child, can bring about monumental changes in every public school system in the country.

HOW TO: Organize for Effective Group Action

Once an advocacy group is formed, and action is being taken, it may seem as if there are no other problems to contend with. But keeping a group together and operating smoothly takes some skill. The following outline, portions of which are adapted from *Parents Organizing to Improve Schools* (published by the NCCE in 1985), is an excellent tool to help you ensure that your group is operating efficiently.

Step I. Identifying Problems

1. List the most pressing problems at your school.
2. Select one problem to zero in on and agree to work as a group to solve one problem at a time, using the following criteria:
   a. Is it a problem that is urgent in the school?
   b. Is it a problem that unites the parents in the group?
   c. Is it a problem that this group of parents can do something about?
   d. Is it a problem that interests each member?
   e. Is it a problem that is OK for each member to work on?
   f. Is it a problem that is soluble in a reasonable period of time?
   g. Is the problem a symptom or a root cause of low-quality education?

Step II. Gathering Information

1. Find out what the community thinks of the problem.
2. Find out what, if anything, has been done already to resolve the problem.
3. Find out the most appropriate school personnel to talk to about the problem.
4. Find out what other groups have done about the problem.

Step III. Setting the Action Goals

1. Agree on what you want changed.
2. Agree on when you want it changed.

3. Make sure group is clear on why goal should be pursued.
4. Is goal specific enough to produce results?
5. Assign fact-finding jobs
   a. get specifics
   b. get documentation
   c. get input from school officials

Step IV. Creating a Coalition

1. Contact everyone who might be interested in your goal.
2. Talk to people who might have different solutions.
3. Work together to determine your real issues.
4. Resolve internal conflicts first.
5. Put your goals in writing.
6. Leave your group open to others — be flexible.

Step V. Planning Strategies

1. Refer back to fact-finding to make sure your information is correct.
2. Refer back to goals to stay on course.
3. Discuss alternative courses of action and decide on which would be best.
4. Develop short-range plans in concrete steps
   a. assign specific people to specific tasks
   b. use people in role they are best suited for
   c. give specific time frame
5. Develop reporting strategy so information can be shared
6. Develop longer-range plans with more generalized steps

Step VI. Evaluating

1. Self-evaluation
   a. How well did group function as a group?
   b. Is everyone in agreement within the group?
   c. What was handled well by the group?
   d. What mistakes were made?
2. Goal evaluation
   a. What did the group do that was effective?
   b. What compromises were made?
   c. What monitoring procedures are in place?
   d. What else can the group do in this or other areas?

HOW TO: Design a School Checklist (*from Parents United for the DC Public Schools*)

A PARENT'S CHECKLIST OF _____

(school name)

My School	N.A.	Don't Know	OK Job	Con-cerned
Staffing				
1. has appropriate numbers of certified staff	_____	_____	_____	_____
2. has unfilled positions existing more than 2 weeks	_____	_____	_____	_____
3. has adequate nurse and athletic trainer coverage	_____	_____	_____	_____
4. has a psychologist	_____	_____	_____	_____
5. has appropriate numbers of counselors	_____	_____	_____	_____
6. has a librarian	_____	_____	_____	_____
7. has an attendance officer	_____	_____	_____	_____
8. has adequate substitute teacher coverage	_____	_____	_____	_____
9. invovles parents in teacher evaluations	_____	_____	_____	_____
10. involves parents in hiring teachers	_____	_____	_____	_____
Programs/Classes				
1. has a well-stocked library and adequate space and facilities	_____	_____	_____	_____
2. has an average class size appropriate to the grade level and discipline taught	_____	_____	_____	_____
3. offers music as part of the curriculum	_____	_____	_____	_____
4. offers art as part of the curriculum	_____	_____	_____	_____

5. offers physical education as part of the curriculum   ____   ____   ____   ____

6. offers foreign language as part of the curriculum   ____   ____   ____   ____

7. offers science as part of the curriculum   ____   ____   ____   ____

8. offers courses that are comparable in scope and sequence to other schools in the district   ____   ____   ____   ____

9. has special reading teachers   ____   ____   ____   ____

10. has special math teachers   ____   ____   ____   ____

11. has gifted and talented programs   ____   ____   ____   ____

12. has many students assigned to remedial or special education   ____   ____   ____   ____

13. has before and/or after school programs   ____   ____   ____   ____

14. is responsive to the needs of my child   ____   ____   ____   ____

Books and Materials

1. has adequate numbers of text-books in good condition   ____   ____   ____   ____

2. has current and appropriate textbooks   ____   ____   ____   ____

3. has appropriate audiovisual and copying equipment (VCRs, TVs, computers, et cetera) that is in good condition   ____   ____   ____   ____

Buildings and Grounds

1. has a good roof (does not leak)   ____   ____   ____   ____

2. has inside walls in good repair   ____   ____   ____   ____

3. has floors in good repair   ____   ____   ____   ____

4. has window frames and panes in good repair   ____   ____   ____   ____

5. has outside doors that operate and shut properly   ____   ____   ____   ____

6. has good safe playground areas   ____   ____   ____   ____

Climate for Parents

1. is receptive to parent involvement   ____   ____   ____   ____

2. has formal parent-teacher
   meetings   _____   _____   _____   _____
3. routinely provides information
   on classroom activities, topics
   covered, and teacher
   expectations   _____   _____   _____   _____
4. routinely provides information
   on school and individual
   student achievement   _____   _____   _____   _____
5. has a strong and effective
   parent organization   _____   _____   _____   _____

General

1. is providing a satisfactory
   educational experience for my
   child   _____   _____   _____   _____

PART II

Issues

Teachers and Administrators

*I*N the 1930s, any prospective applicant to teach in southern public schools had to sign a contract obliging her "to get at least eight hours of sleep while maintaining a healthy diet, and to consider herself at all times a willing servant of the school board and the townspeople." She had to promise not to go out dancing, not to dress immodestly, and "not to fall in love, become engaged, or secretly married." And she was in better shape than her counterpart in seventeenth-century America, who was often offered for sale as an indentured servant!

Teachers have come a long way since then, but there remains a residual sense that the men and women who teach at the elementary and secondary school level chose that career because they were unable to do anything more challenging. As Tracy Kidder says in his book *Among Schoolchildren*, "There is a modern stereotype — it has not been quantified, but every teacher knows about it — that depicts teachers as numbskulls who work short hours, get long vacations, do lousy jobs, and then walk picket lines whining about how badly they are treated."

Just how far off the mark is this popular misconception? Let's look at some current statistics concerning today's public school teachers and see. There are over two and a half million elementary and secondary school teachers, about 70 percent of whom are women. Their median age is 41. Three quarters of them are white, married, and have at least five years' teaching experience. Their average annual salary is a little over $28,000 per year, and 78 percent of them say they work over 40 hours a week to earn it.

More than half of U.S. public school teachers have at least a master's degree. Over 90 percent of them responded to the question "Why did you become a teacher?" by answering "Because I wanted to help children grow and learn." And over a quarter of them say they are likely to leave the profession to go into some other occupation within the next five years. Yet six out of ten American adults agree that one particular teacher made an important difference in their lives through his or her individual attention and concern. These statistics, and others given here, were provided by the National Education Association–published Research/Gallup opinion polls (spring 1987) and by the U.S. Department of Education's *Digest of Educational Statistics* (1989 edition).

Teachers may not be the indentured servants they were generations ago, but they certainly don't get the respect they deserve. And yet we expect our children's teachers to provide them with an education sufficient to send them out into the world prepared for college or for demanding careers. We ask that they provide counseling, discipline, socialization skills, and loving attention — all according to our own personal visions of how they should be provided. We expect them to amplify our own dreams for our children, and to provide them with the means to attain those dreams. We invest our faith in their ability to give our children the tools they'll need to succeed, even if we ourselves don't have those tools, or don't know how to pass them on.

Teachers are closer to parents on the power pyramid (see Chapter 3) than any other group. Unfortunately, neither teachers nor parents have yet recognized that by forming a coalition with one another, they could become a major power force. Parents and teachers are the only groups who have daily contact with children — the only groups who are directly responsible and directly answerable for an individual child's success. That fact alone should help us to overcome real and perceived barriers and join forces to work toward increased decision-making power in the schools.

But the barriers are strong. Why, for instance, do we demand so much of our teachers and administrators, yet refuse to honor their efforts with monetary and/or social rewards? Why are teachers feeling so put upon by society, and parents so betrayed by teachers? Why are administrators perpetuating a bureaucracy they know is counterproductive and resisting change at the expense of their staffs and students?

There are several possible answers to questions such as these. Teacher training programs are outdated and lack the means to provide teachers with the real tools needed to teach today. Control of schools and classrooms is bifurcated so that teachers are forced to operate in a frustrating vacuum. Teachers unions have grown to such great proportions, and become so politicized, that they are in danger of not responding to the needs and demands of their members. And above all, parents and teachers suffer from inappropriate perceptions of one another that make their respective jobs all the more difficult to carry out.

THE MAKING OF A TEACHER

The sad truth is that in recent years we have been attracting fewer prospective teachers than ever into our teacher training programs, and those who do come are being drawn from among the bottom quarter of all prospective students. According to Emily Feistritzer of the National Center for Education Statistics, the number of entrants into American teacher training programs dropped by 33 percent in the decade from 1976 to 1986. In that same period, the number of teaching program graduates dropped 53 percent, while the number of medical degrees rose by 74 percent, engineering degrees by 90 percent, and law degrees by more than 100 percent.

More recently there has been a reversal of this pattern, with teacher training program enrollment soaring in the years 1986–88. But as school budgets enter into fiscal shock, teachers all over the country are being laid off or not hired in the first place, which is very discouraging to prospective teacher candidates. Continuing math, science, and special education teacher shortages are being met by moving other tenured teachers into those classrooms rather than hiring new teachers who may have specialized in those fields.

Economic reality is, of course, the simplest explanation for the teacher drain: despite crowded classrooms, the demand for teachers has dropped over 14 percent in the past twelve years. Moreover, as other careers become available to women, who traditionally make up the majority of our teachers, there will naturally be a drop in teacher training program enrollment. But there are also more personal economic realities behind the decision to stay out of teaching programs: teaching simply doesn't pay enough to attract the best students. We are also having trouble attracting qualified minority students to teach in our increasingly multiracial and multiethnic schools, and so we have an even more severe shortage of well-trained minority applicants in our urban schools, where such teachers are vitally needed.

Admission into teacher training programs has traditionally been a poorly defined process. Most would-be teachers attend at least two years of college before enrolling in a teacher training program, but some programs take students right out of high school while others require a four-year college degree. There is no standardized preadmissions test such as those for law school and most graduate school programs, so many teacher colleges simply devise their own, if they require any examination at all.

But foggy admissions procedures are only the beginning of the confusion. The process of teaching prospective teachers how to teach is one of the most poorly defined tasks undertaken by American colleges. And no wonder: Teachers have no absolutes to go on in terms of *how* they teach. We can give our teachers plenty of curriculum guidance — that is, we can tell them exactly what we want them to teach our children, and exactly how we are going to measure our children's progress — but we can't tell them how to impart this information successfully. Consequently, teacher training curricula emphasize content over method, giving our teachers knowledge without giving them the skills to impart that knowledge.

Education research, what little there is of it, is naturally inconclusive about what makes a successful teacher. Part of the reason for that is legitimate — we don't know how children learn, so it is difficult to tell our teachers how best to teach them. Even if we could, children learn in so many different ways that we would have to teach our teachers many different methods in order to render them able to cope with all the children in their classes. But there's another reason, says Stanford University education professor Myron Atkin: Teachers are often cut off from education research. "When teachers are denied major roles in research," he writes, "they are taught . . . that worthwhile innovation comes from outside the schools. [But] certain knowledge is available only to people who work within a system." Researchers who have never taught in an elementary classroom are not going to come up with viable solutions to problems such as how to teach a subject more effectively, how to handle disciplinary issues, or how to manage communications with parents. By involving teachers directly in the process, researchers can draw on real experience to develop theories and evaluate their impact on the classroom.

At California's Grover City Elementary School, the principal and teachers are working closely with university professors and student teachers from the California Polytechnic Institute in nearby San Luis Obispo. The innovative program attempts to put education teachers right out there in the public schools so that the information they impart to their students is relevant to the real world of the classroom.

Unlike student-teaching components in most teaching colleges, the CPI student-teaching module involves the student teacher's supervisor from the university in the public school classroom. Suggestions on how to deal with curriculum issues or specific students flow both ways — from the classroom teacher to the student teacher and from the university professor to the classroom teacher. Perhaps even more importantly, the classroom teachers get to provide input to the university professor on what really works in the classroom.

These suggestions are being brought back to the university level, where courses are being redesigned with an eye to making them more relevant, thereby preparing prospective teachers to be better equipped in the classrooms. The project is one of several in California and other states that are attempting to put teacher training programs and public schools together in order to improve both. In a similar program in Seattle, University of Washington faculty members are working with Seattle public school teachers to redesign the teaching courses at the university. In an even more dramatic departure from the usual teacher training schedule, where students don't go into classrooms until the end of their training, UW student teachers go into the middle schools in Seattle and begin working with public school teachers there before they've taken any classes on campus.

At the moment, there is more resistance to suggested changes by school administrators than by university teachers. Some school districts don't like working with student teachers, and some prefer to use their own in-house experts rather than those from the teaching colleges, who they see as not having relevant information to offer. But college and university faculty agree that working with their local schools is the only way to train teachers to deal with the real-life issues that will arise once they get into the classroom.

Even with plenty of practical training, there is no guarantee that a graduate of a teacher training program will be a better teacher than someone without formal training. That's because teaching is something of an art, dependent on the personality of the teacher and the "chemistry" between teacher and students. Each teacher brings into the classroom his or her own values, strengths, and experiences. And once there, today's teachers are largely left to their own devices, for better or for worse. Teachers get little feedback from other teachers or even from administrators simply because those professionals are locked into their own classrooms and offices, isolated from one another by the rigors of the daily schedule. What little planning time there is is usually spent frantically Xeroxing, grading, or preparing for the next class, leaving no time for teachers to bounce ideas and concerns off one another.

Such isolation wouldn't be so terrible if all teachers came naturally equipped to handle the problems of all children. But as the student population diversifies, and as education itself becomes technologically more complex, that is no longer even a remote possibility. Teachers have to cope with children of all sorts, not only "average" kids who learn in different styles, but malnourished kids, kids who do not speak English at home, kids with behavior or learning problems, gifted kids, and kids with unlimited combinations of the above.

Attempts are being made to address these issues, at least to sensitize our teachers so that they can spot the differences in their students. But how can we educate our teachers to be able to deal with such a vast educational, cultural, and social diversity when we can't even figure out how to teach them to teach to the "average"? These days, says education researcher Joyce Epstein of Johns Hopkins University's Center for Research on Elementary and Middle Schools, "You can't just teach a teacher how to teach math — you have to teach him or her how to deal with families about math education. We can impart knowledge, not skill. Sensitization, like teaching itself, is a difficult skill to teach."

There's yet another obstacle to be overcome. Assuming that we can equip our teachers to go into the classroom with the appropriate skills, we still have to get them certified by the state in which they teach. Unfortunately, there is no centralized certification procedure, and the requirements vary wildly, even within states. Some states have virtually no requirements, while others have dauntingly complex procedures.

Many states do have teacher competency tests and in-service training (programs that teachers who are already teaching must attend to maintain certification) to be fulfilled. But in times of severe teacher shortages — such as is expected to hit the United States in the mid-1990s — statewide certification exams often fall by the wayside in favor of hiring warm bodies to fill empty classrooms. Even more problematic is the fact that each state operates in isolation, and qualified teachers are discouraged from moving from state to state because of the need to take additional exams. Only recently, for instance, did seven northeastern states enact a reciprocal certification agreement.

The lack of a unified standard for certification is a problem that has educators as worried as parents. American Federation of Teachers union leader Albert Shanker, among others, has proposed a national certification exam to be developed by a National Board for Professional Teaching Standards by 1992. But educators warn that a standard exam, while it will go a long way toward simplifying and professionalizing the teacher certification process, cannot be used as the sole source of certification. After all, the exam will still emphasize curriculum mastery over teaching style, which can only be observed in the classroom. Interestingly, while 77 percent of all adults in a recent Gallup poll indicated that they felt rigorous exams for prospective teachers would improve the quality of teaching in American public schools, only 41 percent of teachers responding felt the same way.

On the other hand, the certification process itself may be a barrier to hiring effective teachers when they are needed. Several states are experimenting with options that circumvent the traditional certification process without sacrificing quality controls of any sort. Having new teachers train for a year under a master teacher is one alternative to traditional certification methods that is gaining respect in several states.

At Boston's Wheelock College, a hundred-year-old teachers college, a 1987 program that provided for intensive interaction between teaching students and working teachers has become a model for other school systems around the country. The program sends Wheelock students into public schools in Boston and in the nearby suburb of Brookline, where they work in a classroom full-time while earning a master's degree at Wheelock.

Each student is monitored by a core planning group comprising the school principal, a veteran classroom teacher (known as the collaborating teacher), and professors from Wheelock. Student teachers work with collaborating teachers all year long, learning everything from how to set up a classroom — something most teacher training programs never teach — to how to conduct parent-teacher conferences.

A modest stipend is provided to the collaborating teacher and principal, and the student teacher is paid as an intern. The college also offers accredited workshops for teachers who want to become collaborators or mentor teachers to students. Wheelock justifies its interest in the collaborative programs with a quote from educator John Goodlad: "The juxtaposition of the action-oriented culture of the school and the inquiry-oriented culture of the university offers promise of shaking loose the calcified programs of both."

Another solution that is getting a lot of attention is the alternative certification process being tested in New Jersey, Massachusetts, New York, and California. Alternative certification — hiring professionals from other disciplines to teach without requiring them to attend traditional training programs — is an explosive subject in education today. The unions, naturally enough, have spoken out against it, and many educators think it will open the door to further incompetency in the profession. Others hail it as the only solution to teacher shortages and to the incompetencies that arise when teachers become entrenched in their methods.

New Jersey's "alternative route" certification program has received national attention since its initial implementation in 1989. Touted by President Bush as a national model, the program has brought more than 1,500 new teachers into the system. Most of them are professionals from other fields such as law or business, or private school teachers who could not teach in the public schools without undergoing New Jersey's stringent certification process.

All have had to take a teachers examination before being allowed to teach, and all are hired on a one-year basis only. They will not be qualified for full-scale certification until they take eighteen education credits. Twenty-three other states have some sort of alternative certification process, but New Jersey's is the most far-reaching.

Naturally, there has been opposition to the program, especially from teachers unions, which feel that the program jeopardizes the professionalism of certified teachers and puts children at risk because alternative teachers have not had the appropriate education training. But criticism has been muted of late, since the program is clearly such a resounding success.

Most of the 1,500 teachers hired under the program are over twenty-five years old, and more than half of them are now fully certified. And 21 percent are minorities, as opposed to only 11 percent in the existing New Jersey teaching force. But perhaps the most telling statistics come from comparisons between the teaching exam test scores: teachers in the alternative programs scored 35 percent higher than their traditionally certified counterparts.

One teacher, one classroom, and twenty-five kids, not all of them reachable in the same manner on the same day. It all comes down to one thing — a teacher's skill at imparting knowledge effectively. That's a very subjective skill — maybe even an unlearnable one. We can define some skills that good teachers possess, even though we can't tell them how to acquire those skills. A good teacher needs to have

- respect for all children;
- enthusiasm for the work of educating children;
- a responsible approach to the children and to the teaching job;
- sensitivity to the variety of individuals in the class;
- a caring attitude toward individual differences in the class;
- fairness in dealing with the class and with the individual;
- friendliness and a good sense of humor;
- unlimited patience;
- skill in communicating to children and adults;
- knowledge of the subject(s) being taught.

Perhaps some training program in the future will be able to impart the importance of acquiring these skills to tomorrow's teachers and will develop ways to teach them directly. But, as everyone who has ever been graced with a gifted teacher knows, there is a special magic that no school, no in-service training, can ever define. And the teachers who have it can change the course of our lives forever.

ISSUES OF CONTROL

Even the best teacher, however, will be useless if he or she has to knuckle under to an uninspired curriculum, a despotic administrator, or a hysterical parent. The most effective teachers may be those who are clever enough to circumvent an often-ineffective school bureaucracy in order to impart the broadest range of knowledge to their young charges.

How much autonomy should a teacher be able to exercise over his or her classroom? How much say should a school principal have in the methods his or her teachers use? What can parents do to monitor what goes on in their children's classrooms without infringing on the teacher's role?

Teachers do have a lot of control over what actually goes on in the classroom, but such control is allotted to them more because administrators have no time to supervise individual classrooms than because they believe teachers are capable of directing their own curriculum. And unfortunately, autonomy in the classroom has little to do with broad curriculum directives, which are handed down by school boards and implemented by superintendents and school principals. In fact, only 63 percent of the teachers responding to a 1987 Department of Education survey said they were allowed any input at all into the curriculum decision-making process. In many schools, teachers feel that they — the most important link between student and subject matter — are totally excluded, which results in a sense of detachment from the material they teach, and in less effective teaching because of it.

Teacher involvement in decision making can work two ways. When teachers use education policy decisions as tools in the collective bargaining process, it can backfire on students and parents alike. But teacher involvement can also work to children's advantage because teachers should be trained to choose what is best, and to have the best interests of the children in mind.

At Cambridge's Graham and Parks Alternative School, a steering committee made up of parents and teachers — with the principal serving as moderator — is responsible for many of the major decisions made at the school level. The group meets on a monthly basis to consider curriculum issues, school rules and regulations, and issues that may arise concerning individual classrooms or the entire school. A separate group, known informally as the A Team, is composed of one teacher representative from each grade level, the principal, specialists, and the staff developer, who meet weekly to discuss classroom curriculum issues and practical details on implementation.

The steering committee also acts as a troubleshooter for problems brought before it by parents, teachers, or the administration. In 1989, for instance, parents and teachers found themselves at loggerheads over the method by which children would be assigned to classes at the next grade level. Parents wanted to be able to discuss the choice of the new teacher and have some say in where their children were placed.

Teachers felt that this put them in the position of having to choose one colleague over another and that it made them vulnerable to parent pressure and open to parent hostility if the parent request was not honored. The principal supported the teachers' position that a lottery system was more equitable and less stressful.

After much discussion and several school-wide meetings, the steering committee came up with a rather complicated procedure that allowed parents to state their choice of receiving teacher (and the reasons for it) but did not guarantee the placement. The plan represented a real compromise: Most parents felt the placement form met their need to have input about their child, and most teachers felt the form reduced the pressure on them to make difficult decisions.

HIRING AND FIRING: WHO SHOULD DO THE JOB?

In most schools, a strict hierarchy of decision-making authority is observed, and teachers must abide by the prevailing methods or risk their jobs. The school administrator is the person with the most power because he or she implements the broad directives from the school board and turns education policy into actual curriculum. The principal also formally evaluates the teachers in the building, which is an even more powerful role. Usually, teachers are hired by a committee made up of principals, teachers, and parents after their résumé has been approved by the central administration. It is over the renewal of individual teacher contracts that principals can exert the most authority.

How is such a decision made? Leaving aside the most obvious reasons for a teacher to be terminated — serious infractions of legal statutes or school rules, abuse situations, and the like, the biggest reason for teacher firing is "incompetence." But what is an incompetent teacher, and how can principals decide who they are? There are no real guidelines, which puts teachers in a bind. And it's difficult to blame a teacher who may have had poor training, or lack of supervision, or who is set in a methodology that is suddenly considered ineffective.

Unfortunately, the fact that principals are the main source of evaluations for teachers has no basis in research. In fact, research has shown that there is no relationship between a supervisor's rating and how much students are learning from a particular teacher. But the courts attach great weight to principals' assessments, as long as they are based on documented classroom observations.

As a matter of fact, student ratings of their teachers were much more consistent with classroom achievement, even on the elementary level. "The only persons in the school system found to be professionally competent to judge the worth of teachers (as measured in gains in achievement) were their pupils," write W. McCall and G. Krause in *Measurement of Teacher Merit.* Test results are another way to gauge effectiveness, but can result in teachers spending all their time preparing students to do well on tests, which have been shown to have little effect on long-term student achievement. More innovative methods have led to radical and effective changes in some communities.

In 1988, Memphis, Tennessee, had more than 100,000 students in 161 schools — many of them in economically depressed areas where the burdens of poverty and racial tension had taken a toll on the children. With the backing of the school superintendent, a group of parents and school personnel undertook a reform experiment that has had sweeping repercussions throughout the system.

In May of 1989, the superintendent announced that seven Memphis schools — three elementary, two junior high, and two high schools — would be closed at the end of that school year. All of the teachers and administrators at those schools received pink slips, meaning they would not automatically be rehired in September.

Each school established a local council, made up of two parents, two teachers, and one community member. Also serving in a nonvoting capacity were the school principal and a student from the school. Together, each council reviewed each teacher and administrator in the school to determine whether they should be rehired. The councils also determined what they wanted each school to teach and how they wanted it to be taught. A task force of parents, teachers, and administrators conducted a needs assessment for each school. Emphasis was placed on the parents' hierarchy of needs as well as the children's. Training sessions were held before the hiring or decision making began so that parents had the necessary skills to make sound decisions on their community's behalf.

The Memphis branch of the National Education Association backed the project and a member served on the hiring and review board to ensure that union contract guidelines were being met. Teachers with tenure were offered the option to switch to another school — if they were not rehired, they were automatically reassigned. The same held for administrators and support staff. Conflicts that resulted from there being as yet no written guidelines for each school were resolved by the local councils with help from the union representative.

In the fall of 1989, the seven schools reopened, with a strong parent-input component in place. Early assessments did not reveal a sharp rise in grade point averages at the schools, but other indicators, such as school attendance, behavior, and participation in extracurricular events, have proven that the experiment has paid off already. According to program director Willie Slater, the benefit of the experiment lay in the attitude toward parents as much as in the school restructuring. "We didn't ask, 'how involved can parents get?' but 'what is it they need and what impediments to their getting it can we remove?'"

In many systems, parents are effectively shut out of the evaluation process, even though alert parents can provide an early-warning system that principals might do well to heed. But parental complaint carries little weight in most school systems. As one court wrote in the case of a teacher who was being accused by parents of rigid teaching methods, "Our legislature has intended to grant to tenured teachers some protection from disgruntled parents. Perhaps such teachers do not win popularity contests, but neither can they be said to be incompetent."

Naturally, teachers deemed incompetent can't get sacked without due process; strong union regulations protect them against automatic termination except in the most extreme cases. And virtually every state has legal restraints on the public criticism of a public servant — private citizens must follow extremely strict protocol when attempting to censure a teacher or administrator. In any case, attempting to get a teacher fired is rarely the most effective way to handle school problems.

Getting teachers to recognize deficiencies and to work on them is a difficult task, as difficult as changing yourself as a result of therapy. At a minimum teachers need to feel supported in the process, have a sense of where they want to go, and be willing to work hard and cooperatively to get there. If they feel judged, forced, or manipulated, efforts to change are sure to fail and ill will is likely to be fanned in the process.

Using parent/student complaints as a guide, the Salt Lake City school district targeted teachers for closer inspection by principals. To avoid the appearance of "witch hunting" the school board's policy was clear-cut right from the start: If a parent or student was unable to resolve a grievance satisfactorily with the person against whom the complaint was lodged, the disgruntled party could file a written request for "Review of Services." The principal would then spend time observing the teacher in the classroom, gathering information from other adults or students who may have the same or opposing opinions, and serving as a mediator in an attempt to resolve the conflict. Over the past decade, one third of all Salt Lake City teachers who were placed on "remediation" were identified through this process.

The process removes the power to directly evaluate a teacher from the parents, but provides them with enough input to have some impact on how and when an administrator looks more closely at a teacher's efforts. And the emphasis on positive remediation for teachers who are found to be falling behind in meeting standards of quality, with its implicit statement that such failures are neither permanent nor irreversible, keeps the review program from being perceived as a terrible threat to job security.

Tenure, the guaranteed security of a job in the school system, is the greatest source of security to teachers, and the greatest source of dismay for parents and administrators. But tenure, like other forms of teacher control, is a double-edged sword. As the source of career anxiety is removed for teachers, so is the source of quality control for the system and parents. Firing a tenured teacher — even if he or she has been found to be incompetent — is a lengthy and costly process, and one that few administrators are willing to go through unless there is an unequivocal need to do so. But the qualifications for tenure have little to do with teaching quality — they have to do with longevity (number of years in the system) and with the number of postgraduate credits a teacher can amass.

If getting rid of a tenured teacher is difficult, getting rid of a principal is an even harder task. To do so, one must be prepared to battle the entrenched bureaucracy of the administration that promoted the principal in the first place. Strong union protection (principals may belong to either the National Association of Elementary School Principals or the National Association of Secondary School Principals, in addition to being members of various other administrative organizations) means that the administration's hands will be tied, and they will at best be able to transfer the individual to another school.

Principals get paid on a scale that can go as high as two or three times that of the average classroom teacher salary. But then, they have a difficult job. In addition to hiring, firing, and monitoring all teacher assignments, they have to prepare the school budget, develop school-wide curricula, and serve as a liaison with district administration. This last may be the school principal's hardest task. Neither labor nor management, principals must constantly balance the needs of their staff and students against the demands of the central system. In a recent survey of high school principals for the Department of Education, 83 percent reported that too much of their valuable school time was spent dealing with unnecessary administrative roadblocks.

But parents can do something. Tenured teachers have been dismissed, even when there was no criminal issue involved. As we have seen, principals and even superintendents have been removed as a result of popular pressure and administrative support. Getting rid of a grossly incompetent educator is not an easy task, and it tends to be the one issue that educators think of first when parent power is suggested. But in fact very few educators are dismissed without every effort having been made to redress the problem in a constructive way first. Often a teacher who is perceived as incompetent is merely in need of support and supervision, or else needs access to new resources to refresh his or her repertoire. These measures are the responsibility of the principal, and parents can take it upon themselves to see to it that principals follow through.

GETTING IN ON THE ACTION

Parents can make assessments of individual teachers on the basis of their interaction with them and on the basis of their child's schoolwork. But as advocates, we want to get an idea about the overall quality of teaching in our own schools and perhaps even in the entire school district. Once we have such information we can use it to determine what changes need to be made in the district's policies regarding its teachers.

The following list of questions is adapted from Terry Frith's *Secrets Parents Should Know About Public Schools*. Frith's questions are meant to be answered by individual parents, but a more fruitful exercise for a parent group would be to assemble the information for each school on a district-wide basis, tabulate the results, and present them to the superintendent or school board along with suggestions for ways in which unsatisfactory answers (such as high turnover rate or high absenteeism) can be addressed.

- How many teachers in the school have tenure? How many are probationary?
- How many possess advanced degrees? How many are working toward further degrees?
- In what way does the school support ongoing teacher education?
- What in-service programs are available, and what percentage of teachers take advantage of them? What rewards are provided for teachers who do participate?
- What is the annual turnover rate?
- How many teachers request transfers out of the school each year? Into what schools, if any, are teachers requesting transfers?
- How does teacher absenteeism compare between schools? How does it compare with schools in other districts?
- How many teachers have been rated "excellent" by the principal? What other methods are used to evaluate teachers? What input, if any, can parents have into the evaluation process?
- How many teachers in each school have received unsatisfactory evaluations, and in what areas?
- What is being done about teachers who are "at risk," or who have not done well on evaluations?
- How are excellent teachers rewarded?
- Are teachers required to set measurable objectives for themselves and to evaluate their own performances?
- Who evaluates teachers besides principals?

- What evaluation forms are used and how well do they assess teacher performance? Is any attempt made to tie teacher performance to student performance?
- Is the evaluation process designed to help teachers improve their performances?

Evaluating teaching caliber system-wide is a valuable way to pinpoint weaknesses. Frith points out that personal opinion about individual teachers does have its place, and she's right. The danger to be avoided is in making that kind of evaluation a personal condemnation. That can be avoided by judging the process of teaching, not the people who are teaching. Frith recommends asking general and constructive questions such as:

- Why are things done this way in this classroom?
- How well are these procedures working?
- What can be done to improve the status quo?

Information gathered by asking questions such as these can also be put to good use in setting up dialogues between parents and teachers that go beyond the usual concerns. Once parents have information about teachers in their system, they can ask the teachers for their perspective on everything from curriculum to classroom discipline methods. The very act of opening such a dialogue will likely clear the air of many misperceptions held by both parents and teachers.

Parents and teachers generally meet in traditional settings — the parent-teacher conference, back-to-school night, or when parents bring their child into the classroom. But such encounters usually deny parents and teachers the chance to really get to know one another. If parents and teachers were to sit down as a group and examine the barriers that keep them apart, they could begin to devise ways to overcome those barriers and work on addressing common areas of concern. Traditionally separated by the barriers they themselves erect, parents and teachers have to seek out new ways to join forces and collaborate on changing the system so that everyone — parents, teachers, and, most of all, students — benefits from the results.

UNIONS

"In the past," writes American Federation of Teachers president Albert Shanker, "when teachers used the word professionalism, it meant paying them more and leaving them alone. Now we're talking about assembling a knowledge base, functioning in the interests of the students, and being accountable for student performance. . . . We want to create more humane schools, and to do that you need a new kind of union."

Shanker's call for reform comes as no surprise to those who have listened to his outspoken views on public education for the past twenty years. But that such calls for reform should come from the president of the AFT, the second-largest teachers union in the country, is a surprise to some.

The National Education Association has 1.6 million members in 9,200 affiliates, while the AFT has 580,000 in 2,100 affiliates, mostly concentrated in large cities. The NEA has a national base, with a strong state-level presence, while the AFT has a stronger presence in many large urban school districts. Together, they represent the largest union membership in the country — the NEA alone is the second-largest single union after the AFL-CIO.

There are other professional education unions. The National Association of Professional Educators (NAPE), with less than 1 percent of total teacher population as members, differs from the two larger unions because it does not support collective bargaining and the right to strike. The NAESP and NASSP represent elementary and secondary school principals. Other unions include the National Science Teachers Association, the National Math Teachers Association, and unions that represent bus drivers, cafeteria workers, and janitors.

Most school districts are represented by either the NEA or the AFT, and teachers in a particular district will be represented by one of these unions. They may choose not to join any union, or they may maintain membership in another union, but only one union will speak for the teachers of that district, and it will speak for all teachers, union members or not. If you go to work in Dade County, Florida, for instance, your legal representative in collective bargaining will be the United Teachers of Dade, an affiliate of the AFT, and you must abide by their decisions.

Teachers unions are fairly recent; collective bargaining, for instance, was not recognized as legal for them until the 1960s, and teachers, as public employees, still do not technically have the right to strike. But nowadays unions are firmly entrenched political machines with vast power, wielded through lobbying efforts, voting power, and financial incentives. They are served by a network of professional union officials, negotiators, and lawyers, many of whom have had little or no contact with classroom teachers. That can mean a loss of voice for the rank and file when outside negotiators from national union headquarters are brought in to arbitrate on behalf of teachers in a district.

Unions can exert a powerful effect on school boards and administrators. What effect do they have on parents? Although the NEA and the AFT both purport to welcome parent involvement, they are not comfortable with the concept of parent power in the decision-making process. The union stance has pretty much been that if parents don't tell doctors how to treat patients, they should not be allowed to tell teachers how to run their classrooms. According to NEA president Keith Geiger, "It is impossible to run a school if a minority — any minority — is allowed to dictate. Parents don't need to be directly involved, since the school board is made up of parents. And yes, there should be room for parents to make decisions at the local level. That's their voice."

But the analogy between teachers and doctors is a difficult one. After all, parents change doctors if they're not satisfied, even in an HMO, where doctors must be picked from among a specific pool. We can't as easily change teachers or schools — except in open-choice systems — so our relationship with our children's teachers is often arbitrarily chosen as well as binding.

Write educators Clete Bulach and William Sharp, in a scathing indictment of unions, "Teachers' unions have become militant in fighting for the rights of their members, resulting in contractual constraints on school boards' ability to respond to criticism [of teachers] and on a low priority assigned to servicing students. Contracts limit the ability of administrators [or parents] to improve the quality of instruction. . . . There is a growing shift in emphasis from serving the needs of students to taking care of the needs of teachers. For example, when school boards propose increasing English and math requirements for graduation, union leaders oppose them, fearing that hiring more math and science teachers may cause other teachers to lose their jobs. Their number one concern is job security."

If professionalism is equated with a desire to serve the client well, say Bulach and Sharp, then there has, indeed, been a decline in professionalism. But it may not be that simple. Without strongly negotiated contracts, teachers could never have achieved a measure of job security or acceptable pay. And it's certainly true that the vast majority of rank-and-file union members are teachers who care desperately about the educational success of their students. Their desire to have more voice in educational policy-making stems from a very real commitment to sound educational practice as often as it does from the need to protect their own futures.

THE POWER OF THE COLLECTIVELY BARGAINED CONTRACT

In great measure, the conflict between unions and parents stems from misperceptions and stereotypes each holds about the other. But the union contract is *still* a legally binding contract, compelling the school to meet the negotiated demands of the teachers union. Those demands are negotiated in what is known as collective bargaining sessions, just as they are in the private business sector. Collective bargaining simply means negotiating between an organized group of employees and their employers. It was established as a legal means of negotiation when the U.S. Congress passed the Taft-Hartley Bill in 1947, making it necessary for both sides to bargain in good faith and come up with a written contract.

As it works in most school districts, the union comes to the negotiating table with a proposal and the school board with a counterproposal. Both proposals are usually well padded so there is latitude for concessions, which are hammered out by professional negotiators for both sides. A master agreement is finally reached that reflects a compromise between the two.

The main points covered by most contracts involve salary levels, job security issues, and benefits. In some districts, it is illegal for the collective bargaining sessions to involve education policy issues. But the lines blur when bargaining sessions involve discussions about how many math teachers can be hired, or how long a school day should be. Nevertheless, teachers unions are gaining power in determining evaluation policy, class size, discipline methods, and hiring and firing methods.

In New Jersey, for instance, the state's "Thorough and Effective Education" law makes it illegal for collective bargaining sessions to include education policy or managerial prerogatives. Since parents are excluded from those sessions, and since the law says they must be involved in those issues, discussion on such topics without parents would constitute a violation of law. On the other hand, some districts find that union-negotiated demands — excluding parents from teacher evaluation processes, for instance — become legally binding statutes, in effect turning union demands into law.

Such a situation effectively excludes those people who are most affected by the outcome of any collective bargaining session — the students and their parents. The most obvious solution to this exclusion would be to institute what National Committee for Citizens in Education director William Rioux calls "trilateral bargaining," which involves not only the employees (the union) and the employers (the school board) but also the "consumers" (the community). But efforts to include a third equally empowered party in the negotiating process itself have not been very successful, since the privacy and bilaterality of the bargaining process is legally protected in the public sector as it is in the private sector.

Some states have programs that at least allow parents to sit in on the negotiations, although not to participate. Two prime examples are Florida's Sunshine Law and California's Rodda Act, which compel negotiators to inform the public of the results of their sessions and allow for public response before a vote is taken.

In Rochester, New York, there is, indeed a trilateral panel, with one appointed parent serving as a full working member of the negotiating team. The parent, elected by community groups, does not carry one third the weight, but can be a valuable and valid contributor nonetheless. In New York City, the Public Education Association and the United Parents Association formed a collective bargaining task force to ensure better public interest representation in union negotiations. But perhaps the greatest effort on behalf of parent empowerment in union negotiating was made by the Philadelphia Parents' Union in 1978.

The Parents Union for Public Schools of Philadelphia (see Chapter 4) has been a watchdog over collective bargaining procedures between unions and school boards for more than twenty years. In fact, the organization got its start during a protracted teachers strike in 1972. Teachers were striking for several reasons, among them more control over classroom size and time, as well as the usual salary and benefits issues.

Enraged that the school board and unions were discussing matters that vitally concerned their children without consulting them, and that the others' decisions would become legally binding, the parents union decided that legal action of its own was the only recourse. So it sued the school board for illegally transferring control over educational policy to the teachers union.

PUPS charged that by allowing contract negotiations to include discussions about numbers of students in each classroom, scheduling, planning time, and other issues, the school board was allowing the teachers union to impose its own demands in areas where it had no legal right. It was the parents union's contention that local and state regulations demanded community involvement in such issues, and that the school board was not entitled to bargain such rights away.

The initial lower court ruled against the parents union, but in 1978 the Pennsylvania Supreme Court reversed its dismissal of the suit. The case was heard in the higher court the following year. The parents union lost the case when the judge decided that parents did not have the right to impose their issues on what was essentially a private contract between employer and employee. Nevertheless, PUPS gained more than notoriety as a result of the suit. It gained clout and respect, and has continued to have a strong impact on all education-related decisions in the city and the state.

By now, even union officials are conceding that collective bargaining needs to undergo some changes. Says the AFT's Albert Shanker, "Traditional collective bargaining has outlived its usefulness by undermining public confidence in schools. We cannot just negotiate for better wages and working conditions, but must accept responsibility for educational outcomes as well." If unions are going to accept responsibility for education policy, then they must also accept responsibility to share those policy-making decisions with the community.

In the 1980s, the small city of Chelsea, Massachusetts, suffered from the lowest test scores in the state, a 50 percent dropout rate, and a staggering 14 percent teen pregnancy rate. The newest school in the system had been completed in 1920, and the classrooms were overflowing with Latino and Cambodian children whose educational needs were not being met by the outdated curriculum and underpaid teachers.

In 1987, the Chelsea School Committee voted to conduct a yearlong examination of the feasibility of having Boston University take over the administration of the schools, and in 1989 the proposal was voted into law. Since then, the university has made a number of dramatic changes in the curriculum, school structure, and governance of the Chelsea schools, and community members are guardedly optimistic about B.U.'s continuing plans to keep parents involved and make their children academically successful.

Chelsea teachers are now under contract to the university, and their 1990 contract institutes a system of merit pay, creates lead-teacher positions, and raises general teacher salaries by an average of 25 percent. The establishment of permanent school-based councils is also part of the ratified contract.

The contract was a welcome antidote to low teacher morale; teachers had been working without a contract since the B.U. takeover, and had not received a raise for three years prior to that. Still, union membership was divided on the value of the new contract, largely because it came at the last possible moment and teachers felt they were being pressured into accepting it. In addition, some teachers feel that merit pay encourages unnecessary competition between teachers, and that the pay raise was not high enough to bring their salaries into line with those in surrounding towns. There is also some resentment of the university's tactic and methods, and some complaints that the real needs of Chelsea teachers and students are being ignored in a flurry of public relations gestures.

But according to union vice president Michael Hiechman, the arrangement is working. "We're hoping we can go forward from here to create a true partnership that includes the teachers, the community, and Boston University together to improve the school system for all the children of the city."

Regardless of how it is achieved, when the bargaining process fails, there may be a strike. In 1961, there was only one teachers strike nationwide. By 1966, there were 203 strikes involving 218,000 teachers, and nowadays the nation's teachers go out on an average of

122 strikes per year. Strikes by public employees are illegal in most states, but that doesn't stop them from happening. Management can strike as well, by instituting a lockout that prevents teachers from coming to work.

When a strike occurs, teachers suffer the disruption of their lives, temporary loss of income, and community disapproval, even if they do not want to strike in the first place. But research has shown that they don't lose much financially because, under the terms of a ten-month contract, they only work a certain number of days per year anyway. And the school board isn't risking the loss of a business, as management would in the private sector. Neither side has much incentive to resolve the conflict quickly.

Of course it's the students who suffer the most, and the taxpayers. There is a big conflict, then, between employee rights, which are clearly justifiable, and public rights, which are often superseded in the bargaining process between school officials and union officials. The fundamental issue is a tricky one, with no easy answer: Does the school belong to the taxpayers or to the employers and employees?

Clearly, the unions serve an important purpose in protecting the rights of the teachers. But parents have the right to hope that teachers unions, which are now basically secure, will initiate concrete steps not only to serve their paid membership, but to serve the clients of the schools — the children. Says Jonathan Kozol, author of an important book, *On Being a Teacher*,

> It is not in the nature of a large well-financed and politically established organization to set out to subvert or excoriate that large social system of which it has come to be an important part. Individual members, on the other hand, need not be restricted by these familiar institutional restraints. Free-thinking teachers, rank and file members of the NEA and AFT, constantly rebel, stand up for moral and political issues, and address . . . matters of conscience. . . . It is precisely these free-thinkers . . . who will redeem the teachers unions in the eyes of history.

THE TEACHERS AND PARENTS SPEAK

Clearly, the union speaks to the general welfare of teachers as a group. But what about the teachers themselves? What do they say about their profession, and about parents' place in it? In a 1988 Department of Education survey of teacher job satisfaction, only half of the responding teachers said they were very satisfied with their jobs — and that's up from 1986, when only a third were. In addition, nearly half of the 1988 respondents have seriously considered leaving teaching, and, as noted earlier, over a quarter are actually planning on leaving within five years.

That's a serious indictment, and there are several legitimate reasons for it. Among the most often reported is *burnout*, a general term used to cover a variety of problems. In *The Coming Parent Revolution*, Jeane Westin lists the chief reasons teachers give for burnout (in order of frequency of mention):

- low morale
- overwork, overstress
- lack of parental support
- additional course load because of budget cutbacks
- too much paperwork
- too much administrative flack
- lack of adequate school supplies
- low image of teachers in community
- poor student response to teaching
- lack of student discipline

In interviews with teachers across the country, however, another word has begun to appear with as much regularity as *burnout: respect*. Teachers don't feel they are getting enough of it; they don't feel they are being given enough responsibility to warrant it or enough recompense to prove it. They feel parents look on them as either servants or cure-alls, not as partners in the education process.

Teachers insist that respect is not only measured in financial terms. But of course, money talks. The average U.S. salary for a teacher in 1988 was just over $28,000. There is, however, a great variation between states; the average is $40,000 in Alaska and only $19,000 in South Dakota. And there are variations within states as well; Rochester, New York, teachers get nearly $50,000 while in nearby cities teachers get paid only $30,000. Such variations usually follow the economic profile of their communities — "good" communities with "good" schools can afford high wages, but low salaries make it hard to keep good teachers in areas where they are most needed, such as rural or urban areas.

When Rochester's ground-breaking teacher experiment began in 1987, it was hailed as the most innovative method around for reversing educational decline through the direct intervention of the teachers themselves. Teachers were given sizable pay increases — up to $57,000 per year — and asked to become involved in the daily lives of all their students. Each school was charged with drafting its own curriculum, geared toward the specific needs of its student body.

Separate middle schools were created for adolescents, and first-year teachers were assigned mentors to help them. Plans are under way to restructure the curriculum in some schools, abandoning the standard forty-minute period in favor of a team-taught multidisciplinary approach. Part of the additional costs of the program were underwritten by large Rochester businesses such as the Eastman Kodak Corporation.

So far, the much-touted program has had mixed success. The head of the Rochester Teachers' Association, Adam Rabansky, has supported the initiatives, and it seems, after two years in operation, that some gains in test scores and decreases in dropout rates have been achieved. But many teachers feel that the program forces too much responsibility on them, and that they have not been given adequate training or time to deal with their students' individual problems.

Critics of the system charge that the experiment offered no strategic plan for achieving its impressive goals, and provided no system of accountability by which it could be judged. There appears to be a growing dissident movement within the RTA as well. "All of a sudden it was just implemented," complained one teacher, "and we had no preparation to deal with the problems the students were having outside the classrooms." But Mr. Rabansky feels that the teachers who are willing to rise to higher expectations are doing just fine. "Some [teachers] would apparently like the pay and the status of a professional without the accompanying responsibility for the welfare of the . . . student."

Since the type and degree of home intervention is determined school by school, there is a great variety in the perceptions of the success of the Rochester experiment. "The whole reform movement is based on the commitment and expertise of individuals," says Catherine Spoto, vice president of the Rochester Board of Education. "I'll get a call from one parent who will say this is the best year her child has ever had, and . . . another who'll say that nothing has changed for his child at all."

"There are still an awful lot of teachers who put their union ahead of their kids," says parent representative Hans DeBruyn. "But if all the reforms on paper actually take place, Rochester's school system will be incredible."

Much as they don't want parents in their way, teachers also blame them for not setting standards and maintaining control of their children. They blame parents alternatively for lack of involvement (in poor schools), or for too much interference (in affluent schools). They feel they are expected to provide a moral and social education as well as an academic one, to be parents as well as teachers for a whole generation of students.

However, teacher resentment of parents is not a one-way street. In a 1988 survey of attitudes of parents and teachers, M. Laurie Leitch and Sandra S. Tagari found that one of the major barriers to positive home-school relationships is the negative stereotypes each group has of the other. According to the teachers interviewed, these barriers included

- parents' unrealistic expectations of the school's role;
- parents' attitude that school isn't important enough to take time from work;
- parents' inability to help with schoolwork;
- parents' jealousy of teachers' upward mobility;
- apathy of longtime teachers and lack of responsiveness to parents;
- absence of activities to draw parents in;
- teachers' resentment or suspicion of parents who are involved.

For parents, the list of barriers reads somewhat differently:

- lack of information about school activities
- lack of time to spend working with child (due to work)
- ill health
- lack of time to spend at school with teacher (due to work)
- conference times scheduled during working hours
- condescending attitude of teachers toward parents
- embarrassment about lack of education
- fear of reprisals against child if complaint is lodged
- inability to communicate effectively in English

But teachers and parents are not as far apart as they seem. In a 1989 Department of Education survey, parents and teachers responded separately to what they thought would be the five most effective ways to improve education (see accompanying table).

% Parents responded	Ways to Improve Education	% Teachers responded
88	Having school notify parents about problems	77
79	Parents limit television until homework is done	80
70	Parents get much more time with children in support of teachers and school	84
80	Providing counseling and support services to children with emotional, family, mental problems	81
73	Developing school programs to involve parents with students who have special needs	67

By sharing their expertise, parents and teachers can overcome the barriers that separate them and begin to work toward common goals.

Since 1965, the Appalachia Educational Laboratory has been involved in upgrading the educational structure in Kentucky, Tennessee, Virginia, and West Virginia. AEL operates a clearinghouse for research and information on rural education and small schools, conducts training workshops on relevant issues, publishes research on effective programs, and maintains a network of schools interested in sharing and learning from one another.

AEL has also established a parent-community school model that is being implemented in several urban areas throughout the region. The model calls for a "greenhouse" located in a neutral area in which parents can meet with AEL staff without feeling pressured by the confines of their child's school. At the meetings, parents are trained in strategies for working with their children as well as with school personnel to assure maximum learning opportunities for their children.

The project works to reduce those barriers that it has identified for both parents and teachers, and to encourage open discussion of the barriers by both groups in an effort to defuse them. Parents and teachers are asked to come up with their own specific goals in separate groups (with help) and then to come together and devise goals that represent their common interests.

AEL sees parents as the primary educators of their children and draws on their expertise as well as on that of local teachers, social service agencies, colleges and universities, and community leaders. The underlying premise of the model is that parents, educators, and anyone else with a stake in the public education process is an equal in the process of creating effective education. All parties must come to grips with their differences, invent and try out new ways of communication, and help each other to help their children succeed.

Clearly, we agree on a lot, although our priorities are somewhat different. The stereotypes work both ways, and only through one-on-one communication can we get beyond them. It's interesting that, in Leitch and Tagari's study, those teachers who did interact often with parents reported much fewer negative responses about parents.

The Southwest Educational Development Laboratory conducted a survey in 1986 that revealed parents and teachers have very different perspectives on what parent involvement means. Parents felt that involvement meant

- taking part in activities that help the school's program;
- allowing the home to enhance school learning;
- assisting the staff in instructional matters;
- assisting the staff in administrative matters.

Educators, on the other hand, felt that parent involvement was limited to

- abetting the school program;
- having the home reinforce school learning;
- staying away from participation in school activities;
- staying away from administrative activities.

"Educators," says SEDL director David L. Williams, "welcome parent participation in the more traditional modes but do not think their involvement is appropriate otherwise, while parents . . . are strongly interested in non-traditional methods of participation."

It's true that parents won't always be "nice" to school personnel if they are allowed more power. But clearly they aren't always nice now, when they are frustrated by their lack of power. The legacy of the "one best system" philosophy remains to haunt us, reducing our ability to perceive education as a shared enterprise.

It is clear that parents and teachers need to learn how to communicate and how to work together in the best interests of the children in their charge. Building a coalition of parents and teachers would probably be the single most important political action any advocacy group could take.

HOW TO: Get More Involved in Teachers Union Negotiations

Before negotiations begin:

1. Organize a parent/citizen group
2. Learn about the collective bargaining processes
3. Gather information about collective bargaining in your district
4. Analyze your district's negotiated contracts
5. Determine present contract costs
6. Evaluate the grievance procedure
7. Report findings
8. Petition for public involvement in negotiations

During negotiations:

1. Obtain and analyze each party's contract demands
2. Request open negotiations or an opportunity to observe
3. Publicize your position on the issues being negotiated
4. Press for more information and work toward a climate of understanding and conciliation

After negotiations:

1. Examine and evaluate new contract
2. If any of its terms clearly involve educational policy, challenge them
3. Observe the administration of the contract through the allotted grievance procedure and assess its effect on school programs, financial resources, and student progress
4. Continue to monitor negotiations as they are resumed for discussion of current board actions

Making Curriculum Decisions

PERHAPS the most difficult aspect of public school leadership for parents to assume is that of curriculum development. It is the area in which we most often assume that the experts have all the answers, that arcane technical skills are required to carry it out, and that all the specifics of what our children learn — and how, and when — is written somewhere in stone.

But our children's school curriculum — the specific content of their courses of study as well as the way in which the material is presented — is the most crucial element in their school career. Success or failure in the adult world may depend on whether or not they have acquired basic skills, pertinent knowledge, and problem-solving abilities while still in school. If nothing else falls into place — if the teachers are merely adequate, the building less than comfortable, the budget meager — a solid curriculum is the single element that would enable our children to survive in a complex society.

As parents, then, we should take a special interest in our school's curriculum, in what students are being taught, how it is being taught to them, when they are learning it, and how their acquisition of new material is being assessed. True, we may lack the technical skills to enable us to develop a course of study on our own, but that doesn't mean we can't participate in establishing curriculum goals and determining the methods used to reach them. The reluctance of many educators to have us participate stems from a perception that curriculum is something as immutable as the three R's themselves. In fact, the way in which reading, writing, and arithmetic are taught is constantly changing, and the information our children can acquire once they have learned basic skills is changing even faster than that.

All the more reason for parents — and the larger community in general — to participate in shaping that kinetic entity we call school-work. If we examine the parameters of a strong curriculum, learn about the materials used to teach it, and look at the ways in which its success is measured, we will be better equipped to become constructive members of a curriculum-development team at the school or district level.

WHO TEACHES WHAT, AND HOW?

The definition of *curriculum* is deceptively simple — it is a specific course of study, including form and content. But the word means different things to different people. Teachers define it according to the materials they are given to teach the course. Unfortunately, teachers are not the ones doing the curriculum development. More and more often, curriculum decisions are being made at the state level, leaving very little room for input from local educators, let alone from parents. Some states even dictate which materials are acceptable for use in, say, a junior high school algebra program or a fourth-grade remedial reading program.

School boards define curriculum according to the goals and objectives they have set for their schools. Administrators tend to define it in terms of packaged programs, while students themselves think of it in terms of papers and tests.

For parents, curricula are defined every night by the answer to the eternal question "What did you do in school today?" Unfortunately, the answer to that question is all too often a lackadaisical "Nothing much." That doesn't mean there is no course of study being offered, but merely that our children are unwilling or unable to report on it to us.

Assuming that they did tell us, however, another problem arises. We all have very definite views on what our children should or should not be taught, on how it should be taught, and even when. Should we concentrate on phonics in first grade, or begin with the whole-word approach to reading? Should we teach the multiplication tables by rote memory or use manipulatives to reinforce them? Should we require a foreign-language course in high school or should it be an elective? When should we begin sex and health education, or should we teach it at all?

Some of us — and this includes teachers and administrators as well as community members — may feel that basic skills should be taught in a basic manner, through drill and repetition, while others feel they should be made more exciting to the reluctant scholar. Still others feel that basic skills should not be taught directly at all, but should be inferred through the creative use of an information-based curriculum, even in the early grades.

Naturally, our views differ dramatically from community to community, from home to home, even from parent to parent. And of course our children's teachers and principals, and the district- and state-level officials who plan our curricula, may have still other views — views that may or may not coincide with those of the majority of the community. That makes it nearly impossible to reach a consensus, even if parents were empowered to shape the curriculum.

It has become crucially important for parents and educators to rethink the current curricula in our schools. Regardless of their prescription for change, everyone agrees that changes need to be made. Curriculum reform may not be the only answer to the problems plaguing our nation's schools, but it is certainly an essential component of any school-improvement plan.

The problem then is not "if" but "how?" How do we decide which curriculum is best for our child and which way it should be taught? More important, how do we determine which curricula and methods are best for the majority of children in our schools, and how to ensure that a broad range of information and methods is available without sacrificing basic skills? The great plight of democratic choice is that such decisions are not easily made. What makes the most sense for a white suburban middle-class child may be totally inappropriate for a recent Haitian immigrant living in a small city or for an African American living in a large urban center. In fact, what may seem the best choice to the parent of one child may be anathema to another, regardless of the family's background or current situation.

DEFINING THE PARAMETERS

There are several general questions on which disagreement over curriculum choices is common:

> Should our children be taught in the fundamental, "classical" style, or should they be given a more flexible, "progressive" education?
> Should they be given a moral, ethical, and social education in school, or should those themes be reserved for home and church?
> Should their curricula be determined at the local level, or should there be a national standardized course of study?
> Should all our children receive the same education, or should we revamp some curricula to redress ethnic, racial, and cultural biases that already exist?

Let's first look at what we *do* agree should be part of any good curriculum. All children, we can safely say, should be well versed in the academic fundamentals, should achieve a minimal level of physical coordination, should be given basic information about their society, and should learn the elementary forms of behavior necessary to deal with others outside the home. We agree that such skills can be taught through many different methods: through lectures and textbooks, through coaching and supervised practice, and by using hands-on question-and-answer techniques.

We agree that all children should graduate from high school with an acceptable level of proficiency in English, foreign-language training, math, science, and social studies, and that they should have acquired problem-solving and critical-thinking skills to enable them to approach college, work, and life with some success. But such generalized tenets tend to translate into a diluted curriculum, which is part of the problem today. In addition, it leads to an inward-looking program of study that focuses on tried-and-truisms and fails to open windows onto the larger, ever-changing world. To counteract this trend, in some communities life skills are being incorporated into the curriculum right alongside study skills.

In Hayward, California, teachers who are participants in the Child Development Project are trying to teach their elementary school students self-discipline, responsibility, and concern for others along with reading and arithmetic. Eric Shaps, project director, says that traditional methods of classroom management may work in the short run, ''but there are long-term costs in the way children fail to internalize the standards and expectations we would like them to become committed to.''

At the beginning of the year, teachers ask their students to write down what rules they feel should be imposed in the classroom. Teachers then help the students devise broader norms of behavior from the rules they themselves have established. Controls are established by the teachers, but the children seem to respond more readily to their own guidelines than to arbitrary rules handed down from above.

While some parents and educators object to ''value training'' in the public schools, the Child Development Project is based on the premise that better-behaved students are better-performing students, and that learning self-control and caring are part of learning to become a useful adult in our society.

Not only is appropriate behavior a goal in itself, but it enhances the academic learning experience for the entire class. For that reason, classroom assignments in the upper grades are listed in terms of academic and social goals: the academic goal of a small-group vocabulary lesson may be to learn the meaning of the words; the social goal is to ''listen to others' ideas.''

As a result of the current preoccupation with improving children's test scores, not enough has been done to improve children's attitudes, or their social development, which is a key factor in adult success. ''It is important for kids to learn to live in a democratic society,'' said Marilyn Watson, another project educator. ''The worst of all outcomes would be to have bright, highly skilled young people without a basic commitment to fairness, justice, and caring.''

In the 1960s, a backlash against rigid or outdated curriculum guidelines led to the development of "relevant" curricula designed to produce students who were better equipped to cope with modern society. Classes in modern politics and culture, self-directed study, and ungraded programs abounded.

Unfortunately, such curricula often became so permissive and student oriented that basic skills were ignored, leaving students as ill prepared as they were with the old curricula.

Of course, the theorists behind those reforms, educators like Jonathan Kozol, John Holt, Herbert Kohl, and Nathan Glaser, were responsible for bringing public education, kicking and screaming, into the twentieth century. Even if the results may have fallen short, their research, and the models they proposed, were intended to make education relevant, for the first time, to both the child and society. They also intended that child-centered curricula be backed with sound basic skills training, a fact many critics have overlooked, and that many educational experimenters did not include in their programs. The accusation of ill preparedness persists in programs like today's bilingual-education programs, which offer non–native speaking students a foreign-language-based curricula but not enough English skills to enable them to thrive on an equal basis in an English-speaking society.

Nevertheless, the call for new basics, which is actually a harkening back to the more classically oriented curricula of the past fifty years, is being heard all over America. It is not necessarily associated with an inward- and backward-directed course of study, nor is it incompatible with the progressive, alternative curricula of educators like Kozol and Holt. In fact, several school systems have instituted "alternative schools," which are really back-to-basics schools.

What is important to remember about the basics versus progressive debate is that the two are not mutually exclusive. In fact, today's most successful curriculum innovations draw on a variety of approaches and allow students to establish a broad base of information in the hopes that they will learn not what to learn but how to learn it.

Brown University educator Theodore Sizer organized the Coalition for Essential Schools after spending years in American high schools trying to reinvigorate their curricula. His 1984 book, Horace's Compromise, *documented Sizer's disappointed journey through schools that had been deadened from educational neglect and abuse, and laid out his then-radical prescription for change: teacher participation in curriculum development, fewer lectures, more hands-on learning through experimentation, cooperative learning by students, parents, and teachers together, and assessment through presentations and exhibitions in which the students would "defend" their work much the way doctoral students defends their theses. Sizer's basic contention is that asking students questions is much preferable, in terms of what they learn and how well they learn it, to giving them answers.*

Since 1983, seventy schools have elected to join Sizer's Coalition for Essential Schools by pledging to shape their own curricula according to his tenets. The schools receive curriculum guidance and teacher training from CES but are expected to follow their own mandates to achieve local educational success. So far, schools in Massachusetts, California, New York, and Rhode Island have become members; Rhode Island and five other states are participating in Re:Learning, another pilot project operated jointly by CES and the Education Commission of the States. In each state, a group of education, business, and community leaders are working together to coordinate school reform.

At Boston's English High, the Fenway Program is a CES school-within-a-school. According to Fenway Program director Larry Myatt, CES schools emphasize that "less is more, small is better, mastery is fundamental. We tried to build the program around those notions." Since the majority of Fenway Program students are classified as "at risk" for a variety of reasons, the curriculum is built around giving them a support system that might otherwise not be there, and then getting them actively involved in their own education. Organizational skills are stressed so the student doesn't just sit around and wait for the teacher to return graded work or make assignments. The idea is to make students feel responsible for their own success, and to make sure that the curriculum has an impact that goes beyond the classroom into their own lives.

The Fenway Program has its problems; because of Boston School Department course requirements, emphasizing depth of study rather than breadth has been difficult to achieve. And so far, the entire English High staff has yet to vote for the CES program with the 75 percent majority that CES requires. But the dropout rate is well below that of Boston's other public school programs, and attendance patterns have improved significantly.

THE LEGAL ISSUES

Despite the vast differences of opinion possible among educators and parents, there are some legally mandated controls on curriculum design. Over and over again, the courts have determined that, while individual groups can control curriculum input for their own children, they cannot demand curriculum changes based on their beliefs. That is, if you don't approve of something that is being taught in your child's school, you can demand that he or she not participate in that course of study, but you can't have the course removed.

There are two types of objections that the Supreme Court has ruled are eligible grounds for removing a child from a portion of the school curriculum: our constitutionally protected freedom of religion or privacy, and our personal beliefs about the value of a particular curriculum. Naturally, the first is easier to document than the second, and therefore appears more often in court cases.

But the court decisions are not always in favor of the parents. In *Wisconsin v. Yoder* (1972), the Supreme Court ruled that Amish parents could take their children out of school after eighth grade because of their religious conviction that children must join the Amish community at that age. However, in a 1974 case, *Page v. Davis,* the Court ruled that the child of Apostolic Lutheran parents could not leave the classroom every time any audiovisual equipment was used, despite the parents' proscription against the use of such equipment. The child, ruled the court, could not be made a martyr to the parents' convictions, and AV equipment was essential to the child's effective education.

Rights of privacy are more problematic. In 1975, a California group called Citizens for Parental Rights sued the San Mateo County Board of Education because they felt their children were being forced to reveal their innermost thoughts and details of family life in a course on sex education and ethics. In a small-group setting, students were asked questions like "What would you do if you knew that your best friend was sexually active?" or "What do you think a boy's responsibility is toward his pregnant girlfriend?" While the course was voluntary, the parents felt their children were being forced to participate through peer pressure, and that the course itself should be dropped. The courts ruled in favor of the schools, and the course remained.

Although the courts have been divided, the teaching of sex, health, substance-abuse, parenting, and family-life education courses have generally been found not to infringe on parents' constitutional freedom of religion or privacy. But the right of parents to determine the education of their own children is also legally recognized, as long as it does not infringe on the best interests of the child. When do a child's best interests supersede the right of a parent to direct that child's education? This issue has proven to be difficult for the courts, which must balance the rights of the parents, of the child, and, in many cases, of the state, which may have its own constitutional right to provide an effective education to all its children. By and large, the courts have placed the burden of proof on educators, who must prove that their proposed curricula provide the child with an important skill or essential knowledge that does not infringe on the parents' religious beliefs in any way.

Citizens for Quality Education, a group of parents in suburban Brookline, Massachusetts, took the school committee to task for what they termed "placing too great an emphasis on values, morals and politics to the exclusion of academics. Too many students," the group claimed, "are being taught to question Western society."

At issue was the removal of an advanced placement European history course taught at the high school. The course, which had attracted between fifteen and thirty students a year, was being replaced with a comparative government course that analyzed the governments of five countries. Two years of European history, along with one of American history, were already being taught, and the school committee felt that substantial portions of the rest of the world were being ignored in favor of a "Eurocentric" bias.

But CQE saw the change as evidence of decline in Brookline's educational standards. The town has traditionally attracted families with high academic standards that are able to pay its high real estate prices, and it has a reputation for a progressive political orientation, although, like the rest of the country, it has become more conservative in the past few years. Says CQE president Bob Costrell, "Our concern was that a group of teachers had been very explicit in . . . promoting social activism," which was held to be inappropriate in a classroom setting. In addition, CQE members felt that, since minority representation had been in place in the curriculum since the 1970s, the school's "classical" academic focus — such as that provided by a course on European history — had deteriorated. In addition, says member Ronnie Gordon, "Part of the program in some of the schools was America-bashing. We found that teachers, at their will, were doing what they wanted because there was no real curriculum in place."

But the CQE itself came under fire when it was revealed that they had asked for access to teacher personnel files and had used articles written by one teacher in an education journal to indicate that the teacher was "politicizing" her classroom. Says school superintendent James Walsh, "There was a lot of concern about the activities of the CQE and the way it went after teachers whose philosophies it disagreed with or trashed curriculum approaches that did not conform with CQE's philosophy."

This example illustrates both the impact parents can have on the curriculum process and the dangers they face in presenting their point of view. In order to be effective when you advocate for a curriculum change, you must first familiarize yourself with the curricular options available and the alternative points of view held about them by different groups. It is also important to choose a few important priorities rather than attempt to cover sweeping issues. An understanding of how decisions are made in your community, whether by curriculum supervisors, school board committees, parent advisory groups, or some other authority, is essential. Whenever possible, it is better to work by consensus, cooperatively, and by informal discussion than by open confrontations. When it becomes necessary to "go public," it is important to understand how media and publicity work, so that your position is represented fairly. You must be prepared to devote long hours to defending your position, and you must be prepared for the possibility, if not probability, that you may lose on your chosen issue. Win or lose, it is imperative that you not draw lines too sharply, because the next year may involve another dispute and you can never be certain just how the lines will be drawn on the next issue.

CURRICULUM MATERIALS: THE TEXTBOOK BUSINESS

One of the most explosive issues any community is likely to face is that of the censorship of books. In 1987, a federal district judge banned more than forty books from school libraries because a conservative religious group found them offensive. That order was later overturned, and a similar case, in New York, went to the Supreme Court, where the judges ruled that the books must remain. In general, the courts have ruled that material offensive to parents' religious beliefs cannot be banned, while obscene material is more likely to be removed from school shelves.

Rulings such as these apply to textbooks as well as to library books or assigned reading materials. But textbooks deserve some special attention from parents. Only 2 percent of the average school budget goes toward the purchase of new textbooks each year. Half of this cost is paid by the school district, half by the state. Because of this financial clout, the state must approve most textbook purchases. Technically, the approved textbook list is subject to public approval, but that's a pretty well kept secret in most states. By forming advocacy groups parents *can* draw attention to perceived deficiencies in their children's textbooks.

In the southern California school district of Hacienda–La Puente, parents have organized a coalition to protest the use of textbooks and curriculum materials that they deem inappropriate. In particular they object to the Impressions language arts textbook series, published in Canada by Holt, Rinehart and Winston.

According to their flyers, the Coalition of Concerned Parents states that Impressions texts "undermine our personal and moral beliefs and parental authority. Historical facts of our wonderful nation are not represented. These textbooks plant seeds of doubt concerning the moral, social and religious values being taught at home. The use of 'situational ethics' is a denial of the absolute values being taught at home. The stories are depressing, confusing and sometimes violent. Negative thinking predominates."

Kathleen Nobbman, a founding member of CCP, objects to the Canadian bias of the literature, which offers tales of "huskies, high country and cold winters. We want 'core' literature to reflect our rich and diverse literary heritage which connects students to social and ethical issues central to our society."

Nobbman has also put together a pamphlet that provides a step-by-step procedure for organizing parents, learning legal rights, evaluating textbooks, and avoiding pitfalls that might cause the group to be labeled "fundamental," "fascist," or "fanatic." According to Nobbman, "There seems to be a trend in many textbooks today of an undermining of traditional values generally accepted universally. How can we today educate ourselves as parents, taxpayers [and] concerned citizens . . . of our rights, responsibilities and options concerning the placement of textbooks in our schools? [We want] to help those who want quality instructional materials in their schools and to help remove textbooks that are inappropriate or detrimental to the moral, spiritual, social or educational development of students."

What makes the $2 billion textbook market such a volatile one? "Textbooks are written for the buyers, who are not the consumers," says Gilbert T. Sewall, director of a private monitoring group, the American Textbook Council. Technically, each state's department of education textbook buyers must provide the public with access — through the state legislature — to textbook purchase decisions, but that rarely happens. More likely, the state will go to teachers, administrators, and legislators to find out what they should be buying.

Textbook companies do the same thing, paying special attention to what teachers want and to the reading level, ethnic diversity, and curriculum guidelines determined by each state. And because they want to sell as many books as possible, textbook publishers must make their material palatable to as many different tastes as possible. This leads to what is known as the "lowest common denominator" approach to textbook writing.

It is not entirely the fault of the publishers. Trends in education are constantly changing, and it can take many years and millions of dollars to develop a complete textbook program, so publishers are naturally wary of programs that might be out of date or too experimental. The need to include all the necessary material in, say, a high school history book can make for long and numbing reading, especially when the text has been written by a number of authors with no common style other than the strict guidelines provided by the publisher.

But critics insist that textbooks could be made more palatable with the use of literature-based material that draws on a variety of styles and subject matter, or that makes use of well-written and thought-provoking essays on a specific subject. In fact, some even go so far as to argue that textbooks are not necessary for an effective curriculum; history can be taught from biographies, diaries, and speeches, science from laboratory experiments, and reading from children's literature. That's assuming, of course, that teachers are willing to give up their prescribed curriculum, with its predetermined units, workbooks, and tests — and that states are willing to allow school districts to use materials of their own choice to teach state-mandated curriculum goals.

On the other side of the fence are critics who charge that current American textbooks are superficial and cater to too many special interest groups to the detriment of the basic educational value of the book. Essential information is the object of a good textbook, and attempts to dilute that information result in a less effective teaching tool. Jeane Westin quotes an Ohio parent who tried to get an American history book pulled from the high school curriculum because of its vapidity. "There are many references to rock celebrities and movie stars — trivia in a textbook! The textbook seems especially to be stretching a point to find ways to be relevant to the women's and civil rights movement at the expense of basic information."

The same argument can be heard from ethnic educators who argue that the Eurocentric bias of most American textbooks trivializes their culture and leaves the mistaken impression that civilization as we know it stems from a Roman, Greek, and Western European history. The Clearinghouse on Educational Choice publishes a newsletter documenting specific instances of textbook bias against religious freedom; their contention is that religious tolerance cannot be taught if religion is systematically excluded from all public school curricula on the basis of the First Amendment.

There is also a growing concern that our textbooks are out of date, poorly written, and insensitive to current conditions in the world. Given the rapid changes in the political geography of the world, it's understandable that publishers would simply not be able to keep up. A geography book written less than a decade ago would be totally obsolete today, and there's no way to overcome such limitations with a printed book. Even more alarming is the fact that a great percentage of books currently in use in our schools are physically deteriorated to the point of uselessness. One parent was aghast to find that the sociology textbook she had used in her Michigan high school was the exact same one assigned to her daughter twenty-six years later, and some communities have had to raise money privately to replace dilapidated books.

Former Cambridge, Massachusetts, mayor Al Vellucci, while visiting various elementary schools during his tenure, remarked that there appeared to be either not enough books or too many shelves in the libraries. When told that no money was available to fill the shelves, Vellucci set about getting the money elsewhere. He first contacted Harvard University and convinced them to donate money. Then he began working the city in general, collecting donations from individuals, corporations, and civic groups with his ''Be a Bookworm'' drive. The Harvard Square Business Association circulated a fund-raising letter on behalf of the project, and Vellucci hosted a Big Pasta Bash at the high school to raise money for its library fund.

At the same time, it came to Vellucci's attention that school textbooks were in sorry shape, soiled and torn, or missing altogether, so that there were rarely enough to go around. Marshaling community support (and ignoring several educators who pointed out that a more effective curriculum might be conducted without textbooks), Vellucci finally prevailed on the city manager to establish a Cambridge Public School Textbook Fund, a dedicated fund — separate from the school board's funding — to be used to replace old textbooks.

Because of strict state guidelines, it often takes extensive legwork, even on the part of an elected official, to make changes in school district textbook policy. In schools where a textbook fee is charged, parents have more control. This practice, however, is under intense legal scrutiny at the moment, and parents in several states have mounted successful challenges to the practice on the grounds that it violates the constitutional right to a free public education. States that do charge fees (for extracurricular activities as well as for materials) must provide an elaborate system of aid to those who cannot afford them.

In order to exert more control, parents need to have more information about textbook alternatives. The Educational Products Information Exchange (475 Riverside Drive, New York, NY 10027) has a computer data base containing information and evaluation on all current instructional material. The Educational Materials Review Center (U.S. Office of Education, 400 Maryland Avenue SW, Washington, DC 20202) also provides reviews of textbooks for a small annual fee, which can be underwritten by parents groups.

COMPUTERS AND OTHER NON-TEXTBOOKS

One way to get around the swift obsolesence of textbooks is to use audiovisual materials that can be more quickly made, more cheaply produced, and shared by an entire class. Today's librarian doesn't just need to know the Dewey decimal system — he or she needs to be a media specialist. How critical are movies, videos, computer programs, long-distance education curricula, and satellite tie-ins to a successful education? Aside from the technical proficiency acquired in learning to use these electronic devices, can such materials provide essential information to our children? Though the cost of developing computer software may be minimal compared to the cost of developing a textbook, the cost of hardware is an insurmountable burden to many schools.

Before such purchases are undertaken, parents need to make sure that the schools have answered some basic questions:

1. Is the new program or equipment worth the price?
2. Can the school afford it?
3. Is there someone qualified to teach it?
4. What is the least expensive way to get it?

When new technologies are purchased and used with care they can provide effective, if sometimes controversial, alternative learning opportunities.

In 1990, the Texas Board of Education, the nation's second-largest educational material market after California, approved the purchase of a statewide laser videodisk system to teach Windows on Science, an elementary school science curriculum. Laser videodisks are twelve-inch platters that resemble phonograph records but contain many thousands of bits of information, both visual and audio, that can be played back via a disk player and television monitor. Information is read by a laser beam, and a remote-control device allows the teacher or student to call up specific material as needed.

Known as electronic textbooks, the advantage of laser videos is that they can be more responsive to students' questions and can provide vivid imagery to underscore narrative information. Simple and quick to operate, they allow far more flexibility than videocassettes or filmstrips. Teachers say it allows them as well as their students to take a more active role in learning, but some critics say it just repackages textbook information in a more appealing way without promoting critical thinking.

Still, the decision to use the system statewide in Texas clears the way for videodisks to compete with printed matter for the billion-dollar textbook industry. Texas state law mandates that instructional material must cost between fifteen and twenty-five dollars per student, and videodisk technology falls in that range. "We are watching the revolution of the textbook," says one educator, adding that "you can put a lot more on a disk than you can in a textbook." But some educators are worried that the technology will cause teachers to ignore reading skills, which they cannot replace. The new technology certainly won't help already plummeting reading scores, but, as one teacher who has used it said, "It's just something else to use to enliven the curriculum. Like any other teaching tool, some students do better than others with it."

Perhaps no electronic equipment in the school engenders as much debate as the personal computer. At what age should children begin to work with computers? Should they master basic skills such as spelling or multiplication before using computer-assisted tools in their work? Is it necessary to have one computer in each classroom — or one for each child? Do we teach computer programming skills to our children or use the machines to teach other skills like language and math?

In 1989, five schools in Indiana began the Buddy Project, which provided all fourth graders in the schools with computers — both in their classrooms and at home. The project was managed by a joint committee of business leaders, Indiana state education experts, and citizens. The equipment was provided by IBM.

The Buddy Project focused on fourth graders first because it was felt that nine-year-olds were not yet gender stereotyped in their attitudes and still communicated well with their parents. In addition, they were old enough to handle regular homework assignments, and no longer in the decoding process of learning to read.

Teachers were trained in the use of the software, paid for their extra time by stipends raised locally, and allowed extra planning time to make the most of their computer-based curriculum. Each classroom received a networked computer with more than seventy programs in everything from computer skills to spelling and math.

After the system had been used in the classroom for about a month, parents were brought in for training by students, teachers, and IBM personnel. Then each student got a personal computer with a twenty-megabyte hard drive, a printer, and a modem. Students helped their parents master the software, and parents got additional software for their own use and for younger siblings to use in the home. The entire system is linked up by modem to instructional support, and the teachers' central workstation made it possible for students to bring in their homework on disk. The use of the Prodigy on-line system made vast amounts of information such as news highlights, financial information, and educational resources available to every family in the project.

The intent of the Buddy system was to allow teachers to use computers to enrich, reinforce, and remediate what they were already doing in the classroom. Teachers have reported more efficient use of time, more student involvement in projects, and more ability to tailor instruction to varying learning styles and speeds. Parents were delighted with their ability to get closely involved with their children's education, and with the entire family's newfound computer literacy.

The following year, the program was expanded to include the fifth grade so that the initial students did not have to relinquish their newfound skills. Student and parent interest in programming ran so high that it was added to the curriculum, and families began expanding their own software libraries to meet their growing skills and needs.

TESTING, ONE, TWO, THREE, FOUR...

Assuming that parents have been able to participate in deciding what is going to be taught in the schools and which materials are going to be used to teach it, the next area for parent participation would naturally be in assessing the success of the curriculum. Periodically we must examine not only how much our students are learning, but whether they are learning what we want them to learn.

Before we can assess our students' progress, we must determine the goals of our curriculum; we have to know what information we expect them to know before we can devise either the curriculum or the tests. Our goals can be as broad or as specific as we like. Generally, parents (and school boards) are responsible for setting major goals, while professional educators determine the specific methods or objectives for reaching those goals. The following two samples illustrate the difference between general goals and specific objectives:

Montgomery County School Goals

- *Reading:* The ability to read and comprehend written material and relate it to other knowledge
- *Composition:* The ability to write with precision, clarity, and acceptable usage, whether to inform, inspire, or persuade
- *Listening and Speaking:* The ability to listen attentively and with understanding and to speak with confidence and effectiveness whether from written material or extemporaneously
- *Mathematics:* The ability to perform computations, to solve common problems of mathematics and logic, and to understand the structure of mathematics so it can be a useful tool in daily living
- *Study:* The development of basic study skills so that students may acquire knowledge efficiently
- *Arts:* The development of some of the basic disciplines and skills in performing and creative arts to be used for communication, expression, and enjoyment
- *Observation:* The ability to identify and differentiate elements of the world around students as they are useful in academic, personal, and artistic pursuits
- *Other goals include:*
  Physical Development
  Intellectual Development
  The Individual and Society

Scientific Understanding
Aesthetic Expression
Career Development
(from *Parents Unite!* by Philip and Susan Jones)

Sample Curriculum Objectives

Elementary School
- Identifies by sight and sound short vowel sounds in a word: a, e, i, o, and u (second grade)
- Associates cardinal and ordinal numbers (1–10/first–tenth) (3rd grade)
- Infers reasonable conclusions from reading selections (3rd)
- Adds all combinations of one-, two-, and three-digit numbers without carrying (3rd)
- Describes the life cycle of a butterfly (4th)
- Uses a globe to locate continents, countries, et cetera (4th)
- Uses guide words to locate words in dictionary (4th)
- Checks the accuracy of answers to addition problems by re-adding and to subtraction problems by adding (4th)
- Diagrams a food chain (5th)
- Compares and contrasts the old and new life-styles of Navajo Indians (5th)
- Subtracts fractions with unlike denominators through ten (6th)
- Classifies rocks by their method of formation; igneous, metamorphic, and sedimentary (6th)
- Compares and contrasts executive, legislative, and judicial branches of government (6th)
- Writes an editorial (5th)
- Applies the concept of molecular motion to solids, liquids, and gases (5th)
- Empathizes with the conflicting feelings of loyalty and patriotism Robert E. Lee felt toward the Union and the Confederacy (6th)
(from *Time for Curriculum* by Henry Brickell and Regina Paul)

Without meaningful objectives, we cannot devise meaningful measurements. Once we have established them, however, we need to decide on the appropriate means of measurement. There are two types of tests to measure academic achievement (aptitude tests, which measure intelligence, and specialized tests are not relevant to this discussion) — curriculum based and standardized. Achievement tests only measure what is being taught, or what is being tested, and are limited by the nature of the scoring mechanism.

The most frequently encountered tests are curriculum based, which are written by the teacher or provided by the textbook publisher to gauge whether or not the student has grasped the material presented in a particular unit of study. In contrast, standardized tests, developed to determine whether a large group of students is performing up to a predetermined standard, are administered to a larger group of children, usually at the beginning or end of certain designated grades (fourth, eighth, and twelfth are the most common).

Standardized testing falls into several categories: tests that measure achievement in a particular area, statewide assessment tests that periodically measure students' progress, and minimum competency tests to measure their level of scholastic achievement at a certain age. Most standardized tests are developed by textbook publishers or by testing companies, both non- and for-profit, in a $200 million-per-year business. Because there is tremendous competition to sell these tests — and because their results can be so powerful in determining a student's future — they are developed with the utmost security, and guarded with military secrecy.

Nevertheless, several states have established sunshine laws enabling parents and community members to see copies of previous tests and requiring testing companies to publicize the nature of the tests, the methods of assessment, and the uses to which it might be put. DE-TEST, a publication put out by the Center for the Study of Education and Politics, is among the few consumer-oriented tools designed to de-mystify testing for the test taker.

Standardized testing of all types has come under fire lately, for a variety of reasons. In 1978, African-American students in Florida successfully charged that the state's standardized minimum competency tests contained material they had not been taught, a violation of the Constitution's equal protection and due process clause. That landmark suit has been followed by years of similar allegations, most of them supporting the theory that minorities are placed at an unfair disadvantage in standardized testing situations.

As the result of such legal precedents, parents can challenge what they believe to be discriminatory school testing procedures. Local or standardized tests are invalid if they incorporate cultural biases that place minorities at disadvantage. Recent studies have shown, for example, that African-American students score an average of one hundred points lower on SATs than their white classmates. Despite recent attention to this problem, most standardized tests still reflect a cultural bias.

When the results of standardized testing are used to place students in college, in advanced placement programs, or in special education classes, we can't rely on the faulty information that such tests provide. Many critics of standardized tests feel that too much emphasis is placed on test scores anyway — that a student's SAT score, for instance, should be just one small part of an overall assessment. On the other hand, some educators believe standardized tests are still the best method available to assess not only an individual's progress in relation to other students but the progress of entire classes and schools.

The tests are easy to use because they give the *illusion* of uniformity. In fact, the minimum competency tests used in every state to gauge the progress of that state's fourth, eighth, and twelfth graders vary widely from state to state, making any interstate comparisons invalid. Most standardized tests gauge only reading and mathematical skills, leaving out all-important writing and critical-thinking skills because they are too difficult to score. The National Assessment of Educational Progress is trying to develop guidelines for tests that would include the writing samples of children being tested. Such portfolio assessment techniques are already in use in some states and districts.

The National Commission on Testing and Public Policy has found that standardized tests are given too frequently to children who are too young for accurate assessment, resulting in improper placement of as many as one third of all children at the kindergarten or first-grade level. The testing companies themselves come up with the "average" scores for their own tests. This process is known as "norm referencing," which means gauging an individual score in relation to the scores of other students. By their own admission, the testing companies only revise the norms every eight years or so because the process is so expensive. University of New Mexico psychiatrist Dr. John Jacob Cannell studied standardized test norms and found that more than 82 percent of all students were scoring above average on the norm-referenced tests. That, he says, is a mathematical impossibility for norm referencing (half the students should be above the norm, half below) and clear proof that today's standardized tests do not accurately reflect the achievement levels they are meant to assess. He calls it the "Lake Wobegon effect," referring to Garrison Keillor's imaginary town in Minnesota "where all the children are above average."

Unfortunately, individual and school-wide test scores are a major determinant in placement procedures and college and job applications. They even determine our perceptions of how "good" a school is, although critics charge that the only thing standardized tests accurately measure is how well students have been prepared to take that particular test. In spite of these pitfalls, standardized tests are still widely used and there is great pressure on students, teachers, and school districts to perform well on them. Naturally, such pressure has led to increased allegations of cheating — by students as well as by teachers, who have been known to obtain copies of the tests beforehand and coach their classes specifically on the test material. This "proficiency-based curriculum" means that students may be taught only what is on the tests. The curriculum is built around the tests, rather than the other way around. Educators who follow test-based curricula are technically doing their jobs, but they are not necessarily preparing students to make academic progress or to think for themselves. Teaching to the test, as it is called, not only throws off standardized scoring mechanisms, but it limits the academic curriculum to that determined by an outside testing agency that has had no input into the school community's choice of curriculum.

The real objective of any testing system is to measure what skills students have acquired over the course of the semester and how well they can use the material they have been taught. And some new testing formats are attempting to do just that.

In Waterbury, Connecticut, a high school biology tester gave his students jars of live brine shrimp. Their test was to figure out the best saltwater solution in which to keep the shrimp alive long enough to be mailed to another state. In a statewide California pilot program, students at a La Jolla high school are passing in portfolios that include samples of writing in the style of famous authors as well as self-evaluations of their own writing progress. In East Harlem, New York, math and science students are being graded on their knowledge of projectile motion on the basis of projects the students themselves designed, using moving objects of their own choosing.

Critics of these new testing alternatives say they are too cumbersome to give and grade as well as too expensive to administer. There may be no single right answer, but multitiered judging standards could be formulated that would make it possible to grade even the most complex test project. And by testing only a sample of any given school population, a school district could easily arrive at an assessment of school-wide progress, which isn't intended to gauge individual progress anyway. Although it may be difficult, there is no reason why standards can't be determined from the careful evaluation of, say, writing portfolios or long-term science projects.

TRANSLATING SCORES INTO ACTION

Accountability may be the major pitfall of standardized testing, but what happens with a child who does not do well on a test? Unfortunately, our remedial programs lag far behind our testing protocols, and it may be up to parents to insist that low scores call not for student coaching on test questions but instead for more long-range programs to boost skills. In many cases, standardized tests reveal too little too late: a student who fails his or her state's minimum competency test in high school has already suffered from many years of educational neglect, and a failing score may only precipitate a dropout if no adequate remedial procedures are in place. If standardized tests have any validity, say some educators, it is to inform parents and teachers about the gaps in a child's education that then need to be filled by remedial instruction.

In order for that use to be fulfilled, parents and teachers need to learn how to decode scores and translate them into effective curriculum choices. That means making individual scores available to all parents, and it's an issue that's worth fighting for, since it provides valuable information even if the tests themselves aren't perfect. Some districts now permit parents to receive their child's individual scores, while others provide only school-wide or district-wide information. Even then, having scores for one district gives parents no information on how their child's schools are performing in relation to other schools in surrounding districts. If tax apportionments are an issue, such cross-district measurements could be an essential tool in determining accountability. Parents can also use broad-based scores to track "cohort" scores, or scores of an entire class year after year. If a consistently high cohort score drops sharply in, say, the fourth grade, that provides a clear warning signal to parents or educators that something is wrong.

But having the scores isn't enough. Parents often feel cowed by the technical language of testing, even though our legal rights under the Family Educational Rights and Privacy Act guarantee that all test materials and scores be explained in language we understand. Test-scoring terms are often confusing and misleading. Some scores will be given in five or six different formats, none of them particularly illuminating. Staninines, or standard nines, divide the test-taking group into nine equal levels. Grade-equivalent scores, which measure a student's performance in terms of the year and month of the grade level, often bear no relation to reality because they are established on a curve and not on the basis of an absolute. Criterion-referencing, an alternative to norm referencing, gauges a child's score on the basis of predetermined "correct" answers that may or may not be valid. Even raw data, the child's actual answers to the test questions, isn't helpful if it isn't accompanied by a clearly written explanation of what those questions were.

TOWARD A WORKABLE, PARENT-DRIVEN CURRICULUM

Maybe it would be easier if there were national standards to which every school in the country had to adhere. Gallup polls in 1989 indicated that the great majority of Americans support a standardized national testing program, with a specific examination required for high school graduation. But the quest for national standards leads inevitably to questions about the desirability of a national curriculum, and most Americans still want to retain local control of school curricula. The National Assessment of Educational Progress decided in 1990 to establish national tests based on absolute standards of what fourth, eighth, and twelfth graders ought to know. They convened panels of parents, teachers, and education researchers to determine what kinds of information and concepts should be tested at each level and then divided the scoring system into four groups: those who would score above advanced standards, those between proficient and advanced, those between basic and proficient, and those who do not meet the basic standard.

The results of such tests could give America its first visible report card on the status of its students. But critics charge that national standards are only politically expedient, and that they do nothing to improve achievement levels at local schools. All the arguments about standardized testing would resurface with a vengeance. A nationalized, standardized testing program might reinforce a proficiency-based curriculum at the expense of critical thinking. Perhaps even more important, such a program would make it virtually impossible for parents to participate in shaping their children's curriculum.

TOWARD CHANGE

How can we make decisions about what to teach and how to teach it? We can work with teachers to overcome the communication barriers that parents and educators experience. We can stop expecting educators to have all the answers and begin to arrive at a consensus with them and with other parents about what we need to teach in our community schools. We can ask for parent-teacher-student-administrator contracts to make us all more answerable to our common goals (see ''How To: Write a Partners-in-Learning Contract,'' at the end of this chapter). We can ask questions about curriculum goals at school committee meetings, about classroom objectives at school classroom meetings, and about our children's performance at teacher conferences.

We can become experts on reading test scores, demanding raw scores and explanations for our own child's performance, and information about our school's performance in relation to other schools. We can convince our school administrators to move toward a portfolio method of assessment that uses samples of our children's writing and thinking as well as standardized test scores. We can keep careful records of our child's education progress and of the progress of our children's schools.

We can lobby for the establishment of a lab school in our district to try out innovative curricula, teaching methods, and assessment techniques that we determine to be appropriate for our children. Lab schools are our testing grounds for education reform.

"I equate lab schools with chemistry or biology labs in the natural sciences," says John Johnson of the National Association of Laboratory Schools. "They are spawning grounds for new ideas and new pedagogy." Despite budget cutbacks and ongoing debates over program efficiency, lab schools are thriving all over the country, providing teachers colleges and school systems with new ideas, new energy, and new possibilities for success.

The granddaddy of all lab schools, established by John Dewey in 1896, is the University of Chicago Lab School, which consists of an elementary, middle, and high school. While many lab schools are situated on college campuses, a growing number are moving into the communities they are intended to serve.

There are over one hundred lab schools now functioning around the country, and a greater number of lab school programs within existing schools. Lab schools focus on a wide variety of educational issues, most of them related to a narrow field of research, but some with broad-based curriculum goals:

- *The University of Chicago's elementary lab school is experimenting with the development of logical thinking in young children and with a writing-based curriculum.*
- *The State University of New York College at Buffalo's lab school focuses on new teaching methods for brain-damaged children.*
- *Carnegie-Mellon is examining the use of Macintosh computers in developing preschoolers' senses of color and shape.*
- *Illinois State University at Normal is studying how technology can help learning disabled students.*
- *The University of Hawaii is trying to make science more alluring by including health, environment, and technology in the curriculum.*

The great majority of lab schools are connected with universities or teachers colleges, although some have been established by school districts themselves.

Parent groups wanting to explore lab schools need to contact school administrators to find out what lab school programs are already in existence and explore the possibilities of creating a program or school in conjunction with local universities and/or businesses. Parents can stay involved with lab school planning all the way through implementation and monitoring to be sure that the experiment continues to reflect the goals of the community. The results of lab school work, according to NALS's Johnson, are encouraging. "Lab schools are a volcano that is showing signs of puffing."

Most importantly, we can insist that our school's curriculum reflects the cultural reality of our neighborhood as well as the world, and we can become involved in the planning, decision making, and monitoring necessary to see that it does. This involves putting into use many of the skills outlined in Chapter 4, but the results are surely worth the effort. Parental involvement in curriculum decision making is working in Memphis, in Boston, in Dallas, and in Dayton. It can happen anywhere parents are willing to organize, research, and act responsibly.

HOW TO: Get Answers about Local Testing Procedures

How and when do schools test students? How can we decide if those tests are valid for our children? How can we interpret the results? The National Committee for Citizens in Education publishes an excellent pamphlet entitled *Parents* Can *Understand Testing.* In addition to explaining the reasons for test giving, types of tests given, and a valuable list of minimum competency test regulations for each state, the pamphlet provides parents with a list of questions they can ask their local educators to determine if a particular testing procedure is valid and/or worthwhile. It is paraphrased here, in condensed form:

I. Questions about teacher-devised tests

1. How many tests are given during the school year, and how time-consuming are they?
2. What are the tests designed to accomplish?
   Valid answers: a) to help motivate student learning
                   b) to provide teachers with feedback
                   c) to help make placement decisions
3. What types of tests are being given? Are they multiple-choice, true-or-false, or essay? Do they assess the student's grasp of the material as well as his or her memory of the fact?
4. How are the tests prepared? Are they designed to be "pop" quizzes or to cover extensive units of study? Do they accurately reflect the material covered and the objectives of the curriculum?
5. How are the tests graded or rated? Is the student's performance evaluated on the basis of his or her individual degree of mastery or on the basis of relative performance vis-à-vis other students? Is the scoring mechanism reliable?

II. Questions about tests purchased from test publishers

1. How often are they given and how time-consuming are they?
2. What are the tests designed to accomplish?
3. What types of tests are being given, and why were they chosen?
4. How and by whom were the tests chosen? Who made the decision

about buying a particular test, and what process did that person use to arrive at that particular choice? What were the chief considerations in making the decision?

5. How are the tests administered? Are the instructions provided by the publisher being followed? Is the test being administered in an appropriate setting (quiet, spacious, comfortable) by trained personnel? What measures are being taken to discourage cheating?

6. How are students being prepared to take the tests? Are they being given adequate preparation about the nature of the tests — what kinds of questions will be asked, how the tests are scored, and what the scores mean? Are they being drilled on the material to the exclusion of other curricula? Have the students' opinions been sought about the degree of difficulty or confusion generated by previous tests, and has this information been incorporated into test-purchasing decisions?

7. How are the tests scored and reported? Has the school purchased a machine-scoring device? How quickly are score reports distributed? If tests are scored by hand, what is being done to ensure accuracy? Do reports provide detailed information on wrong answers for teachers and students? What methods are used to convert "raw" scores into scoring systems that students and parents can understand?

8. How are the tests interpreted and used? Who is responsible for seeing to it that teachers, parents, and students understand their scores? Are decisions based on test scores made accurately, accounting for margins of error and other academic information besides the tests? Are scores used to help teachers and students evaluate their progress, and are measures taken to remediate any educational weaknesses that the tests reveal?

III. Questions about tests supplied by the state education authority

1. What is the nature of the state's testing program? What subjects does it cover in what grades? What types of tests are used?

2. How are the test scores used? For guidance, minimum competency, graduation, promotion, state fund allocation, and/or state college admissions?

3. Is the testing mandatory for all students in the state? If not, why are some students excluded?

4. When are the tests administered and by whom? How much time do they consume?

5. Who does the scoring, and how are scores reported to schools and/or individuals?

6. To what extent do local school personnel participate in the development and/or selection of tests?
7. What evidence is available on the tests' validity for the purposes chosen?

IV. Questions about miscellaneous testing matters

1. Individually administered IQ tests: Are they administered by trained individuals? At what age are pupils tested, and how are the results being used? Are the scores entered into the student's cumulative record?
2. Tests of attitudes, interests, self-concept: Are they administered individually or in groups? Are they used for counseling? What specific tests were used and why? Are some students exempted, and why? Are results entered on cumulative records?
3. College admission tests: Which tests are offered to college-bound students? What is done to prepare them for tests, to help them register, and to advise them of the need to take such tests? Is the school calendar set up to avoid conflicts with major test dates? How do the scores compare with grades students receive on classroom work or on locally designed tests?

HOW TO: Write a Partners-in-Learning Contract (*adapted from the Maryland Public Schools*)

We know that learning can take place only when there is a combination of effort, interest, and motivation. As we are all committed to _____'s progress in school, we are going to do our best to promote his or her achievement. This agreement is a promise to work together. We believe that this agreement can be fulfilled by our team effort. Together we can improve teaching and learning.

As a student I pledge to

- work as hard as I can on my school assignments;
- discuss with my parents what I am learning in school;
- follow the code of student conduct established in school;
- ask my teacher questions when I don't understand something;
- go to my public or school library at least once a week;
- limit my TV watching and read books instead.

As a parent I pledge to

- provide a quiet study time at home and encourage good study habits;

- talk with my child about his or her school activities;
- reinforce the code of student conduct;
- find out how my child is progressing by attending conferences, looking at schoolwork, or calling the school;
- encourage my child to read by reading to him or her and by reading myself;
- limit my child's TV viewing and help him or her select worthwhile programs.

As a teacher I pledge to

- provide motivating and interesting learning experiences in my classroom;
- explain my expectations, instructional goals, and grading system to parents and students;
- explain the code of student conduct to students and parents;
- communicate and cooperate with each parent to ensure the best education possible;
- find out what techniques and materials work best for the student and employ them;
- guide students in their choice of TV programs.

As a principal/administrator I pledge to

- create a welcoming environment for students and parents;
- communicate to students and parents the school's missions and goals;
- ensure a safe and orderly learning environment;
- reinforce the partnership between parent, student, and staff;
- act as the instructional leader by supporting teachers in their classrooms;
- provide appropriate in-services and training for teachers and parents.

*Signed*_____

Most important, we all promise to help each other carry out this agreement. Signed on this _____ day of _____ 19____.

The Other Curriculum: Making and Breaking the Rules

B ACK in the "good old days," parents could send their children to school confident about what they would be learning: reading, writing, arithmetic, history, science, and social studies. Graduates of most American public schools could be counted on to know certain things, regardless of where they went to school: where Abraham Lincoln was born, what the Bill of Rights stood for, the capital of North Dakota, and the square root of 144.

But schools weren't just about the three R's and their companion curricula, even back in those allegedly simpler times. Parents were sure that once their children had completed twelve years of school they would have the requisite skills necessary to make them proud and productive members of American society. Their political, moral, and social education was not explicit in most cases, but it was consistent with the values that parents themselves held at home. There was no question of conflict between home and school curriculum, because everyone was supposed to believe in the same things.

Of course we know that such a myth was never the case; parents have been absorbing, debating, or rejecting school-infused values since before there were public schools. The history of public education, like the history of the country itself, is fraught with tension between the status quo and the avant-garde, and it is the fruit of that tension that creates change. Nevertheless the popular image of schools was that they created sound citizens, and their factory-like structure reinforced the sense of homogeneity both among schools and between family and school.

Today we can labor under no such delusions — our society is as fragmented as our school systems, and the idea of commonly held principles about what children need to learn is as unlikely as the idea of commonly held visions of what our society needs to be. We cannot agree on whether or not our children should learn Spanish, new math, whole language experience reading, or multicultural approaches to history, let alone on what we should do to teach them to be "good" and "productive" citizens.

Yet our schools, in addition to teaching a dazzling array of explicit curricula, are also being asked to teach social skills, moral values, ethical rules of conduct, and basic survival skills. They are being asked to provide health and sex education, driving and street safety skills, nutrition and substance abuse education. They are being asked to monitor our children in the classrooms and hallways, on the playgrounds and in the streets, and even, in some cases, at home when parents aren't there.

Critics of this all-inclusive curriculum of life — and many public school educators are among them — argue that such survival skills are not the province of the schools but should be taught by parents, church, and family. Some parents agree, while others feel that the schools must rise to meet the demands of a more-complicated-than-ever world, and recognize that some children need more help than others to render them equally likely to become good and productive citizens.

Schools do need to teach much more than the three R's — in fact, it is unlikely that the three R's could be taught if students didn't first learn the appropriate mode of conduct in the classroom necessary to education. Issues of behavior management, safety, classroom control, and discipline are not part of the explicit curriculum, but they are central to the success of any school. They also provide us with a sharp insight into the kind of school our child attends, and tell us more than any academic curriculum about whether the school-infused values will clash with our values at home.

Equally important is the question of how, and what, to teach those students who do not fall into the general student population. Learning disabled, handicapped, gifted, bilingual, or at-risk children require special education, and the schools are legally responsible for providing it. But mandated special education does not necessarily mean successful special education, and parental impact on such programs can be the deciding factor in their quality and effectiveness.

The question remains, though: Who teaches what, to whom, and how? Can schools teach our children how to behave even if we do not approve of their behavior code or their methods of enforcing such codes? Can we expect them to provide all our children with the appropriate education so that they all graduate with an even chance of joining our polyglot society? The way in which schools conduct the business of educating their students is as important as — perhaps more important than — the actual education itself. It is the way in which schools act most clearly "in loco parentis" — in the place of parents — to create socialized adults.

It is this second curricular agenda — the agenda of rules and regulations and special cases — that is most often controlled by schools and district regulations, by state and federal laws. Parents may feel stymied by rules that make it seem as if changing the suspension procedure or a special education regulation is much harder than changing the math curriculum. But parents can make — and have made — essential contributions in these areas; in fact, their guidance is more likely to be sought than it is for more explicit curriculum issues.

By examining school approaches to behavior and discipline codes, due process issues, and safety procedures, and by looking at the gains made by parents in several areas of special education, parents can begin to get a picture of how far they can go to control this "hidden" curriculum. They can work to eliminate friction between the values imposed at home and those at school, and they can make sure that the school is teaching the whole child — and every child — to become an equally proud and productive member of the adult community.

LEARNING THE RULES IN SCHOOL

Anyone who has walked into a room full of rambunctious second graders knows that getting their attention — and keeping it — is an uphill battle. Parents often wonder how a teacher can manage a class of twenty-five when handling one or two can seem so overwhelmingly exhausting. As a matter of fact, teachers often wonder how parents can manage children at home, since they seem to be so difficult even in the structured confines of the school.

Children can be difficult to manage, and it goes without saying that unmanaged children are more difficult to teach. Educators' philosophies about child discipline range from extremely permissive ("Let the child do what he wants; his natural instincts will help him focus on whatever work is important to him") to extremely controlling ("The child is an unruly creature who must be contained and tamed so that she can learn information necessary to civilize her"). No one disputes that children learn better when they are able to concentrate on whatever it is they are learning, but discipline is about more than creating a maximal learning environment. It's also about value setting, whether we acknowledge it as such or not. When we ask a child to defer to the teacher, we are saying something about the relative values we place on children and adults.

When we ask a child to raise his or her hand before speaking we are making a value judgement about the needs of the group over the needs of the individual.

Nowhere is this more apparent than in the methods a school or teacher chooses to enforce a behavior code. Such codes are usually determined on a school-wide or district-wide basis, although classroom teachers have a great deal of latitude in determining how to apply them. A behavior code covers the ways in which children are expected to conduct themselves in the classroom, in the hallways, on the playground, and in the school's public spaces. It also entails the consequences of inappropriate behavior. The goals of behavior codes are to promote a positive and receptive learning environment, instill appropriate group behavior, and protect other children and adults from disruptive or unsafe behavior. While we may differ on what we judge to be acceptable, most parents and teachers agree that these goals are necessary for an effective school experience.

Expectations vary from school to school; an acceptable learning environment may be a quiet classroom where everyone faces the teacher and listens, or it may be a classroom where children talk to one another in small groups. They also vary from space to space; what we expect of children during a spelling test is different from what we expect of them during a class discussion or on the playground.

Learning the appropriate behavior in each instance is not an easy job, especially for five- and six-year-olds, to whom the very idea of large groups in large spaces may be daunting. But learn them they do; kindergarten teachers often comment on the vast difference between the behavior of their students in September and the following May. Some schools make behavioral expectations quite specific — notices are sent home, contracts between parents, students, and schools are signed, and regulations are clearly posted in classrooms and halls. In others, the code must be deduced more informally. Most states have laws stipulating that students cannot be punished for breaking rules not clearly stated beforehand.

In some cases, parents or students themselves provide input into the code-making process. Some schools even allow students to determine the appropriate discipline for infractions of the rules they have helped design. Such self-determination works best with older students and plenty of guidance from adults, but it can be an extremely successful way to promote cooperation. It can also be a valuable lesson in group decision making and the democratic process.

Interactive methods of determining codes and enforcements can also act preventively to deter misbehavior. Other preventive methods, such as rewarding positive behavior and creatively channeling potential misbehavior, have also been very successful in reducing classroom management problems. These measures are very effective with younger children, and, though they require a great deal of adult control, they can make children feel like active participants in determining their own behavior, which is certainly the goal of any behavior code.

Located in central Los Angeles, the George Washington Preparatory High School has a 65 percent low-income/minority population. For years, the school was notorious for its drug use and gang violence as well as for its low academic performance. More than half the nearly 2,000 students had requested busing to other schools.

Then George McKenna was hired as the new principal. He added the word preparatory *to the school's name and to its curriculum model and set about pursuing a vision of academic excellence through the use of magnet classes, new teachers (hired with parent input), a parent advisory group, and an enforced discipline code.*

McKenna also instituted training in nonviolence for his students. Modeled on the teachings of Martin Luther King, Jr., and Mahatma Gandhi, the training emphasized compromise, coexistence, and conflict resolution as successful means of working out problems in school and out.

The training was opened to the students' families as well, so that parents could become involved in using and monitoring the new nonviolent techniques. Parents and their children were asked to sign Contracts for a Nonviolent Home, promising that they would not physically or verbally abuse one another.

George Washington Prep is now one of the safest schools in the district, with high college admission rates, low absenteeism, and a waiting list for entrance.

Most schools determine behavior codes at the administrative level and decide upon enforcement mechanisms in the same way. This method has the advantage of being clear and consistent throughout the school or system. Such mechanisms have a wide range of severity, usually dependent on the nature and number of times the infraction has occurred. They include, in ascending order of severity:

- public acknowledgment
- reprimands
- loss of privilege
- extra work
- detention
- removal from classroom
- suspension
- corporal punishment
- expulsion

Except for the last three (to be discussed later in this chapter, in the section on schools and the law), the use of these punishment mechanisms depends a lot on the teacher's personality and the child's response. If you feel that your child will benefit more from extra work than he will from classroom removal, you certainly have the right to discuss that with his or her teacher. Most teachers will welcome the opportunity to explore more effective methods of discipline.

Such measures are usually reserved for an infraction of rules governing classroom behavior or behavior in a larger supervised group. What about controls on behavior of students in unsupervised settings such as playgrounds and hallways? Although such areas are technically supervised, it is often difficult for adults in charge to keep track of everything that goes on in a crowded area where children are not expected to be paying attention to a specific activity. Many parents feel that their child's safety is compromised by such situations, and some school districts have responded by providing students and parents with clear-cut behavior guidelines that delineate unacceptable behavior and specify the consequences of an infraction.

In October of 1990, after several threatening incidents at area elementary schools, the Cambridge School Department issued a K–8 weapons policy to every child in every school. The policy said, in part: ''bringing a weapon to school, using a weapon on school grounds, or having a weapon in your locker, pocket, or while you are at school, on the bus, or at an after-school activity, is a grave offense and is against school rules and regulations. It is also against the law.''

The policy delineated two types of weapons — those that were clearly threatening, and ordinary objects used in a threatening way. It clearly stated the mandatory suspension periods for an infraction: two days suspension for grades K–1, four days for 2–4, and ten for 5–8. Meetings to consider further action would also be a part of the punishment process.

The policy arrived with a cover letter describing the seriousness of the problem, and asking parents to become part of the education process by stressing the dangers of weapons to their children, regardless of age. In addition, each policy came with a contract that was to be signed by both parents and child indicating that they understood both the regulations and their punishment. Although there was some question about the appropriateness of the mandated suspension for very young children, the policy received widespread support from parents throughout the city.

The National Committee for Citizens in Education provides a list of ways in which parents can monitor the level of violence in their children's schools. Indicators of escalating violence include:

- growing absenteeism
- complaints or stories of problems (in lunchrooms, et cetera)
- increasing false alarms (fire alarms, bomb threats, et cetera)
- verbal abuse of teachers
- minor thefts
- a significant drop in achievement levels
- the presence of nonstudents around the schools

Any perceived rise in the level or frequency of violent interactions should be dealt with immediately. If parents are not satisfied with the action taken at the school level, superintendents or school committee members should be notified of confirmed cases. Failing that, civil authorities may be brought in by parents to take control.

LOOKING READY TO LEARN: DRESS AND HAIR CODES

Behavior codes are not the only area in which schools feel the need to control their students. Another issue that attracts much scrutiny is that of school dress codes. At first glance dress codes seem to be an insignificant issue, but educators point out that the ramifications of clothing and hairstyle can be great. In southern California, for example, excessive gang violence has led to the banning of certain colors in school dress, since the colors are associated with gang allegiance and can be incendiary. The feverish rush to keep up with the latest styles, and the economic pressures that many parents reported as a result, led to the establishment of a school uniform code in a Connecticut school district. Some parents and educators are pushing for a uniform dress code because it removes the status-or-stigma effect of wearing regular clothing and emphasizes that the purpose of the school day is to learn. But students in a number of schools have initiated strikes and protests to challenge dress codes they see as restrictive.

In 1989, five hundred students in Henry County, Georgia, picketed the board of education to protest a newly established dress code. They felt the code was out-of-date, excessively restrictive, and limited their constitutional freedom of expression (more on constitutional issues later). While the protest did not result in any changes, it did illustrate the ongoing debate between those supporting freedom of expression and those who feel that such expression needs to be limited in a school setting.

The rules below applied to grades six through twelve:

- *Hair will be clean, neat and well groomed. Extreme hair styles that, in the opinion of the principal or designee would cause a disruption in the educational environment or that would be a safety or health hazard are prohibited.*

- *Girls' hair length and style will not be such as to cover the eyes or interfere with the learning of other students.*
- *Boys' hair will not cover the eyes or extend below the bottom of the shirt collar.*
- *Girls' skirts, split skirts, and dresses must come to the top of the knee. Slits in skirts or dresses must not be considered extreme or unreasonable.*
- *Boys' clothing that is too tight or immodest is prohibited.*
- *Proper undergarments are required.*
- *Jewelry or clothing that has pictures, logos, lettering, writing, or other symbols that the principal or designee consider vulgar, offensive, profane, suggestive, disruptive, reflecting sexual or obscene overtones, or advertising controlled substances is prohibited.*

The director of management services at the Henry County Board of Education defended the code by noting that it reflected the values of the communities in which the schools exist. ''Obviously, any rule is inhibiting a child's freedom or his ability to explore and grow. But obviously, you cannot run a school without any rules. The Board of Education feels that the community values call for an environment conducive to learning. Standing by themselves, dress codes do not necessarily affect the educational environment. But together with other standards (freshly painted halls, clean bathrooms, uncrowded classrooms), they do.''

In most cases, reasonable dress cannot be prohibited unless it is unsanitary, unhealthy, disruptive, or obscene. Of course, making such a determination is a subjective matter with much room for dispute. If you have concerns about the validity of school dress codes — whether you feel those codes go too far or not far enough — you can bring up the subject at school committee meetings or at school-wide parent meetings. If enough parents feel that changes should be made, school officials may be responsive to constructive suggestions for change. Remember, though, that the students themselves can be a potent force for change and, in matters of personal appearance and grooming, involving the students themselves in the decision-making process will make for a more realistic and enforceable dress code.

HOW IT'S DONE HERE: LEARNING SCHOOL PROCESSES

Other school regulations may seem less potentially explosive, but they may be even more important to your child's educational success. Learning about school policies concerning attendance, class size and composition, promotion and retention, tracking, and school transfers is essential for parents who want to be actively involved in the education process. Making changes in those policies can be a difficult proposition requiring careful research, effective organization, and patient lobbying at the district level. Let's look at some of these and see how our schools stack up.

School Attendance

State law determines the number of days a child must attend school each year in order to be eligible for graduation, but the states leave enforcement up to the local districts. Since there is a clear connection between attendance levels and school budgets (state funds are often disbursed on the basis of the average number of children in daily attendance in the district), it is in the best interests of each district, educationally as well as financially, to see to it that as many children as possible attend school.

But how do schools encourage good attendance or penalize poor attendance? And how do they determine what is an excusable absence and what is considered a "truant" or unexcused absence? In some schools, perfect attendance is rewarded with a certificate or a ribbon, either to an individual student or to an entire class. In others, poor attendance can result in a lowering of a student's grade-point average. Dealing with truancies has usually been left to law enforcement officers, but some schools have been experimenting with other ways to discourage unexcused absences.

A controversial state law in Wisconsin ties the disbursement of state welfare checks to the number of unexcused school absences of a family's teenage children. Milwaukee parent Geneal Fengier, whose husband is disabled, was shocked when she learned that she would receive no check because there had been more than two truancies during the previous month. The law allows the state to withhold up to two hundred dollars a month per child for such absences after a limit of ten is reached for the year.

With the program, known as Learnfare, the state hopes to encourage students to stay in school, reasoning that students who finish high school are statistically less likely to become welfare recipients themselves as adults. By holding the parents responsible for the children's attendance, the state also hopes to encourage parents to stay more actively involved in their children's daily lives. "People bear responsibility for the money they receive. The point is to keep these kids in school so they can get a job, get off welfare, and break the cycle of dependency," says State Social Service Secretary Patricia Goodrich.

But parents like Mrs. Fengier, who says she was unaware of the program until she received the notification of no payment, think that's unrealistic. "I knew what the problem was," she says, "but I'm not there in school with them. If a kid's going to cut, he's going to cut.'' Her son's absences, she says, were a result of serious problems, and she was getting no help with the problems even though the family was being penalized for them.

Other critics, citing instances where parents have made up excuses for their children's absences to avoid the loss of income, say the program gives teenagers troubling economic power over their parents. A lawsuit has been filed on behalf of the parents who have lost benefits as a result of the program. Inaccurate record keeping in school and lack of support services are two of the program's problems that Goodrich says will be addressed before the law is extended to children between the ages of six and twelve.

Grade Retention

Perhaps no issue incurs as much emotional upheaval as the subject of retention — having a child repeat a grade in which he or she has not acquired the requisite skills. Educators have been debating the subject for years, and the current thinking is that retention has proven to have no positive results and several negative ones for the child. Since repeating a grade most often means going through the same material in the same way, there is little chance a child who has failed to grasp the material the first time will do so only because he or she is seeing it again. In fact, the low self-esteem that results from retention makes it likely that the child will do more poorly.

There is an ongoing debate about the abuse of grade retentions along racial and ethnic lines; African-American and Hispanic students are retained nearly twice as often as white students. But the reverse side of that coin also provokes argument: social promotions, which push a child on to the next grade even if he or she is not ready to handle the material, have also grown over the past decade. Just as they are wary of the ineffectiveness of retention and charge that retention is often racially based, parents accuse teachers of promoting children who are unruly or hard to teach simply to get them out of their classrooms. Several school boards have been sued by parents (and students) who have charged that students were promoted when they were not adequately prepared to go on.

Parents most often get involved in the retention/promotion issue when it affects their children. By then it is often too late, and, if a school policy is in place, there may be little that can be done. A more effective solution would be to monitor your child's progress carefully and make sure that he or she is getting the appropriate help during the year if he or she is not performing successfully in class. If retention is discussed as a possible option, the possibility of letting your child go on with special help may be a good option to raise. If retention is a virtual certainty, you can make sure that the repeated grade is not simply a year of the same work but that changes in curriculum are made to allow your child to succeed the second time around. As always, grouping with other parents who have similar concerns will ensure that the general issue of the school's retention/promotion policy receives the attention it deserves.

Tracking

Tracking is the policy that allows schools to place students in groups according to their ability. It has been widely practiced in American schools for the past several decades, and is only now coming under scrutiny in many school districts for its exclusionary implications. A recent study done for the Boston Public Schools by the Massachusetts Advocacy Center, for example, revealed that tracking systematically excluded African Americans and Hispanics from advanced placement courses, college preparatory curricula, and the city's prestigious "exam" high schools, which require a rigorous entrance examination for admittance.

The National Committee for Citizens in Education has studied tracking policies in a number of middle schools and shown conclusively that children in lower tracks receive inferior instruction, inferior learning materials, and less stimulation and encouragement. Tracking not only deprives those in the bottom tracks of an adequate education, but it also isolates those in the upper tracks, depriving them of the chance to interact with students whose abilities may not match theirs, but who have other skills to offer. NCCE found that collaborative learning groups, combining students of varying abilities and skills, is a far more effective solution for children of all levels.

Despite these findings, some parents feel that heterogeneous groupings deprive the more advanced child of the opportunity to accelerate. Like parents who argue for the removal of tracking, those parents in favor of it must communicate with teachers, administrators, and other parents about their concerns at teacher conferences, school council meetings, and other available forums.

DUE PROCESS: WHEN POLICY PROBLEMS BECOME LEGAL PROBLEMS

What happens when school policy blends into local, state, or federal law? A child may be kept after school for breaking a school rule (such as cheating on a test or not handing in an assignment on time), but if a child breaks a criminal or civil law (if, for instance, he or she attacks a teacher or uses drugs in school) he or she becomes eligible for stronger disciplinary methods, and, in some cases, for civil punishment as well. In addition to discipline issues, there are laws governing class size, school attendance, testing and placement, and safety issues that can also come under the jurisdiction of local, state, or federal law as well as school policy. While we have legal protections regarding our children's education, we (and our children) also have legal obligations to meet, and some of the changes we seek to make may come up against these legal obstacles (see Chapter 2).

Let's look at the disciplinary issue first. The line between school policy and civil law is particularly blurred here. Most schools have disciplinary policies that reflect civil and criminal law, and, in some cases, augment it. In general, the same rights that citizens (teachers as well as students) enjoy on the street are extended to them in the classroom, and anything that is not sanctioned by law in the larger world is also proscribed in the school. This protects both teachers and students, although court rulings in the past few years have limited students' rights somewhat.

In addition to ensuring a more effective learning environment and training productive citizens, school disciplinary policies are created to support and augment civil law, just as state policies are often created to support and augment federal law. But when students break this dual set of laws, they may find themselves being punished in both the legal and school systems. Some parents take issue with this double jeopardy and have argued successfully that dual punishment is unfair. Still, in both cases, the student is protected by his or her constitutional right to due process, and that's what parents must make sure of when a child does get involved in a disciplinary procedure. According to federal law, all children have a right to an education, even if the nature of that education is left to the states, and any attempt to deprive a child of that education must follow clearly prescribed procedures to ensure that the right is not unjustly removed.

Some legal issues can arise to complicate or clarify school policy in areas that we've already examined. School discipline, for example, leaves the realm of local policy and becomes a legal issue when corporal punishment is used. Corporal punishment, the use of physical force on the body of the offender, has been tested in several state and federal courts across the country, and the results have been mixed. Corporal punishment is illegal in some states, but most states allow it under ''reasonable'' conditions as long as the punishment is not considered ''excessive.'' Of course, such terms leave much to the discretion of the teacher or administrator, so parents need to make sure that their school's rules concerning such punishments are made clear, either in a school handbook or by the school principal.

The basic legal principle behind corporal punishment is that ''an educator may use such force as is believed to be necessary for proper control, education, and training of the child.'' Exceeding those standards is grounds for civil and, in some cases, criminal action against a school employee. According to the law, school employees can always use reasonable force to protect themselves and/or other students. In other cases reasonable standards include:

- forewarning the student
- taking less drastic steps first
- meting out the punishment in the presence of a school witness and with the reasons clearly stated
- providing a written explanation to parents
- ensuring that the punishment does not exceed the limits of state law

In some states, those standards are met and children have been struck with paddles, forced to stand for long periods, forced to consume obnoxious substances, thrown against walls, forced to do excessive exercise, pushed, punched, dragged, choked, and deprived of meals. Parents who find such "reasonable" standards to be excessive need to work together to make specific changes in local or state law to proscribe tactics they feel to be inhumane.

Unlike corporal punishment rules, a school's suspension and expulsion rules are not governed by any civil law. Suspension, the enforced exclusion of a child from school on a temporary basis, and expulsion, or permanent exclusion, are generally meted out according to the dictates of local policy. School districts are required to make their suspension/expulsion policies available to all parents, listing the infractions for which these punishments might be handed down, the number of suspension days related to each infraction, and — most important — the procedure that must be followed before enforcing such punishments.

In general, due process requires that you be notified of a pending suspension/expulsion in advance, that your child be given the opportunity to defend himself or herself, and that there be a procedure in place to allow an appeal. Short suspensions — from one to ten days — may be given fairly regularly in some schools without formal prior notification, provided the school has already notified all parents and students of the terms under which such a suspension would be issued.

Longer suspensions — over ten days — require due process before they can be initiated, and several states have laws requiring that suspended students be given work to do at home so that they don't fall behind in class and further jeopardize their school success. Technically, though, your child, unless handicapped, has no right to an education during the time of his or her suspension.

Students who are involved in suspension/expulsion hearings have rights of their own under due process. They have the right to legal counsel, to cross-examine their accuser, to present evidence in their own behalf, and to an appeal. David Schimmel and Louis Fischer, authors of *Parents, Schools and the Law*, provide the following breakdown of events as they should occur in such proceedings and list what each should include:

1. Notice of hearing with parents, child, accuser, administrator (and counsel, if available)
   - time and place acceptable to parents
   - clear statement of alleged infractions
   - notification of the right to counsel
   - description of proposed procedures or punishments
   - adequate time to prepare for hearing
   - access to available evidence
2. Hearing
   - advisement of student's right to speak or not to speak in his or her defense
   - presentation of evidence
   - opportunity to confront and cross-examine
   - written record of proceedings
3. Findings presented within an agreed-upon period of time
   - accurate reporting of proceedings
   - recommendations
4. Appeal
   - prompt application of disciplinary procedures, if applicable
   - right to appeal and availability of procedural information
   - right to prompt action on appeal

If your child is being considered for suspension and you cannot be reached, the school cannot suspend him or her. If you have not been contacted by phone, you must receive written notice. The conference, if it is necessary, must be held before the suspension itself is over. Once the suspension is over, you may be asked to come to school with your child the first day, but, if you refuse, your child cannot be kept out of school beyond the agreed-upon suspension. If you are appealing, your child has the right to stay in school until the appeal is resolved. In such a case, your child may be placed on an in-school suspension and prohibited from attending regular classes.

If a situation presents an imminent danger to other students or teachers, a student can be removed from classes at once as long as the notification process takes place as soon as possible after removal. From a parent's perspective, the longer the suspension, the more carefully these due process procedures should be handled. If an expulsion is being considered, every alternative option should be considered. In general, you should do everything you can to get your child back in school as quickly as possible. Here are some questions to think about:

1. What disciplinary actions were taken to help my child deal with this problem prior to the current action?
2. What other school support services were offered to help my child with this problem?
3. Why wasn't I notified of the problem earlier?
4. What alternatives to suspension could be offered?
5. What constructive efforts can be made to rectify the situation so that it doesn't happen again?
6. Were my child's rights respected during the proceedings?
7. Were my rights respected during the proceedings?
8. Was the hearing conducted in my native language, and at a time convenient to me?
9. Was my child given ample opportunity to state his or her case and present witnesses on his or her behalf?
10. Was the recommendation arrived at fairly?
11. Were my rights to appeal made clear, and was I notified of the right to counsel?
12. Was I given several options for advocacy support?

Situations do occur in which children are wrongly condemned, and appeals have been made to overturn unjust suspensions and expulsions. But the law also provides the opportunity for parents to initiate their own disciplinary action in certain cases. If parents can prove negligence in evaluating or placing students, or excessive and malicious treatment by an educator with evidence of an intentional cover-up, then it may be possible to institute criminal proceedings against the school. (Parents can also institute civil or criminal cases against individual teachers who they feel have broken the law.) But educational malpractice suits cannot stem from a perceived failure of the schools to provide the students with adequate instruction.

CRIMINAL PROCEDURES: WHEN THE COPS ARE CALLED

The same due process procedure must be followed if your child is suspected of conducting an illegal activity at school. Illegal activities include damage, theft, or destruction of property, endangering or harming school personnel or students, and possession of illegal objects or materials such as drugs, weapons, or contraband. Conviction resulting from an arrest on school property could lead to expulsion from the system, so parents need to make every effort to ensure that due process is followed — and that the child in question is receiving plenty of constructive help in addition to the disciplinary measures.

As long as there is reasonable cause for suspicion, educators can conduct widespread searches for illegal materials, looking in students' lockers and desks as well as in public areas. Law enforcement officials, however, need a search warrant to look in students' handbags, although several courts have allowed police to look in students' lockers and desks on the grounds that they were school property. Since the schools can turn the contraband over to the law enforcers, who can then use it as evidence, the distinction between school and civil authority is moot in most cases.

If your child is arrested, he or she will be taken to the nearest police department. Every effort will be made to contact you beforehand, but it is not necessary that you be notified before the arrest takes place. Parental assent must be sought, but not given, before your child can be questioned. He or she will be assigned a juvenile officer if under eighteen and then booked and told to attend a detention hearing. A public defender is usually assigned to detention hearings, but if the hearing finds your child needs to be held over for trial you may want to arrange for your own lawyer.

The schools cannot help you protect your child if the law has been broken, and may cooperate in seeing that he or she is brought to justice. It is your job to see that the process abides by his or her constitutional rights — and yours — and to see that your child gets the help he or she needs.

DISCRIMINATORY PROCEDURES AND SAFETY ISSUES

Another area where school policy and practice enters the realm of due process is when it is discriminatory. You can challenge any practice that you believe to be based on bias of any kind. If, for instance, you think your child is being singled out on the basis of race or because he or she has a learning disability, you are entitled to take legal action on his or her behalf. This includes discrimination in disciplinary actions, in classroom placement or tracking, in testing procedures, or in the child's general treatment in school. Nationally, twice as many African-American students as whites are suspended — a figure that lends itself to speculation about the selective reactions teachers might have to the behavior patterns of African-American versus white students. Students may also find themselves being punished for misbehavior that they themselves perceive as culturally acceptable — rowdy play-fighting or name-calling, for example, or seeming disrespect for authority.

Discrimination on the basis of race, gender, ethnic origin, or handicap is illegal in every state. For example, you can challenge practices you believe to be biased against minorities or handicapped children, or work to create discipline codes that take cultural discrepancies into account. The first step is to raise your concerns with local school officials and attempt a local resolution. If that doesn't work, you can file a complaint with the state or federal office responsible for enforcing antidiscrimination laws.

Federal intervention into school discrimination is also possible if the program is one that is partially or fully funded by the U.S. government. Call the Director of the Federal Office of Personnel Management within ninety days of the alleged discrimination and it will be investigated confidentially. If discrimination is found to exist, federal funds will be withheld to bring the program into line with the law.

Discriminatory testing — tests that are biased against members of a particular group — is another grounds for legal action. Minority groups score much lower on standardized tests than non–minority groups, and several court cases have found evidence of bias in the questions on the tests themselves. Such skewed test scores can result in tracking and placement programs that exclude minorities and perpetuate a system which places them in the lower tiers of the American social structure.

Dress codes have come under legal scrutiny, too. While schools cannot constitutionally compel short hair and long dresses, the courts have ruled in favor of such regulations. Currently, about half the states have laws on the books allowing schools to regulate dress and hygiene codes in some way.

With the vociferous support of parents, Frank Mickens, the principal of Brooklyn's embattled Boys and Girls High School has taken steps to ensure what he believes will be an atmosphere more conducive to learning. He has instituted a dress and behavior code that includes bans on gold jewelry, removable gold tooth caps, expensive shearling coats, and portable tape players.

He also has told his male students to begin wearing ties to school, although no similar code has been imposed on girls or on teachers. To ensure that even the poorest student can afford to live up to the code, he has asked local retailers to provide ties and button-down shirts. Those students who do not wish to comply with Mr. Mickens's policy are offered transfers to other schools.

The legality of his policy is debatable. Legal advisers have said that, according to New York City law, Mickens can only request compliance, not demand it. If he does, the chancellor's office has indicated that Mickens would be ''invited in for discussions.'' But Mickens is undaunted by such minutiae. ''We make the law here. This is the law, and yes, I have made decisions after consultation with parents and students.''

While academic performance has not yet improved, even the board of education has noticed the new atmosphere of law and order at Boys and Girls High. And according to a member of the PTA, parents from all over the city are "knocking at the doors to get their kids into the school."

There are other areas where the law intrudes onto school property. Sex discrimination is illegal. Harassment of students on the basis of gender is grounds for legal action, as is exclusion on the basis of sex from extracurricular activities, although some courts have upheld single-sex intramurals if equal opportunity to play is provided to members of both sexes. Girls can try out for noncontact sports if there is no comparative girls team, and some states have adopted broad-ranging equal rights amendments stating that anyone can try out for any team, regardless of gender.

The legality of intramural sports extends to safety issues as well. Reasonable care must be taken to ensure the safety and well-being of students on and off the playing field. Lawsuits have successfully blocked schools from allowing games to be played without protective gear or without proper training of the students by the coaches. There is, however, a certain assumption of risk involved in allowing a child to participate in sports, although even if you sign the release statements required from parents by most schools, you would be able to sue if your child was injured as a result of teacher or school negligence.

Safety is an issue elsewhere, particularly on school buses. While state laws regarding school bus safety vary widely, most states do not yet require the simple expedient of seat belts on all buses, and even those that do often have trouble enforcing their use.

School bus accidents injure over 6,000 students a year and kill several hundred. In Parents Unite! *Philip and Susan Jones offer the following list of questions to check that your school's transportation system is as safe as possible.*

1. *What is the licensing requirement for drivers?*
2. *What background checks are conducted on drivers?*
3. *What training is provided to drivers?*
4. *How often are they retested?*
5. *What is the driver turnover rate?*
6. *What is the procedure for reporting accidents?*
7. *What happens when a driver gets a traffic citation?*
8. *How old are the buses?*
9. *What is the regular maintenance schedule?*
10. *Is the driver responsible for a daily pretrip check?*

11. *Do buses have seat belts, energy-absorbing seat backs, reinforced seat anchors, et cetera?*
12. *Are exhaust levels checked for possible leakage?*
13. *Are standees allowed?*
14. *Is an adult other than the driver on the bus each day?*
15. *If the bus is subcontracted by a private transportation company, who in the school department is responsible for bus safety?*

SPECIAL CASES, SPECIAL LAWS

In perhaps no other legal area have parents had the impact that they have had on special education law. Parents were instrumental in the passage of Public Law 94-142, the landmark 1972 federal legislation entitling all children to an equal education regardless of their handicap or disability. Parents were critical to the passage of various state laws that reinforced and expanded the provisions of the federal law, such as Massachusetts's Chapter 766, widely regarded as a model program in terms of services and delivery. And parents remain crucial members of local organizations fighting to retain those rights under current budget crises.

Currently, between 12 and 20 percent (depending on who's counting) of all American schoolchildren fall into the category of having special needs. That's a large number, but the category is surprisingly broad. Special needs can mean children who are physically or mentally handicapped, children with learning disabilities, or gifted children. It can mean children who are poor and undernourished, non-English-speaking children, or children otherwise at risk for school failure.

It's logical that the parents of children with special needs should become deeply involved in their children's education — after all, their children often require a great deal of their time and attention just to make it through the day, let alone make it through school. Parents of such children are used to advocating for their own child's needs — whether it is for special access to a science classroom for a child in a wheelchair or extra reading time for a child who reads English more slowly than he or she reads Spanish.

It is when parents who are already advocates on an individual level get together in groups to discuss their common interests and goals that their real power can be felt, and that is exactly what happened with special needs parents. In many states, special education parent advisory councils for each school district are required by law, and the school district is required to provide a meeting place and some administrative support. In other states, such councils have sprung up on their own and have begun to serve in an advisory capacity to state departments of education on special education advocacy issues.

Parents were involved in both the enactment and implementation of federal and state special education policy. They educated themselves about the issues involved, held conferences to spread their information to a broad network of parents and professionals, organized local, regional, and statewide chapters to lobby and educate others, and created an information system that allowed for quick mobilization of forces in the event of a crisis.

In 1970, even before the Massachusetts special education law was written, the Massachusetts Advocacy Center published a shocking report titled The Way We Go to School: The Exclusion of Children in Boston, *which detailed the systematic exclusion of special needs children from public schools. The report resulted in a strong coalition of advocates, parents, and legislators who then worked together to write and press for the passage of what became known as Chapter 766, the state's ground-breaking special education law.*

Chapter 766 highlighted the need for every special needs child to receive an individual and multifaceted assessment and education plan. It also stipulated that all children, regardless of disability, must be educated by the public schools if their parents so desire. A due process system was instituted for grievances, and schools were given a two-year phase-in period.

Once they had lobbied to get the law passed, MAC realized that its main focus would have to be to monitor implementation throughout the state. They asked the state to conduct on-site ''audits'' of individual districts. They publicized the new regulations to parents and provided for their involvement in those audits. They maintained their own independent auditing and advocacy procedures as well.

As a result of MAC's efforts, the exclusion of special needs children from public schools was virtually eliminated. But problems persisted. The resulting rise in the numbers of children being served — and the rise in local special education budgets — strained both local and state education agencies. Monitoring continued to uncover individual infractions. More disturbing was a continuing trend toward discrimination against minority special needs children. MAC continues to be a force for advocacy in these areas.

Once PL 94-142 became a reality, parents were invited to participate in the actual drafting of the law's regulations. As a result, not only are the terms of the law particularly responsive to the constituency it was meant to serve, but parents were able to write themselves into the implementation policy. In other words, parents made it illegal for any special education program to operate without constant parental input and supervision.

As a group, then, the parents of special needs children serve as a model to other parents who want to organize around any issue at all by beginning individually and then drawing on the knowledge and resources of other parents and groups. If your child is being considered for a special education evaluation — or if you feel that your child should be given an evaluation, which you have the right to request — your first move should be to get the name of the local parent council in your district (your school should provide it for you).

Some basic information to remember:

- No child may be classified as handicapped without an evaluation, or on the basis of only one means of evaluation.
- You must give written permission for your child to be evaluated, or you may request an evaluation, which your school must provide if there is just cause.
- You may request an evaluation in your child's native language, and you may insist that the results be given to you in yours.
- The evaluation must be conducted within a reasonable time frame, as dictated by state or federal law.
- You may review all the results of those evaluations, question or demand clarification on any of them, and demand retesting if you do not agree with the recommendations that result from them.
- You may ask for a hearing if the school does not agree to provide the services you deem appropriate for your child.
- If you agree to the IEP (Individualized Education Plan) proposed by the evaluation committee, you have the right to be kept informed of your child's progress and to request changes if you don't feel he or she is making appropriate progress.

The number of children with special needs has grown dramatically in recent decades, partially because of demographic changes in our population, but also because the public education system in our country is the only public service agency legally responsible for caring for such children. For instance, if a child is severely physically handicapped, the public school in the town in which he or she lives is legally responsible for paying for that child's education (even if it means a residential home), for medical care while the child is in school (even if it's for twenty-four hours a day), and for special transportation to and from school.

In other words, the tremendous success of parents in getting special education law mandated has also been responsible for the tremendous financial burden many school systems suffer because of it. In fact, some special education groups feel that the time has come for parents to lobby, along with school employees, to have that burden shared by other social service agencies and health care providers.

TITLE I/CHAPTER 1: FIGHTING TO STAY INVOLVED

Title I of the Elementary and Secondary Education Act of 1965 provided federal funds to state and local education agencies to enable them to provide compensatory education services to disadvantaged school-children. Initially, there were three categories for determining who was entitled to compensatory education:

- low-income children
- migrant children
- neglected or delinquent children

From the start, Title I was intended to help parents as well as their children. Parents were given direct "constituent involvement" in Title I programs, which meant that they served on parent advisory boards and were themselves eligible for some education benefits. School-level and district-level parent councils were mandated by law, and direct involvement was one of the reasons for Title I's early success.

In 1981, Title I became Chapter 1 under the Educational Consolidation and Improvement Act. Enforced parental involvement was excluded from the new law, and districts were required only to "consult" with parents before making program decisions, rather than include parent councils in the decision-making process. It wasn't until 1986, when the federal Department of Education reinstated some parental-involvement clauses by forcing the local education agencies to develop written policies for their inclusion, that parents were invited back into the Chapter 1 fold.

Historically, compensatory education was supposed to provide services for poor parents as well as poor children. But the danger in such a well-intentioned policy is that such parents were often deemed unfit because they were poor and uneducated. In addition, regulated parental involvement often meant involvement on institutional terms, and parents sometimes found themselves rubber-stamping the school district's agenda because they were unaware of other options.

Today, Chapter 1 parents are represented by the National Coalition of Title I/Chapter 1 Parents, a Washington-based organization that provides parents with a bimonthly newsletter, regional training conferences, on-site technical assistance, and financial assistance to enable them to maximize their input into compensatory education programs.

BILINGUAL EDUCATION:
THE FORKED-TONGUE DEBATE

Just as today's society is becoming more polyglot, so today's school-children are becoming more diversified. It is not unusual for a medium-sized elementary school to host children from half a dozen countries, and some urban schools can count more than twice that number in their English-speaking student body alone.

It is when those students do not come to school equipped with enough English to learn in that language that multicultural education hits its first snag. Rather than boasting of a mini–United Nations in the schools, many school districts are now complaining about the variety of non-English-speaking children whom they must educate in their native tongue as well as in English.

The Bilingual Education Act of 1974 provided federal funds for local education agencies to plan and develop bilingual education programs and for states to train teachers in those programs. In 1985, the act was amended to provide for more direct information dissemination to parents, including the right to decline a bilingual placement. The goals were to achieve proficiency in English as well as to maintain respect for the child's native culture. Neither the 1974 law nor the 1985 amendment requires bilingual education by federal law but merely for transitional programs until the child can enter an English-speaking program. Some states also offer native-language maintenance programs as well.

The federal programs were certainly well-intentioned — serving to provide children with an education in the language they best understood while at the same time offering instruction in English so they could eventually be "mainstreamed" into regular English-speaking classrooms. Another agenda concerned the respect for the native cultures brought to the schools by foreign-born or non–Western European families. Not only were the bilingual students to be taught in their native tongue, but the customs and culture of their native land were also to be made part of the curriculum.

Several problems emerged. The first was that bilingual education programs tended to segregate members of non-English-speaking groups — from each other as well as from the English-speaking majority. The result has sometimes been that racism is exacerbated rather than alleviated. Non-English-speaking children did not get a chance to learn the social skills of their English-speaking peers, and vice versa. As a result, when the two groups got together in a mainstreamed setting, the non-English-speaking children often found themselves pariahs, the new kids on the block, even though they had been in the school for a number of years. Another problem was that while native cultural values were taught to the children in the bilingual classes, no attempts were made to teach those values to the students in the rest of the school. Again, children found themselves segregated by ignorance as well as by language.

Nevertheless, non-English-speaking parent groups have been adamant in their support of bilingual education. Advocates — many national minority-rights groups among them — believe that bilingual education represents the best possible chance for non-English-speaking children to be able to participate fully in American society. They believe that by developing multilingualism in the schools, we will also develop multiculturalism, and that the only chance for cultural parity among races in the future lies in such diversity at the school level. This view is supported by the U.S. government as well as by a majority of local education agencies.

In 1973 a group of parent and community leaders in rural Center, Colorado, a town with a large Mexican-American population, formed the Chicano Education Project. They started with local issues but soon grew into a statewide group concerned with Colorado's discriminatory education policies, which CEP believed were largely responsible for holding Chicanos in a second-class status.

CEP members traveled across the state and discovered that many Mexican-American students were being instructed in English when they spoke only Spanish. CEP advocates responded by helping parents file lawsuits against their districts charging that the failure to incorporate Spanish-language instruction in the school denied them equal educational opportunities under the law.

The suits failed, but working with state legislators CEP drafted the state's Bilingual-Bicultural Act of 1974, one of the first such state laws in the country. The act required that districts offer a full-time bilingual program in grades K–3 if 10 percent of the students in those grades were ''students with linguistically different skills.'' A community committee was given a strong role in program planning, and bilingual teachers were to be hired.

There was strong opposition to the passage of the new law, especially in the poor rural communities where ''Anglo'' control was threatened. CEP provided support to those parents who were waging uphill battles to win approval for the bilingual programs. They provided training in advocacy tactics, held information workshops, and investigated the districts' failure to use state bilingual funds effectively. Parents were discouraged by the long battle, but by 1979 changes in district administration led to a sudden shift in favor of bilingualism. Mexican-American personnel were hired, and the programs finally began to be implemented as CEP had proposed. The center still maintains an active monitoring and advocacy program, and works on national issues as well.

But there are those who dissent — who feel that bilingual education is more likely to exacerbate current tendencies toward racism and an ethnic underclass.

Learning English Advocates Drive (LEAD), based in Burbank, California, is a grass-roots group of educators and concerned citizens who advocate reform of the existing bilingual education laws. The focus of such education, according to LEAD, should be to teach all students in English as quickly as possible. Children are "being held hostage by the bilingual lobby that reaps millions, calls all opposition racists, and has become a Spanish maintenance plan." Research purporting to support the efficacy of bilingual education, says LEAD, is in fact published by bilingual educators who personally profit from the programs they support.

LEAD proposes an alternative curriculum that, while supporting cross-cultural understanding, would immerse non-English-speaking students in an intensive ESL (English as a Second Language) program designed to bring them up to proficiency level as quickly as possible so that they can then be educated in the mainstream English-speaking classroom. Foreign-language classes would be offered as enrichment.

LEAD president Sally Peterson says that the power of the bilingual lobby is such that many teachers and even non-English-speaking parents are afraid to speak in opposition to it. Even so, Los Angeles teachers voted in 1987 to support LEAD's drive to reform bilingual education. But the legislature was unwilling to adopt any changes, and so the state's Transitional Bilingual Education program still stands.

Critics charge that the LEAD proposal forces education back a decade, to the time when children were forced to sink or swim in English-taught classes. They further accuse LEAD advocates of racism and of trying to protect their English-speaking union jobs by excluding bilingually trained teachers from the system.

But Peterson points to local changes such as those in Berkeley, where the mandatory bilingual education program was replaced by several alternative programs among which parents and schools could choose. And LEAD is taking its campaign national, exhorting school systems all over the country to look into alternatives that do not "segregate non-English-speaking children and delay their assimilation into the mainstream of American life."

Today, innovative bilingual programming takes the concept of bilingualism at face value — it is truly bilingual rather than monolingual in intent. Spanish-speaking children, for instance, are taught English while English-speaking children are taught Spanish — often in the same classes. Multiculturalism is also a part of such programming, allowing children of both cultures to benefit from one another's experience as well as to gain a broader perspective on their own.

Like many educators, parents have always had strong views about bilingual education — they either love it or they hate it. Federal and state bilingual education laws are legally enforceable, but the debate that rages on the topic is not silenced by legal precedent, and new cases are appearing almost daily that challenge one or another assumption about the efficacy — and the legality — of bilingualism in our schools. What do we do when our children are forced into English-speaking programs before they are ready? How do we handle bilingual programs in which children are never mainstreamed, where they remain segregated for up to eight years? What about the charge that bilingual programs prepare non-English-speaking native children for second-tier educational careers, thus perpetuating the race/class system that is already rampant in our society?

Such questions are being raised, both informally, in groups of parents and educators, and formally, in court challenges around the country. The danger lies in bilingual and monolingual parents being forced to compete with one another for the same funding, causing them to see one another as enemies rather than allies. And the dangers of racism and cultural myopia are ever present in any bilingual debate, making it an area fraught with tension.

If you feel that your child is not receiving an appropriate education through his or her bilingual program, trust your own instincts. Discuss your impressions with teachers and other parents. If a general problem exists you may well discover allies in your community and be able to raise a united voice when approaching the administration with ideas for change.

TOWARD A CONTINUITY OF VALUES

All of this discussion about parents and legal issues leads to what Harvard educator Sarah Lawrence Lightfoot has termed "a continuity of values. Without continuity between home and school, children find it increasingly difficult to integrate their separate experiences, with the result that both home and school are rendered less effective in shaping the child." Do we work toward cultural pluralism for our children, or toward assimilation and homogenization? Do we allow our schools to demand that our children do things we wouldn't expect of them at home, or work to ensure that our home values are respected at school? Do we challenge our school in areas where we feel our rights are infringed upon, or rely on ourselves to provide what the schools cannot or will not?

Increasingly, parents are finding the wherewithal to pursue issues of law and conscience, to come together in groups or work alone, to ensure that their children, and all children, benefit from the best education possible under the law. And failing that, they are willing to work to change those laws.

For thousands of years, the Pueblo Indians of San Felipe, New Mexico, have lived in the same place, raised the same crops and livestock, and followed the same time-honored traditions. But lately the Pueblo parents are defying tribal tradition to send their children to the nearby public elementary school instead of to the reservation school.

Their reasons are simple. "We want our kids to learn to adapt to the world out there, rather than the world in here," says Bonnie Candelaria, whose five-year-old attends the school six miles away in Algodones. Although the San Felipe reservation school conducts its classes in English, the language heard in the hallways and on the playgrounds is Keres, the Pueblo tongue.

"What you get when you put Keres speakers with Keres speakers is Keres speakers," says Algodones principal Shatron Alt. By the time a Pueblo student reaches the public middle school, he or she may be linguistically handicapped by the lack of English spoken in the Pueblo school.

Tribal leaders see the defection as a threat to the continuity of the millennia-old Pueblo culture, and point to the rising loss of young people as evidence that a non-Indian education will lead young adults away from Pueblo mores, further diluting an already weakened community. All over the Southwest, Native American leaders are struggling to keep collective control of their children, and are often surprised to find their authority challenged from within by parents who normally would never think to question it.

But parents are leaving in growing numbers, in spite of alleged threats and taunts and the perception that, in doing so, they are radically denying their entire Indian heritage. Eight years ago, there were no Pueblo children at Algodones; now there are sixty-four — nearly half the total enrollment. "My feeling," says Alt, "is that no one has the right to coerce anyone. Parents should have supreme power over their kids' education."

And the parents who send their children there do not intend for them to lose their heritage. "My father teaches them the Indian ways at home," says Candelaria. "At school they'll get the English way. They can go by both. I want my daughters to be ready to go out into the world on their own."

HOW TO: Improve Discipline at Your School (*from the Parents Union for Public Schools, Philadelphia, PA*)

1. Schools can have an open house for parents to go over a school discipline code booklet with principal and teachers.
2. Students should receive a copy of the same booklet and discuss it with teachers.
3. Schools should have a positive atmosphere and focus on learning.
4. Parents and teachers should communicate regularly to prevent suspensions, class cutting, lateness, and incomplete schoolwork.
5. Parents and staff should work to get at the cause of students' misbehavior, not just punish it.
6. Schools and communities can have "Student Pride" campaigns to reward positive behavior on an individual and classroom level.

7. Suspensions should be used only as a last resort.
8. Organize parent patrols of trouble spots like bathrooms, lunchrooms, and playgrounds.
9. All members of the school family should feel responsible to enforce discipline rules.

Guidelines for discipline at home and at school:

1. Give attention and praise for good behavior.
2. Throw out all rules you are unwilling to enforce and be willing to change rules if you determine it is reasonable.
3. Explain rules, but don't feel you must justify them.
4. Allow the child to assume responsibility for his or her action.
5. Don't expect children to show more self-control than adults.
6. Be honest with children.
7. Teach children to have respect for themselves and others.

HOW TO: Conduct a Special Education Checkup (*adapted from the NCCE*)

What Federal Law Requires in Educating Your Child

An appropriate education at public expense has been declared a civil right for every handicapped child in this country. The setting must be as normal as possible for each child or, as the law says, in the "least restrictive environment." Federal funds are available to help pay for some of the extra costs involved in providing these special services. With this assistance also comes the requirement that the child have an Individualized Education Program (IEP) to be developed with the participation of the child's parents.

The federal laws giving you and your handicapped child these specific rights are:

- Public Law 94-142, the Education for all Handicapped Children Act, a federal program (20 USC § 1401), requires that all public schools provide every handicapped child with an appropriate education and related services.
- Section 504 of the Rehabilitation Act of 1973, a civil rights amendment (20 USC § 794), prohibits discrimination against handicapped persons.

Most states also have laws about handicapped children; they must conform to federal law, but may have additional provisions which the schools must follow.

Your Child's Education Plan

Under current law, the parents of handicapped children have substantial rights to be involved in their individualized education program. As you go through the IEP process, be aware that the school must follow these procedures:

	True in my school?	
	Yes	No
• A meeting to develop the IEP must be held within thirty calendar days of a determination that the child needs special education and related services.	☐	☐
• Parents are to be notified of the meeting in a timely manner.	☐	☐
• The meeting should take place at a mutually convenient time and place.	☐	☐
• Participants at the IEP meeting must include: evaluation personnel, a representative of a public agency, the child's teacher, the child's parents, the child (where appropriate), and others at the discretion of the parents or agency.	☐	☐
• The IEP should be implemented as soon as possible after it has been written and approved.	☐	☐
• The IEP must be in effect at the beginning of each school year.	☐	☐
• The IEP must be in effect prior to the provision of services.	☐	☐
• A copy of the IEP must be given to parents who request it.	☐	☐
• The IEP must be reviewed at least once a year.	☐	☐
• A complete evaluation of each child must take place every three years.	☐	☐

School District Policies

All public schools are required to set district-wide policies and procedures that conform to the requirements of PL 94-142, to state guidelines, and, in the case of a child's school records, to the federal Family Educational Rights and Privacy Act (20 USC § 1232g). To be within the law, a school district should be able to demonstrate that it has the following policies in force:

True in my school district?

Right to an Education Yes No

• PL 94-142 requires that all handicapped children be provided with a free, appropriate education ☐ ☐

Eligibility for Services

• Children are eligible for services if they have one or more of the following handicaps: hearing, speech, vision, learning disabilities, chronic or long-term health problems, emotional disturbance, mental retardation, and/or physical impairments. ☐ ☐
• Services are to be provided to all handicapped children and youth from ages five through seventeen. ☐ ☐
• Services for handicapped children from birth to age five are currently being expanded. ☐ ☐
• Services will be extended to all children ages three to five by 1993. ☐ ☐

Child Identification

• All handicapped children living in the district are to be identified, located, and evaluated, according to policies and procedures prepared by the local school district. ☐ ☐

Services Required by Law

• The IEP can include a wide range of related services to be provided at no cost to the parents. This may include: speech and language therapy, social work services, psychological services, school health services, physical therapy, occupational therapy, transportation, vocational education, and parent counseling and training. ☐ ☐

Least Restrictive Placement

To comply with the requirements of federal law, a child must be placed in the "Least Restrictive Environment," with nonhandicapped children wherever possible.

True in my school?

	Yes	No

School districts should have a number of alternative placements available for handicapped children such as:

	Yes	No
• Regular classes	☐	☐
• Special classes	☐	☐
• Supplementary services provided together with regular classroom instruction	☐	☐
• Special schools	☐	☐
• Hospitals and institutions	☐	☐
• Home instruction	☐	☐

The placement should be:

	Yes	No
• Determined at least annually	☐	☐
• Based on the IEP	☐	☐
• As close as possible to the child's home	☐	☐
• If possible in the school the child would attend if not handicapped	☐	☐
• Made by those familiar with the child's needs	☐	☐
• Unlikely to result in harm to the child or to the classmates	☐	☐

Each handicapped child should participate to the extent appropriate with nonhandicapped children in nonacademic settings, including lunchtime, recess, extracurricular activities, and other group and school-wide events.

School Records

	Yes	No
• Parents are to be given an opportunity to examine their child's complete school record.	☐	☐
• The child's school record may not be released to anyone outside of the school system without the parents' permission.	☐	☐
• The school must maintain a list, available to parents, of all those who have examined the child's record.	☐	☐
• If the school intends to destroy any of the old records, they must inform the parents and give the files to them if requested.	☐	☐
• The school must follow the procedures outlined in the Family Rights and Privacy Act to allow parents to challenge material in the child's record that may be inaccurate, misleading, or deemed an invasion of privacy.	☐	☐

Parents' Rights and Parent Involvement

True in my school?

Testing   Yes   No

- Parents have the right to request testing and evaluation to determine their child's eligibility for services.   ☐   ☐
- Parents' permission must be obtained in order for testing to take place.   ☐   ☐
- Parents have the right to an independent evaluation for their child if they disagree with the school evaluation.   ☐   ☐

Individualized Education Plan

- Parents must be consulted and involved in the preparation and adoption of the IEP.   ☐   ☐

Placement

- Initial placement cannot be made without the agreement and signature of the parents.   ☐   ☐

Appeal

- Parents are consulted concerning changes in placement, and given the opportunity to appeal if they disagree.   ☐   ☐
- Parents have the right to challenge the school's decisions concerning testing, classification, placement, services, school records, through an appeal and hearing.   ☐   ☐

Due Process Procedures

The school district must develop procedures to assure parents the following due process rights:

- Prior notice, in writing, and informed consent for the initial evaluation and placement; prior notice, but not consent, for placement changes.
- An appeal of the hearing decision to the State Department of Education, within thirty days.
- Hearings at a convenient time and place.
- Surrogate parents must be appointed if parents are unavailable or if the child is a ward of the state.
- If decision of the hearing officer is in the parents' favor, they are entitled to be reimbursed for attorneys' and legal fees.
- If parents wish to contest the outcome of due process procedures, they may pursue civil action — bring suit.

HOW TO USE THIS CHECKLIST

This checklist is for you to determine whether your school district is following the law and providing all the opportunities to which you and your child are entitled.

Here are some ways to use it:

- Call a meeting of parents and ask members if they feel the district is living up to the law.
- Request a meeting of your group with the superintendent and/or director of special education. Go over the list item by item, requesting documentation if necessary, to check the district's compliance.
- If you are dissatisfied, ask the superintendent to remedy the situation by a certain day and request a follow-up meeting.
- If you feel the responses are unreliable or uninformative, ask the Special Education Director at the state level for any monitoring reports they have on your district. Check them against the answers you received.
- Once you feel that the responses are reliable, you could, depending on how serious your findings are, send the filled-out checklist, along with a letter identifying yourself and any others you represent, and describing how you got the information, to:

    The Special Education Office at the State Department of Education

    The regional Office for Civil Rights, U.S. Department of Education

    Your local newspaper. If there is an education reporter, call him or her and request a meeting.

    The National Committee for Citizens in Education — call on the toll-free Help Line, 1-800/NETWORK (638-9675)

PART III

Answers

C H A P T E R *8*

Making Choices

*N*OW that we have examined the state of our schools and looked at some of the school issues that demand our attention, we can consider some answers to the problems we experience there. Clearly, answers have been available all along, as the examples in the previous chapters attest. But let's look critically at the major tactics being employed by parents (and schools) to increase parental control over local schools and over the quality of their children's education.

First among these tactics is school choice. Choice, along with school-based management (see Chapter 9), is the current "hot topic" in American education. Parents aren't necessarily the instigators of these concepts, and there have certainly been cases of parents being co-opted by school administrators who have used the structure of choice or SBM as mere carrots to entice parents to participate in a mediocre system. But parents are becoming increasingly wary of pseudo-reforms that offer them titles but no power, and school officials in several cities have been surprised to find that their puppet parent councils have taken matters into their own hands.

WHAT IS CHOICE?

On first reading, the idea of choice is crystal clear. School choice confers on parents the ability to decide which school is most appropriate for their child and the freedom to send their child to that school. The per-pupil expenditure for each child follows him or her to the school of choice, whether that school is across town or across the state.

Beyond that basic definition, however, lies a rat's nest of contradictions and questions: Does choice include nonpublic schools? What happens when choice is constricted by racial balancing or when a good school is filled up? Who pays for transporting poor children to faraway schools? How do poor schools get funds to improve if they lose money when children leave? What happens to the balance between state and local funding if children can move between local districts? How can we ensure that choice is based on valid decisions?

One thing is quite clear: The concept of choice irrevocably changes the social relationship between parents and school. Instead of the education institution being the paternalistic autocrat, decreeing what gets taught and how, it becomes the service provider to a savvy client who can shop elsewhere if unsatisfied with the service. The National Governors' Association 1991 Report on Education was eloquent on the implications of this change:

> Today, the public school system controls both the production and consumption of education. The system tells the students what they will learn and at what speed. Students and their parents have little to say about it. A more responsive system would incorporate what students and their parents say they need with the education services necessary to meet those needs. We propose an idea in the great American tradition: that you can increase excellence by increasing choice.

Certainly choice is the essence of democracy. It provides the greatest possibility for institutional responsiveness to the people. And most Americans are used to having options everywhere, from their choice of political candidates to their choice of sandwich bread. But public education has labored under the massive burden of having to be all things to all people. The unfortunate result has been a lowest-common-denominator approach to education.

Choice would change all that. Choice would force schools to compete for the dollars necessary to operate by forcing them to compete for students. Schools that must compete, according to choice advocates, are schools that will improve and tailor their programs to meet the needs of their student body and parent community. According to the National Governors' Association, "Choice is the deregulation move needed to make schools more responsive."

Choice turns schools into marketplaces. It allocates resources to those schools that are most responsive to parents' and students' real and perceived needs. It enables parents to determine the course of their own child's education, and the direction of education in the community as a whole.

According to the U.S. Department of Education, which is pushing choice as an imperative for improving the nation's schools, choice has well-documented benefits. Choice programs can

- bring about basic structural changes in schools;
- recognize individuality and better serve each child's needs;
- foster competition and greater accountability;
- improve educational outcomes;
- keep potential dropouts in school;
- increase parents' freedom;
- increase parents' involvement in and satisfaction with schools;
- enhance educational opportunities, especially for the disadvantaged;
- encourage racial and economic integration;
- provide extra challenges for students who may be dissatisfied or doing poorly in a traditional program;
- raise the morale of educators who are allowed to create distinctive programs from which parents can choose.

But all choice programs are not created equal, and achieving those desired effects requires more effort than simply opening the doors and telling parents to pick any school they like. According to educator Joe Nathan, who coordinated the governors' report mentioned earlier, choice programs, in order to be successful in meeting those goals, need several components. They are worth listing here because they provide a clear checklist against which you can measure your own local choice options. Policymakers who wish to implement effective choice programs must insist that

- a list of skills and knowledge that all students are expected to develop is created to apply to all schools, regardless of the instructional method or special emphasis they have chosen;
- transportation is provided, especially for children from low-income families;
- student assignments and transfer policies are fair, widely understood, and legally sound. Desegregation must be a consideration, which generally means that unlimited choice will not be possible in metropolitan areas. Selection should not be based on a first-come, first-served basis, which favors the most informed, aggressive families;
- an effective system of parent information and counseling (in appropriate languages and in a generous time frame) is established;
- families are allowed to enroll their children in schools in neighboring districts that have room as long as this movement does not harm desegregation efforts;
- in states with small, rural districts, a financial cushion is available to those districts for the first several years to help them adjust to possible net losses of students;

- states move to equalize funding among districts and reduce reliance on property taxes;
- planning, in-service training, and program development funds are available to teachers to allow them to create and improve programs in response to state guidelines and parent priorities;
- surveys of parent priorities and an assessment of what the system is providing are used to help develop programs and monitor progress;
- provisions exist for continuing oversight and correction so that choice does not produce unintended problems.

One of the earliest and most comprehensive choice programs in the country was developed in Cambridge, Massachusetts, where all the K–8 schools in the city were changed from neighborhood schools to schools of choice. Since Cambridge had a strict racial balance policy, parental choice was limited by the need to ensure that all schools (and all classrooms) were balanced racially, ethnically, and in terms of gender.

Cambridge parents can choose any one of the district's thirteen schools as long as those balances are met. More than 90 percent of the parents get one of their first three choices out of a possible six choices on a citywide kindergarten application form. Preference is given to siblings of children already in the school, and provisions are made for older children to transfer between schools at a parent's request.

Every school did not establish a magnet program — many relied on their already strong identities to attract parents. There are small schools, large schools, schools with traditional academic methods, and several alternative programs. There are schools with large bilingual populations (Hispanic, Haitian, Portuguese, and Asian) and schools that emphasize computer learning.

In 1980, right after the program began, some schools experienced a drop in enrollment as a result of the choice plan. New principals and/or new curricula were provided so they could compete for students, and test scores at even the weakest schools have improved dramatically since the program went into effect. Even more encouraging is the fact that the discrepancy between the scores of white and African-American students has decreased under the plan, proving that socioeconomically integrated education enhances the achievement of all students.

Problems do arise when there are not enough places available in those schools that historically receive the most requests for kindergarten admission. The school committee has responded by opening new kindergarten classrooms in those schools and, in some cases, by opening popular programs in additional schools.

Crucial to the success of the Cambridge choice program is the Parent Information Center, which provides information on school choices to parents in a variety of languages, and which helps parents set up school information nights and parental visits to all the schools in December and January of each year, prior to kindergarten application.

MAKING CHOICES ABOUT CHOICE

Not all choice programs are the same. It's up to parents to know enough about the options available so that they can participate in designing the school choice program that most closely reflects the community's needs and goals. Is desegregation without busing the prime cause for establishing a choice plan? Has there been increasing parental pressure to offer schools with alternative curricula? Is transportation an insurmountable problem for a large rural community? Is funding available to support effective change in undersubscribed schools?

Answers to questions such as these will help choice plan designers narrow down their options considerably in designing programs to meet the criteria the community sets. Basically, though, there are four approaches to dealing with choice: open enrollment plans, magnet schools, controlled choice, and tuition tax credits. We'll define each here and then discuss potential problems later on.

Open Enrollment

In an open enrollment plan, anyone can go to any school, as long as there is room and the schools remain balanced for race, ethnicity, and gender. Most open plans allow parents the option to choose their neighborhood school or one of the specialty programs within the district; others allow them to choose from schools with similar programs on the basis of staff, school size, or proximity to parents' workplace. Preference in nearly full schools might go to neighborhood residents or be filled by lottery.

Minnesota, one of the first states to adopt statewide choice policies, has a multifaceted choice program that has been available to public school parents across the state since 1985. One aspect, the Postsecondary Options Program, allows high school students to take college-level courses at state expense. The High School Graduation Incentive Program encourages potential dropouts to seek alternative forms of education outside of their district high school.

The elementary and secondary Open Enrollment Program allows parents to choose any school in the state for their child as long as that district has room and the racial balance of the school will not be disrupted by the placement. The money that would have gone to the child's home district is transferred to the district of choice. Such a policy is possible because the state pays over two thirds of the per capita school costs for each child, so that elaborate interdistrict transfers of funds are not necessary.

At first, participation by each district was voluntary; in 1990, participation became mandatory for all districts. Districts are also encouraged to promote choice from within by offering magnet programs, which emphasize a particular course of study. In St. Paul, for example, about half of the district schools offer magnet programs in subjects such as Spanish, Chinese, creative and perform- ing arts, and humanities. Test scores have risen dramatically, say St. Paul administrators, and the district's desegregation policy is being met.

Detractors of the Minnesota policy, however, point out that the number of children taking advantage of the statewide program is minuscule; even with mandatory open enrollment, only 2,000 students out of the state's 700,000 are participating. While attending an out-of-district school is free, transportation is not, leaving many poor parents without the option to choose a faraway school. And some critics worry that choices are being made for trivial reasons — better sports programs, less demanding courses, even proximity to girlfriends.

Still, the program has created a different mood in Minnesota schools, and parents know that their complaints about a local school are being taken much more seriously by administrators who stand to lose money if they don't listen.

Magnet Schools

Magnet schools concentrate on a particular strength or specialty to draw students, and parents may choose the program that most closely meets their child's needs or interests. The great majority of existing choice programs employ some version of the magnet concept, often in conjunc- tion with an open enrollment policy for its nonmagnet schools.

The concept of the magnet school is not new — for years, school systems have been creating special programs that concentrate on a unique or alternative perspective. Such schools were made available to all students in the district, either through an open enrollment policy or on an examination basis. Manhattan's High School of Music and Art, the Bronx High School of Science, and Boston's Latin High (the oldest public high school in the country) are prominent examples of long- standing magnet school programs. Elementary-level magnet schools have long been available as well, usually providing accelerated study programs or specializing in basic studies or alternative models of educa- tion.

But with the advent of parental choice programs, the magnet school concept has had to expand dramatically to meet the needs of parent- consumers. School systems using the magnet approach must offer a wide variety of programs, retailoring the curriculum at each school to make it fit the particular emphasis of that school. School districts cannot afford to make all their schools magnet schools, but the program has even forced educators at traditional neighborhood schools to clarify their educational philosophy in the hope of making it more appealing to newly savvy parent-consumers. Some school systems offer the same magnet programs in several schools to reduce transportation costs or overcrowding.

There are many types of magnet programs. Some concentrate on a particular area of study while others focus on alternative methods of delivery. Some of the most common magnet school specialities are

- science and technology
- math and computer studies
- fine arts/performing arts
- foreign-language/international studies
- basic curriculum (classical)
- open or alternative curriculum
- vocational/technical training
- future studies (high technology)
- continuing schools for dropouts or at-risk students
- special education programs for learning disabled children

Different types of magnet programs can be offered throughout a school system, giving parents the broadest possible choice. With proper management such programs can turn schools around.

District IV in East Harlem, Manhattan, was once best known for its drug dealers, high dropout rates, and for having the lowest reading and math scores in the city. In 1974, district superintendent Sy Fliegel, with support and input from East Harlem parents and the powerful Harlem Parents' Union (see Chapter 9) initiated one of the earliest magnet school choice programs in the country.

District IV established over fifty magnet programs based on curriculum thematic content and delivery style. They ranged from the Jose Feliciano School of Performing Arts to the Academy of Environmental Science, from the Isaac Newton School for Science and Mathematics to the School of Science and Humanities. There is even a parochial-style school where students wear uniforms and follow a strictly classical curriculum. The staff at each school is responsible for designing the programs, creating the schedule, and hiring personnel to teach it.

The magnet concept is implemented in elementary as well as junior and senior high schools, and some programs have been so successful that they attract out-of-district students from more affluent communities. Overall, test scores have risen dramatically, truancy is way down, and teacher and student morale is high. Best of all, says Harlem Parents' Union director E. Babette Edwards, the system has allowed for parent control and pride, which has greatly increased parental participation in the schools overall.

Some systems provide popular magnet programs in several different schools, and many combine magnet programs with traditionally run neighborhood schools to give parents that option as well. Magnet systems are often combined with open enrollment systems so that parents can choose to send their child to a specialty school or to a "regular" neighborhood school.

Controlled Choice

Unfortunately, open enrollment/open magnet programs often flounder because of practical problems. Transportation is always difficult, especially across districts or within large districts. Supply often can't meet up with the demand for particular programs. A natural segregation may render the program invalid because it doesn't conform to federal desegregation statutes. Controlled choice is an option that allows school districts to offer some choice to parents without jeopardizing legal limitations or inviting total chaos. Some districts implement regional-choice programs to allow for more freedom of movement within a restricted area of a large district. Others provide district-wide magnet programs that are situated purposefully to break the mold of segregated housing patterns.

In the spring of 1989, parents of Boston schoolchildren began choosing schools under a new student assignment plan that allowed for controlled choice. The city was divided into three zones for elementary and middle schools (only one for high schools) and parents were allowed to choose a school from within their assigned zone. Some magnet schools such as the Raphael Hernandez School, a two-way bilingual school where elementary children learn in both English and Spanish, were open to children in any zone. Others were limited to students within that zone.

Although the purpose of the plan was to reduce the need for desegregation busing, it had other benefits as well. Parents were given a broader choice of schools than they had under the rigid court-ordered desegregation policy that had previously existed. If students wanted to stay in their old schools, they were allowed to do so, with transportation. Neighborhood school choices for young children were given special consideration, although they could not be guaranteed.

The program initially affected kindergarten, first, and sixth graders, and was extended to all grades the following year. East Boston, an isolated geographic district separated from the rest of the city by Boston Harbor, was exempted from the program, although East Boston parents could voluntarily send their child to out-of-zone schools. Parent information centers were set up in each zone with information and applications provided in several languages and free shuttle buses available to take parents around to the school fairs that described the school programs in each zone.

Tuition Tax Credits

Unlike vouchers, tuition tax credits do not put money (or chits worth money) in the hands of parents. They work by offering state or federal withholding allowances on taxes to parents who want to send their child to a school outside of the public school system. And unlike vouchers, tuition tax credits do not apply to public schools in other districts, only to nonpublic schools. The amount of the credit is low (the current maximum is $650 or 50 percent of the total tuition). Tuition tax credits offer a broader base for parental choice than vouchers, although voucher advocates say vouchers should be usable in any kind of school. The legality of tuition tax credits is still being debated, since the question of the use of public funds to support private and/or religious institutions is still being debated. A statewide ballot question calling for a tuition tax credit program in Oregon was defeated in 1990. (See the section "Problems with Choice," later in this chapter, for more on these controversial choice options.)

WHICH SCHOOL IS RIGHT FOR MY CHILD?

Education can be seen as both a consumer service and an investment. It's good to understand how choice improves education and what constitutes a decent choice program, but what we really need to know is how to make the best school choice for our children. Let's assume that a program of parental choice has been instituted in your community, and that parents have been instrumental in designing it. The program carries the stamp of local community needs, transportation is provided, racial equity is achieved, and interim financial support is given to those schools that need to alter their programs.

Once such a choice program has been designed and put into effect, you are faced with another set of questions. How can you make the right choice of schools for your child? Unlike the job of creating a choice program, this decision is not a group effort. Although communication among parents is essential to get the maximum information about schools, you must examine your own child's needs and your own ideas about education very carefully, and make your choice based on what works best for your family alone.

Such a decision is not an easy one to make. Convenience, tradition, and peer pressure undeniably affect choices about where to send a child to school. But it is a decision you are ultimately qualified to make if you take the time to consider your options carefully. The U.S. Department of

Education publishes a pamphlet called *Choosing a School for Your Child* that is very helpful as you wend your way through the decision-making process. The step-by-step section on choosing a school is adapted here — it could be applicable to any school choice program or to families who are moving into new school districts and want to learn more about the schools. A school-quality checklist is provided at the end of this chapter:

Steps for Choosing a School

Step I: Think about your child and your family.

A. Consider your child's personality. What are his or her strengths and weaknesses? Does he or she have special interests or talents that can be exploited or special needs that should be addressed?

Children who thrive on exploration and responsibility might flourish in an open school, while others fare better in more structured or traditional settings.

Another factor is your child's school experience to date. A child who is bored in school may need more challenging work, while a child who has difficulty keeping up will want a school with a strong commitment to helping individual students.

How does your child respond to small and large groups? Some youngsters might fall through the cracks in a large school while others might benefit from the variety available in a larger setting.

B. Consider your family's beliefs and values. You may want a school that will work with you to develop the values and character traits you want your child to acquire. You may want your child exposed to a variety of beliefs and values, which would mean looking for a school with a broad spectrum of families. Your own philosophy of education also plays a role in determining which kind of school you choose for your child. Do you believe that children need a teacher who represents an authority figure or one who works more collaboratively with children? Do you feel that schools should concentrate on the basic academic skills or that they should encourage children to explore their own interests?

C. Consider community ties. Children learn better when their school is supported by a strong community. Your family's community ties can be an important factor in your choice. If your family has many friends who live close to your home, a neighborhood school might be a wise choice, or your religious community may be the deciding factor. Community ties can be established in other ways, too — old friends, a group of like-minded students, a strong school leader or a great after-school program can all help define a strong community.

Step 2: Collect information on all available schools.

A. Start early, ideally a year before you want your child to enroll in a new school. Some schools stop accepting applications as early as January. You have written information to read and school visits to make before you can make a decision.

B. Collect information about the schools' curriculum. Consider elementary schools that stress reading, writing, math problem solving, and hands-on work in science, history, geography, and civics. Good elementary schools should also offer computer literacy, a foreign language, music, art, and physical education.

   High schools should ideally provide thorough training, including, at the very least, comprehensive programs in
   - 4 years of English
   - 3 years of mathematics
   - 3 years of science
   - 3 years of social studies
   - 2 years of foreign language study
   - $\frac{1}{2}$ year of computer science

   In addition to a rigorous core curriculum, good high schools should offer advanced placement classes that are available to all qualifying students, and a wide variety of electives to encourage independent courses of study. Training in study skills should also be available, along with vocational training classes open to all students.

   Some schools emphasize specific fields of study, such as performing arts, ethnic studies, science and technology, or have a particular religious affiliation (parochial schools), and the quality of programs should be clear from written material available to parents.

   A written declaration of the school's educational philosophy should accompany information about the curriculum. What kind of learning does the school consider most important? Is the curriculum taught by traditional methods or is there an emphasis on alternative styles of teaching and learning? How does the school believe students can learn best, and does it offer a variety of options? What programs exist to reach out to at-risk students? If a written statement is not available, talk to teachers or principals and get them to describe their goals.

C. Find out about important school policies, particularly about:
   - discipline codes
   - homework expectations
   - grades and classroom feedback mechanisms
   - school staff policies, such as opportunities for teachers to control curriculum and teacher incentives
   - admission policies, if applicable

D. Get proof of results by asking to see:
   - information on test scores for the past few years
   - attendance rates
   - turnover and graduation rates
   - postgraduation activities such as career and college counseling
   - special achievements, awards, grants, et cetera
E. Get information on the quality of school facilities such as:
   - library and media centers
   - classroom materials
   - computer laboratories or computers in classrooms
   - lunchroom, gym, and auditorium facilities
   - informal gathering places for children, such as playgrounds or lounge areas
F. Get information on school staff. Ask about the student-teacher ratio, total staff numbers, the education level and number of certified teachers, the number of specialists and their fields, and the relationship between teaching staff and administration.
G. Get information about community resources. What other institutions, such as local libraries, universities, businesses, and social service agencies does the school draw on for extra input into their program? What provisions are made for parental input on all levels, from parents as teachers to parents as school decision makers?
H. Talk to other parents, community leaders, and local residents and find out about the school's reputation. Collect enough data so that you get a range of opinions but still retain a sense of the real quality of the school. Ask people to explain why they have the opinion they do, and try to get specific details.

Step 3: Visit the school.

A. Arrange a visit by calling the principal's office and making a date that is mutually convenient. You will want to spend an hour or so, visiting several classrooms and specialists while school is in session, as well as scheduling time to talk to teachers and/or administrators.
B. Ask yourself these questions as you take your tour:
   - Do I feel comfortable in this school?
   - How are the adults treating the children?
   - How are the children treating the adults?
   - Is there an atmosphere of study, discovery, and concentration?
   - Is there an opportunity for a variety of kinds of study?
   - Does the tour guide seem to be avoiding certain rooms?
   - Is the building tidy and well maintained?
   - What opportunities exist for parent involvement, and how open is the staff to parent input?

C. Ask questions of the staff to confirm what you have learned about the school through written information and interviews with outside adults.

Step 4: Get your child into the school you choose.

A. Find out about the admissions process. What happens if there are more applicants than available spaces? Are there any admissions requirements, such as tests or interviews (usually the case with private schools or public examination schools)? Is there any financial help available to pay for public school transportation, if needed, or private school tuition?
B. Monitor the admissions policy to make sure your child is being treated fairly, and that preference is not being given beyond the school's stated admissions policy.
C. If your child does not get into the school or program you choose, find out about a waiting list, or about any grievance procedures available to help you plead your case with district officials.
D. Find out about transfer opportunities and the district's policy regarding moving your child to another school. Some states have rules governing school transfers if a parent feels there is a legitimate reason to make the move. Some successfully argued reasons:
- My child has special education needs.
- My child is failing at his current school.
- The current school's program is not appropriate.
- The school I want my child to attend is much closer to home.
- Moving my child will improve the racial balance of the district.

WORK-BASED ATTENDANCE

One unusual choice option is a work-based attendance program. Under this type of program, parents can choose to send their children to a school that is closer to their place of work than to their home, even if their workplace is in a different school district.

Proponents of work-based attendance programs point out that the concept of strong neighborhood identification no longer exists, and that when it does it often exacerbates racial and social segregation. They also point out that such a program would enhance school/business cooperation at a time when neighborhood-based schools are often strapped for resources. Work-based attendance would increase parental control over schools because parents would be closer to their child's school and therefore more likely to participate in school programs.

Work-based attendance programs would have to contend with the same problems as any choice program, particularly if they involved out-of-district placements. Transportation would have to be coordinated, since parents might not always be able to take their children to and from school. Before- and after-school programs would have to be initiated because the parents' workday is usually longer than the school day. Eligibility would have to be closely monitored to prevent overuse of the program by those who can afford it, leaving those who cannot without the work-based choice option.

Several large corporations now provide on-site or nearby day-care services to employees, and a few have offered space in their buildings to small public school programs on an experimental basis. Thus far, however, work-based attendance has not been widely tested and its future is not clear.

THE SCHOOL AS A MARKETPLACE: BUSINESS INTEREST IN EDUCATION

The basic philosophy underlying all choice programs is that the school is a marketplace, and that schools must compete with one another to provide those services most in demand by parent-consumers. Schools that can offer programs parents like will thrive, and schools that cannot offer such programs will wither. While such a notion is clearly beneficial to parents and students, representing a major change in the traditional perception that schools are autocratic factories offering no choice to their clients, we should examine the concept more closely.

Describing education in business terms reflects a new interest in education on the part of American corporations, and they have reason to take notice. Millions of high school graduates are entering the work force without the basic skills necessary to perform their jobs; American corporations are spending $25 billion a year on remedial training — reading, writing, and basic math skills as well as basic job training. Further, corporate America is steadily losing ground to foreign business, a fact that is also blamed on the poor performance of American workers at all levels. In response, businesspeople and corporations are offering creative solutions to the problems in education in the hope of improving performance at all levels.

In one of the poorest urban pockets of Chicago's North Lawndale district, a small school has been thriving for three years thanks to the investments of several area corporate giants — Sears, United Airlines, Quaker Oats, and McDonald's. They are underwriting the Corporate Community School (CCS), a mostly African-American school run mostly by African-American teachers and administrators who believe that the city's public school system sells poor minority children short.

The school is the brainchild of Chicago businessman Joe Kellman, who saw the deterioration of his old neighborhood and was appalled by the waste of human potential represented by area children. Believing that corporate practices could bring any school up to snuff, he engineered the project, which is now headed by principal Elaine Mosley. Self-discipline is stressed to reduce the time teachers spend on behavior management and increase their academic effectiveness. Parental information and education is provided so that parents become partners in the school's educational philosophy. Students are chosen by lottery, with special efforts made to inform those families least likely to respond to such invitations.

The school also provides social services to help the predominantly single parents find a way out of the dead end of poverty that grips so many of them. "Wellness" — of body and mind — is stressed rather than the usual attention only to problems. Teachers are paid about 10 percent above Chicago's public school pay scale to ensure professionalism. In a city largely ignored by politicians and educators, the CCS consortium believed that a "self-tax" on the future of Chicago's children was a sound business investment in the future.

With such great investment at stake, it's no wonder American businesses have begun to look closely at public schools and to see what can be done. And it's not surprising that business leaders choose to reform schools by making them more like businesses. Business leaders see the public school system as a failed monopoly, a bloated and mismanaged administration that is free to ignore the legitimate interests of its consumers. Each of the 15,000 districts operate in isolation from the others, providing "customers" with no opportunity to sample alternative "products."

This political model must be substituted by an economic model. In the private sector, argue businessmen like former Xerox CEO David Kearns (whose book, *Winning the Brain Race*, cowritten with educator Denis Doyle, set down many of the tenets of the "school as a marketplace" philosophy), you get what you pay for. At Xerox, the most important customer is the one who got away, the dissatisfied consumer who chooses to buy non-Xerox products. Xerox concentrates a great deal of energy and money on winning that consumer, and Kearns feels schools must do the same thing.

According to these theorists schools run like businesses would be much leaner, with streamlined administrations and more emphasis on school-based control. Building principals would have tremendous autonomy, and central administration would provide services only. A "lockstep, myopic management," says Kearns, results in a lack of professionalism and an emphasis on bureaucratic convenience over academic results.

Kearns and Doyle are foremost among a group of businesspeople and educators who advocate a radical change in our education delivery system. Their plan provides for unlimited choice, in which schools must compete with one another for faculty as well as students. Under such a plan, states would fund children's education without regard to local tax bases, and teachers would be able to market themselves to any school in the district. All large school districts would have universal magnet programs, so that all schools would be free to implement new teaching strategies and learning methods as well as special programs.

Students would be able to complete their education at their own pace, moving as fast or as slowly as they needed to in order to master the skills in each subject. The traditional grade structure would be abolished, although states would provide annual minimum competency testing on which promotion to the next level would be based. Teachers would set curriculum, choose texts, and share in staff and program development. Schools that were unable to attract teachers and students would be forced to reduce their staffs and programs, and would, if they did not provide more competitive programming, eventually be phased out.

Proposals such as Kearns's, and those proposed by Arthur Anderson in his widely read *A New System of Education: World-Class and Customer-Focused*, are seductive in their energy and simplicity. But some educators believe they are dangerously deceptive, because they create an atmosphere of intense competition in which many students, and many poorer schools, would not fare well. In addition, such a plan might foster the kind of well-trained work force that American businesses desperately need, but it would not lend itself to the development of critical or creative thinkers and problem solvers, which the country really needs in the long term. As Harvard professor Charles Willie asserts, "Educators don't know how to run businesses, and businesspeople don't know how to run schools." Besides, students and parents are not products like widgets, they must cooperate and participate in the entire process rather than just sit back and choose from among the schools offered to them by administrators.

The debate between business and education interests rages on, but it is clear that the once comfortable distance between the two has been bridged. Just as businesspeople now take a growing interest in test scores and curricula, so educators now talk in terms of making an investment in education. The benefits of early-childhood programs are argued in terms of cost-benefit analysis — for every dollar spent on the famous Perry Pre-school Project in Ypsilanti, Michigan, in the 1960s, it was estimated that seven dollars would be returned to society in terms of higher tax contributions from grown students and lower expenditures on welfare, remedial training, and crime. Educators point out that money spent on education pays off in the range of 7 to 11 percent — after inflation (according to the Committee for Economic Development's 1986 report *Investing in Our Children*). In language that sounded as much like an annual corporate report as an education manifesto, the committee said that "there are substantial opportunities for yielding very high returns from improvements in quality rather than from increasing the number of years of education completed." While investing in our children is obviously in the best interests of everyone, the potentially rewarding alliance between the business and education establishments is often an uneasy one.

Chelsea, Massachusetts, is a working-class city near Boston with high dropout and teen-pregnancy rates and the lowest test scores in the state. In 1989, desperate for a solution, the city of Chelsea contracted with Boston University to manage its schools (see Chapter 5). Basic components of the B.U. plan included:

- *a focus on early-childhood programs, especially on English-language training for non-English-speaking toddlers;*
- *clear curriculum goals with particular attention to studies that relate to the students' lives and community;*
- *individual learning plans for each child;*
- *a mentor system for single-parent children;*
- *year-round, daylong day care,*
- *enhanced professional help for teachers;*
- *community involvement;*
- *adult literacy programs;*
- *prenatal nutrition and health programs.*

In September of 1990, B.U. began its experiment. The legal web allying the public schools with the private institution was tangled, but legitimate. B.U. had been chosen by an elected school committee, it could be dismissed by a majority vote, and all meetings were open to the public. B.U. officials touted the experiment as the spearhead of a real education revolution for failing schools. B.U. President John Silber said that educational expenditures "are not consumer expenditures, they are investments in educational capital . . . the moral and intellectual capital of the nation."

It seemed a marriage made in heaven — a needy public school system and a wealthy private institution with unlimited theoretical expertise. Right away, though, there were questions about financing; if B.U. couldn't raise the enormous amount of money needed to support the program, would it back out altogether? The program went on, although several key components were not implemented right away because of funding problems.

More basic questions were raised by the local teachers union. Teachers were concerned that the university would have the right to hire and fire them, and wondered how it would treat their seniority and promotion rights. They were concerned about being accountable, as public servants, to a private institution. Some teachers wondered if the university could really come through with the changes it was touting. American Federation of Teachers president Albert Shanker, whose union represents the Chelsea teachers, angrily accused the university of ''making promises that are irresponsible . . . like going to a doctor who promises to cure your cancer.''

Other groups were also concerned. Hispanic parents worried that their children's needs were underrepresented and that the emphasis on early English proficiency was unrealistic and unfair. Other parents were suspicious of B.U.'s motives and skeptical that their children's education would really be improved by the face-lifting measures. Parents who had been instrumental in supporting the initial proposal felt they had been left out of the implementation. Even some school committee members were disillusioned by B.U.'s ''high-handedness'' in dealing with a new teacher contract in the fall of 1990.

Nevertheless, the plan is still in effect, and B.U. promises that its motives are honorable and its intention is to promote the best education possible for Chelsea children. Critics are watching closely, hoping that B.U.'s definition of the ''best'' approximates that of Chelsea's families.

PROBLEMS WITH CHOICE

Choice is not a new concept. Back in 1925, a landmark Supreme Court case, *Pierce v. the Society of Sisters*, determined a parent's right to choose a parochial school over the state-mandated public school. The right to choose private education, whether in parochial schools or independent schools, has been accorded to all parents ever since. But the government has never attempted to address the issues of equity raised by this decision: only those parents who can afford to pay for private education have the freedom to choose it. All the ruling has supported is the right of any parent to choose the appropriate education.

Since then, courts have decided that the purposes of education may, at times, be broader than the interests of the individual child or family, allowing states and localities more say in determining what is best for their future citizens.

Certainly choice has made for strange bedfellows, allying liberal educators who value the variety of curricula available through choice with conservative fundamentalists who believe that the best education for a child is one that strongly reaffirms the religious and moral values taught in church.

But the great debate about choice centers on several fundamental problems, both legal and ethical. Chief among them are questions of financing and equity: What do we do with all those kids who want to go to overenrolled School A, and what happens to poor underenrolled School B? Even more important, what happens to those kids who don't have the wherewithal to apply to School A, and couldn't get there even if they got in?

Many choice systems were designed specifically to combat racial segregation by offering an alternative to forced busing. If parents throughout the district could choose schools based on what they needed for their child, and if the "good" schools were open to all children regardless of what neighborhood they lived in, segregation should disappear naturally. The theory makes a lot of sense, but in reality segregation is often exacerbated by an ineffective choice program. Lack of funding to provide transportation to children whose parents cannot afford it is the biggest stumbling block.

Another is the lack of adequate information on good programs for parents who are not aggressive enough to seek it out. While some parents with the time, energy, and connections thoroughly research all schools, other parents don't because of language or cultural barriers, lack of time, or because they aren't aware of their options. Effective choice programs must be carefully designed to combat these pitfalls to desegregation or else risk the loss of federal funds.

Another insidious problem with choice is that it is usually more available to those who can afford it. The reality of most school systems is that affluent parents can send their children to private or parochial schools, or they can move to communities with better schools. For families stuck in the cycle of inner-city poverty, choices may be limited to those schools readily available in the immediate neighborhood or district. The poor may not have ready access to all the resources available to them. In their case, an open-market system works to their disadvantage, since they are often shut out of popular schools simply because they don't know about them until it is too late.

A study released by the Institute for Independent Education in 1986 said pointedly that "black children who choose to apply to magnet schools are often denied the available spaces. Most are actually forced to remain in schools catering to remedial programs, rather than those accelerated and challenging programs in magnet schools." And a 1990 study done for the city of Boston found that African Americans and Hispanics were more than twice as likely to be "tracked" away from college preparatory programs and into vocational training programs. Even those minority students who managed to get into Boston's prestigious exam schools often languished because their elementary and middle school programs had left them ill prepared for the rigors of such schools as Latin High.

Overcrowding is a problem in many schools. What will happen to good schools that are weakened because they are so popular that too many students want to enroll? Either they will become less good because of overcrowding or they will become less open because students get turned away. Another concern is what happens to the schools left behind — those schools with low scores and unsuccessful programs. Are they unsuccessful because they have poor programs or because the school doesn't have the resources to make the program work to meet the needs of a needy student body? Says California educator Ed Foglia on the scenario of further exodus, "Already poor schools would have less money than they had before. And less money does not buy more or better equipment, textbooks, supplies or materials, much less hire more or better teachers."

Inner-city schools are more likely to be viewed as having negative programs than suburban schools, a perception that is as much a function of the location and local population as it is of actual school quality. That's blaming the student body for the failure of the school. Says AFT president Albert Shanker, "The prospect of losing a dissatisfied customer may incite a school to change, but will that dissatisfaction be as acute if the family is poor, and the child no prize?"

How can such a school rebuild its image along with its program? A committed staff and community can go a long way, but not without additional resources, which are often not there in a local tax-based fiscal system. Besides, if the district offers parents and teachers the opportunity to move to a more desirable school, who will be left to implement the changes? Clearly, money has to be made available for these struggling schools so they can compete on the open market and not be outmaneuvered before they even have a chance to offer an exciting program.

The question of financing raises the knotty legal issue of who will pay for choice programs. If money stays within the district, the issue is fairly cut-and-dried: The money spent annually to educate each child in the system follows that child regardless of where he or she goes to school. But what about districts that encompass a wide variety of tax bases? And what happens when parents demand the freedom to choose a school outside of the district? What if District A depends on 40 percent state funding per child and District B depends on the state to pay for 80 percent of the expense? Who pays the difference?

Tuition tax credits and vouchers have come under attack for the same reason. Proponents insist that the only way to improve education is to create true competition, and the only way to do that is to open choice to all schools, public, parochial, and independent. Critics of both systems, on the other hand, argue that the effect of vouchers or tax credits will be to sap the financial resources of public schools, rendering them even less able to compete in an open market. They point out that tax credits will offer little financial relief, especially to low-income families.

Do vouchers and tax credits really foster competition? Although the U.S. Supreme Court (in *Mueller v. Allen*) upheld Minnesota's statute permitting tax deductions for private schools, a Wisconsin judge overturned a statewide open choice program on the grounds that it jeopardized the state's public education system. Competition is fine when it focuses on differences in quality among schools. But offering parents a choice between a Catholic school and a public school is like offering them a choice between purchasing an oven or a stereo system — they are not comparable. Voucher advocates point out that choice is not really an option without a voucher system; many families would be able to afford their choice of schools if a large chunk of their income were not already being paid out in taxes to support public education. Those parents are forced by law to pay into the public system, regardless of where they may choose to educate their children.

Still, the trend toward private education is growing, and the issue of choice, except as it affects parents' ability to pay for educational alternatives, seems to be tangential to the decision to educate publicly or privately. The problems with choice are by no means insurmountable. But they are serious enough to demand that parents pay close attention to the kind of choice program being offered in their district, and participate in every level of its implementation.

ALTERNATIVES

Let's pretend that vouchers and tuition tax credits did not exist, and that the question of affording one school over another was not a problem. Open choice programs were universal, and you could send your child to any school, anywhere, without regard to districting, racial balancing, or transportation. Where would you send your child to school? Obviously, you would use the criteria mentioned earlier in this chapter to choose what you believed was the best possible choice for your child.

But choice does not guarantee quality. Some parents feel that choice merely gives them the option to choose between several mediocre schools. Others feel that their child has special needs that cannot be met by the public school system, or the family has special requirements of education that public schools cannot fulfill. For families like these, alternatives to public schools are worthy of serious consideration.

Much has been written on private — or independent — school options and on the recent surge in independent school enrollment. Of an estimated 46 million enrolled in U.S. elementary and secondary schools in 1989, about 12 percent were at independent schools. Of those children, 15 percent attended private nonsectarian schools such as elite preparatory academies, special interest schools, or experimental programs. More than 50 percent attended private Catholic or parochial schools, and of that number less than 70 percent are Catholic. The rest attended other religious schools. These numbers reflect an increase of 15 percent since 1970, when independent school enrollment had dropped to an all-time low.

That renewed surge in nonpublic education is most often explained by parents' growing dissatisfaction with the quality of public schools — with curriculum content and accountability, with conflicts about teaching methods, and with discipline, drug, and violence problems in the schools. Parents who have been unable to make satisfactory changes in their own child's school situation have begun to opt out in large numbers — alarming numbers — even in systems that are not considered overly stressed by those problems.

It's true that independent schools perform better than public schools according to several measures. The National Center for Education Statistics reports that independent school students perform one grade level higher on standardized testing than do public school students of similar backgrounds. This superiority becomes even more marked in children from disadvantaged backgrounds, perhaps because the public schools available to such children have traditionally been lacking in adequate staff, programming, and resources.

Another reason for the high performance of independent schools is that such schools attract families who believe in their approach to education, and thus are more likely to invest in it at home. "Independent schools," says the NCES report, "are an agent of the family and an extension of the parents' will." For parochial schools, that community is religiously defined; for private schools it is defined more individually, by the school's credo or concentration.

Obviously independent schools — and their students — benefit from increased parental involvement. But the quality of such involvement also differs from the public school version. It's more likely to be supportive and centered around common interests, which create strong positive bonds. Public school parental involvement, as we have seen, is more often orchestrated by the school's needs than by the parents', and is more liable to be nonproductive or downright hostile.

Independent schools also have the advantage of being able to offer smaller classes, a distinctive learning style, and a clearly delineated curriculum. They can cost well over $10,000 a year or less than $500. They can have hundreds of children on a perfectly groomed campus or a dozen kids in a rented room. Independent schools are not bound by state law concerning curriculum standards, teaching accreditation, or even number of days spent in school. That freedom can translate into innovative programming or individual attention or into a dogmatic adherence to traditional academic models, but whatever the style of the school, it is one that parents understand and approve before their child ever walks into a classroom.

One criticism of independent private schools is that they favor white, upper-middle-class families and foster the kind of elitism that perpetuates racism and classism. It's true that the minority population of most independent schools is small (the national average is under 10 percent), although many are doing what they can to offer scholarship opportunities to qualified minorities and many are actively seeking to diversify their student bodies as well as their curriculum. However, it's often difficult for nonadvantaged families to have access to information about independent schools, and, with a history of inadequate education at a poor inner-city public school, a bright child may not make the grade even if he or she is able to apply to a private school.

Parochial schools are receiving their share of the disaffected public school market, too. While some Catholic schools have been forced to close because of shrinking church membership, others are thriving because they accept non–church members. This is particularly true in urban areas where minority parents, mostly African American and Hispanic, have chosen the structured, well-disciplined and traditional curriculum style of the Catholic schools. These parents have felt particularly disenfranchised by inner-city public schools that sell their children short and leave them vulnerable to inner-city ills like drugs, pregnancy, and violence. They see the Catholic schools as a true sanctuary for their children, and agree to the religious training provided because it more or less fits in with their value system, if not their particular religious persuasion. Most Jewish schools and Bible schools, while they do not attract the numbers of Catholic schools and tend to cater more exclusively to families of similar religious background, can boast the same high performance records as Catholic schools. Parochial schools have the additional advantage of costing far less than independent schools — an average of less than five hundred dollars per year.

In a poll conducted by the Louisiana Association for Business and Industry in 1986, more than twice as many respondents felt that the state's private or parochial schools were better than its public schools. They based their opinions on the belief that private schools offered a "better education" by "better teachers" despite the fact that the majority of private school teachers were paid less than their public school counterparts and fewer of them had state accreditation.

Over half of the parents of public school children said they sent their children to those schools because it was free and convenient, or because they couldn't afford a private education. Less than one fifth said it was because public schools were the best choice. Private or parochial school parents strongly believed that their child's school offered a better education than that available in the public schools.

In a separate, nationwide poll, such sentiments seem to be showing up with greater frequency. In a 1986 Gallup/Phi Delta Kappa poll on public attitudes toward public schools, 49 percent of parents whose children were attending public school said they would send their children to private or parochial schools if they had the means. Forty-two percent said the same thing in 1982, the first year the question appeared on the poll.

Some parents don't accept the independent school model any more than the public model. For these parents, home schooling is another alternative. States cannot constitutionally require children to attend public school, but they can require them to attend *a* school, so many parents educate their children at home.

Technically, all home-schooled children are subject to the same state education requirements as their public school counterparts, but methods of monitoring their academic progress vary widely from state to state. Some states require annual exams and have a high school graduation standard. They mandate, for instance, that multiplication be taught in the third grade and geography in the fourth. They cannot mandate teaching methods or materials, however, and have little legal recourse if parents choose to follow their own curricula. Other states exert little or no control. In several states, there is no provision at all for home schooling, and parents may even risk violating state truancy laws if they keep their child at home. Check with your state office for education to find out what the guidelines are in your area.

When home schools begin to attract a group of children, they run the risk of being identified as an independent school, which would be subject to more rigorous scrutiny. Home schools that educate more than the children of the family in that home can be monitored in terms of teacher competency, teaching methods, subject matter, length of school day, and methods of assessment. However, the state cannot rule on the motivation of the parent who chooses to keep his or her child at home, and the home school is not bound to provide a curriculum identical to that of public school as long as the child masters certain basic skills before he or she can be issued a high school graduation certificate.

When parents do choose one established school over another, either among public schools or between public and independent schools, they become accomplices in the system that rates schools and ultimately determines their survival. In spite of the recent trend away from public schools, some parents are making the decision to stay and fight — to work harder to make their public schools better rather than abandon them. Such a decision hinges on some very personal considerations: Should you protect your children from the ravages of an inadequate system and provide them with the very best you can find for them, or should you support public education and work aggressively to improve your children's school experience (and thus their school and school district)? Should you set your ideals aside and give your children the best education money can buy? Or should you give them a public school education for the sake of society, because they (and you) will make that school a better place?

Opting for the former makes a lot of sense to parents who see their children's schools as presenting real dangers in addition to a lack of quality education. What it does not address, of course, is the helplessness of parents who see the same real dangers but don't have the same access to alternatives. The latter course of action may require an inordinate amount of time, energy, and vigilance, but if it works the benefits are real on both the personal and societal level. And of course, that's the real foundation of any choice program — that it work.

HOW TO: Choose the Best School for Your Child (*adapted from* Choosing a School for Your Child, *U.S. Dept of Education Office of Research and Improvement 1989*)

Prepare separate checklists and fill one in for each school you consider.

Curriculum

1. Thorough coverage of basic subjects? Yes _____ No _____
   If not, which subjects are not covered completely?
   _____

2. A special focus to the curriculum? Yes _____ No _____ What is it?
   _____

3. Elective offerings (if appropriate)
   _____

4. Extracurricular programs to enhance learning and character development?_____
   _____

Philosophy

5. Emphasis on a particular approach to learning and teaching?
   Yes _____ No _____ What is it?
   _____

6. Belief that every child can learn in his or her own way? Yes _____
No _____
7. Encouragement of attributes of good character? Yes _____ No _____

Important Policies

8. Discipline _____
9. Violence/Substance abuse _____
10. Homework _____
11. Homework hotline? Yes _____ No _____
12. Tutoring available? Yes _____ No _____
    If yes, by whom? _____
13. Grades, feedback, and recognition _____
    What type and how often? _____
14. Teacher opportunities and incentives _____

Proof of Results

15. Standardized test scores: Current _____ Past _____
16. Attendance rates: Students _____ Teachers _____
17. Graduation rate: _____
18. Dropout rate: _____
    Reasons for dropouts/transfers: _____
19. Special achievements or honors for the school?
    _____

School Resources

20. Staff backgrounds and qualifications _____
    _____
    Available specialists? _____
    Staff development and support? _____
21. Library? Yes _____ No _____
22. Classroom books for independent reading? Yes _____ No _____
23. Auditorium or other meeting facilities? Yes _____ No _____
24. Physical education facilities? Yes _____ No _____

Parent and Community Development

25. Parent volunteers in school? Yes _____ No _____
    Doing what? _____
    Parental participation in decision making? Yes _____ No _____
26. Teachers enlist parent cooperation? Yes _____ No _____
    If yes, how? _____
27. Other community members involved in school? Yes _____ No _____
28. Partnerships with local businesses or other institutions?
    _____

Reputation

29. Views of parents with children in the school _____

_____

30. Views of friends and neighbors _____

_____

31. Views of community leaders _____

_____

CHAPTER 9

School-Based Management

IF parental choice is the medicine for poorly run schools, then school-based management is the surgery that is intended to excise such schools from the system. School-based management — sometimes called site-based management, shared decision making, or decentralization — opens the door to local control of local schools. Under this system, school principals and teachers have a much greater say in how the school is run, both in terms of short-term management and long-term goals. And to varying degrees, school-based management (SBM) presupposes parental and community involvement in all of the decisions affecting a school — curriculum, building care, staff, and student-body decisions.

Clearly, SBM is an option that offers parents the chance to participate, on a very active level, in the education of their children. When SBM allows for full parental participation, it is one of the strongest solutions to the problems that plague our schools, since it allows parents to find specific answers to specific problems according to the needs of their local community. But when SBM merely shifts administrative power from the central office to the principal's office, it makes for few changes in the status quo.

In this chapter, we'll examine the positive aspects of SBM and look at some of the pitfalls school communities around the country have encountered while trying to implement it. We'll look at some of the school-restructuring ideas that have come out of decisions to manage schools locally, and at the new role of central administrations in SBM programs.

We'll also explore the role of the school board in running the schools, and see where parental input can change that role to make school boards more accountable locally as well as centrally. And we'll look at the problems that arise when parents (and teachers) are handed the keys to the school without being given appropriate training to allow them to manage it efficiently.

LOCAL POWER, LOCAL RESPONSIBILITY

There are three components of a successful SBM program (according to the National Committee for Citizens in Education):

- Schools have the authority to make major decisions.
- All important decisions are made by teams.
- The system's central office facilities work with the teams.

By definition, SBM places maximum educational planning responsibility in the hands of individual school councils. That responsibility should include all aspects of running the school, from decisions about replacing old desks to decisions about what is taught, how, and by whom. Such an arrangement, where maximum control rests at the bottom rather than at the top of the pyramid, is radically different from the traditional school structure that we examined in Chapter 3. The key unit of management is the community school, not the centralized bureaucracy.

What is most radical about the SBM structure (when it is working well) is that it encourages everyone who is most concerned with educating local children to get involved in the *process* of educating them. It offers parents, teachers, community members, and local school administrators the incentive to act, because direct action brings direct results. It deeds ownership of — and pride in — the local schools to those who use them, and work in them, and benefit by them most. Since "our" children (as parents, teachers, and administrators) are the beneficiaries of the education process, the management of that process should be "ours" not "theirs."

The Harlem Parents' Union was created to represent parents and students just as all school employees have union representation in the school system. It is not directly connected to the districts' decentralization policy, but reflects the philosophy that the voice of the community is a powerful one in determining the direction of the Harlem public schools.

In fact, it was the HPU's concept of community control that, in the mid-1970s, became the basis of the New York City Board of Education's decentralization policy. But because New York was so large, even decentralization left much of the management of the local schools in the hands of smaller district administrations. The HPU has been instrumental in moving decentralization a step further and delivering authority to the local communities that are served by the local schools.

E. Babette Edwards, the HPU's charismatic director, is eloquent on the particular need for minority parents to achieve a measure of control over their children's education. "I have always believed that parents are consumers with a vital interest in their children's academic achievement and must exert a controlling presence in the public school system. I submit that the record of the public school system in teaching black children is nothing short of disgraceful, and that the schools make every effort to discredit significant parent participation."

To this end, the HPU has an impressive agenda: to challenge the notion held by many educators and social service providers that home conditions are responsible for the poor academic achievement of African-American and Hispanic students; to fill an information vacuum that exists for Harlem parents in terms of how the school system works and what they can do to improve their child's performance in it; to encourage parental involvement on all levels; to monitor student achievement and offer tutorial programs for students and parents; and to provide advocacy services when needed.

ESTABLISHING A WORKABLE SBM COUNCIL

There is no doubt that SBM — and school choice — provide active forums for parents to participate effectively in school decision making. Parents whose children attend schools where no such programs exist have several options to try to get them initiated. You can meet with other parents and teachers who share your interest and make a proposal to the school superintendent. You can work with your local school board to put the SBM agenda up to a vote. You can legislate to get cities and states to mandate SBM programs — provided, of course, that adequate parental input is allowed in designing the program. Or you can go after corporate or foundation grants that might provide the resources to study such a program without taxing the school system.

If you want to be directly involved in shaping the schools of the future — if you want those schools to reflect the changes in America's educational, social, and political fabric — then you must get involved directly in decision making and coalition building at the local, state, and national level.

SBM is not a new concept, of course. Cooperative schools have been operating for years, and enjoyed a heyday in the sixties. In the mid-seventies, the concept of local control of unwieldy urban school systems gained attention with several successful experiments. Salt Lake City, Utah, for instance, instituted a two-council system in all its public schools — an improvement council to make academic decisions and a school-community council to make general steering decisions. Tulsa, Oklahoma, and Jackson, Mississippi, followed with similar programs.

By the late 1970s, thirty states had passed laws requiring greater local participation in school decision making. Unfortunately, many school councils offered parents only figurehead status, or made sure they were in the minority in the voting process. Still, the idea that locally made decisions were apt to be more effective has taken deep root in America's public schools.

But the freedom to make basic decisions entails a great deal of responsibility. How can we be sure we're making the right decisions? Once we have the power to guide our schools, how do we know which direction to take? Parents, teachers, and administrators need to examine their motives as well as their methods before embarking on any SBM program.

The same questions can, of course, be asked about a centralized administration. In fact, many large centralized school systems have been accused of a lack of accountability and challenged for making decisions that were not in the best interests of the students. SBM programs can avoid that pitfall in several ways:

1. By allowing each member of the council to offer expertise in the area he or she knows best. Local administrators have experience in dealing with management, and know the needs of the general population. Local teachers know the academic and social needs of the students in the community and have the most information about teaching methods and materials. Local parents know their own children and their own education agendas. Local community members know the community's agenda and have a broad understanding of its needs. Local (high school) students know how programs will be received and can help design programs to focus on at-risk peers.

2. By providing for a coalition-based group to ensure that attention is paid to all aspects of any school issue.

3. By recognizing that confidence and capability increase with power and training, and by providing both to all members of the coalition so that everyone is educated about everyone else's needs and no one is made to feel less powerful or less valuable to the group (see below for a discussion of training).

The Graham and Parks Alternative Public School, one of the choice elementary-middle schools in Cambridge, Massachusetts, was established as a consolidation school binding a traditional neighborhood school and a small open-classroom-model alternative school. The 1983 merger required a careful realignment of two very different populations — the multicultural, neighborhood-based Webster School and the innovative cooperative-education model of the Cambridge Alternative Program School.

Right from the start, the Graham and Parks policy called for active and equitable parent involvement. The merger document clearly stated that ''parents and teachers will exert the same (fifty-fifty) control over hiring, retention in the program, curriculum, student admissions, and school policy which parents and staff of CAPS currently enjoy.'' All staff, including the principal, were hired by a committee that included an equal number of Webster and CAPS parents. Special attention was taken to ensure that the membership reflected the ethnic diversity of the school population.

This committee is, under the bylaws, ''the final decision-making body of the school.'' On the staff side sit the principal, the parent coordinator (a paid liaison between parents and staff), and five staff members. On the parent side sits the chair of the parent council (a school-wide group open to all parents) and six additional parents elected by the parent body. Each member gets one vote at all times, even in the event of a tie.

The committee was initially charged with making final recommendations regarding teacher evaluations, but a teachers union grievance put a legal stop to that power. The committee is still responsible for making all operating-policy decisions and instituting all long-range planning for the school. Most issues are discussed separately in parent-teacher meetings and their recommendations are brought to the committee.

Disputes do arise that polarize the committee. Teachers, who meet weekly, have expressed concern that their power to determine the day-to-day course of the curriculum is undermined by the strong parent presence. Some parents see the initial mandate of the school as being eroded by time and complacency. Issues such as these are resolved by school-wide discussion. The procedure is lengthy, and sometimes acrimonious, but parents and staff remain committed to the process.

What constitutes a workable SBM council? The optimum membership is between twelve and eighteen members, with the same number of school personnel as community members. An "ideal" council might consist of:

   1 administrator, usually the principal
   4 teacher representatives
   1 or 2 support-staff representatives
   4 parents
   4 students (on high school councils only)
   1 or 2 community members
   1 optional nonvoting member of the central administration

It is important that the membership represent the diversity of the total population; if there are several ethnic groups in the community, they should be represented on the council. Parents of students with strong academic records should share seats with parents of academically at-risk students, and so on. The methods by which each member is selected can vary, including:

- appointment by the administrator
- appointment by a member of the represented group
- election by the represented group
- election by the general population
- a combination of appointment and election

When an SBM council first convenes, several things should happen before any issues affecting the whole school are addressed:

1. Members should provide one another with information about their strengths and weaknesses — what they plan to bring to the council and what they need to learn. Cooperative education would allow members of the council to learn from one another the skills needed to be effective council members.

2. Leadership of the council should be determined by election, with the school administrator serving in an advisory capacity but not as a more powerful voice than anyone else on the council. The administrator should provide other members with orientation about the function and role of the council without attempting to influence the decision-making process.

3. Time and space should be allotted for members to work out internal issues before they can begin to agree on their common goals. Communication between parents and teachers, for instance, may be strained by unresolved tensions or discomfort with their newly equalized roles. Until these internal conflicts are resolved, the council will not be able to work toward a unified goal, or even define which issues are most important to the school. Getting the group to act as a group in the best interests of the school should be the first goal of any council.

4. Bylaws or a constitution should be written to set out the purpose of the council and delineate its powers with regard to the school and the central administration. Regular meeting times should be established and the minutes of the meetings should be made public to everyone in the school community.

WHO'S IN CHARGE: ISSUES OF ACCOUNTABILITY

Even when an SBM council has achieved these difficult goals — defining itself and its agenda — there remains the question of accountability. To whom does the council answer when there is a question about poor test scores? To whom does it appeal when there is a need for additional money to fund a new program? Who gives permission to develop that program in the first place?

In addition to monitoring individual schools, the differences between schools must also be monitored to see that they do not become liabilities. Who ensures that the students in School A are getting enough math, or that the students in School B are not being shortchanged because they can't afford computers?

The obvious way to make sure that roles are clearly identified and powers clearly defined is to set up some kind of written agreement between the central administration and the local council. The terms of this agreement should, of course, be decided jointly except in cases where legal or fiscal restraints apply. The Boston public schools, for instance, have a Memorandum of Agreement to delineate the relationship between both parties. The first part offers a statement of intent; in the second and third sections, the central administration and the local councils lay out their goals and methods so that there are as few surprises as possible.

One important item to be included in such an agreement is the process by which local councils can apply for waivers of system-wide regulations. In some SBM systems, there are even provisions to apply for waivers of state regulations, such as those concerning the number of school days per year or hours in the day. Such waivers are granted when the local council can prove that they would have a clearly positive effect. The agreement should also provide for a grievance system should such a request be denied, and to ensure that unforeseen conflicts can be resolved fairly.

It would seem that conflicts between local councils and central administrations could easily be avoided by eliminating the latter. After all, many critics of public schools argue that bloated administrations are one of the largest stumbling blocks to effective education. But to eliminate the central system altogether would be self-defeating. In order to prevent schools from becoming dangerously isolated, or from having to compete with one another for limited services, there needs to be some degree of central organization.

Chaos would result from a total lack of bureaucracy. But how much centralized monitoring is too much? What is the legal responsibility of the SBM to the central authority? And where does the power of the school board or the district headquarters come from? Many parents and educators believe that the answer lies in using the central administrative facility in a new way — as a resource instead of a power source. The central office should be charged with controlling procedures instead of outcomes, with providing services that the local councils can use at their discretion. Such services would include counseling and special education services, textbook and material clearinghouses, library and media services, building maintenance services, and union contract negotiations. The central office would also be responsible for providing technical information and assistance to local councils, answering questions on state regulations, or providing the council with sources of information, funding, and assistance for local programs.

Another important job for the central office would be to coordinate interschool services so that School A, for example, can participate in School B's new computer programming course, or students from School C can take Japanese at School D. The need to integrate activities remains a real one despite the trend toward local school management. It's far more efficient for six schools to participate in one specialized program than for all six to try to develop their own.

And of course, the central office must see to it that all students in all schools are performing up to the standards set locally and statewide. While assessment methodology should be designed with plenty of local input and tailored to the specific aims of each school, there is a need for some degree of standardization, if only to provide parents with information about the strengths and weaknesses of one school over another. If School A's students consistently perform well in math, there may be a good math curriculum worth looking into. If the writing portfolios are strong at School B, the language arts curriculum is probably strong. By coordinating programs, an active and supportive central administration can be the key to a well-thought-out and smoothly running system.

In 1985, the U.S. Department of Education rated only one comprehensive (i.e., system-wide) school improvement program as "highly effective." That program was the Johnson City Central School District, a small factory town in upstate Broome County, New York. Although there is no formal SBM program in the system, its remarkable effectiveness lies in the fact that it is system-wide and developed with full participation and enthusiasm by the central administration as well as by local school personnel and parents.

Johnson City's program is "outcome-based"; that is, the curriculum and instruction methods are designed to create maximum learning by the greatest number of students. But those outcomes are not just measured in test scores,

*although Johnson City students perform remarkably well on standardized tests
in reading and math. In addition, the system measures its students' achievements on the basis of five ''exit behaviors'':*

- *Students are to have high self-esteem as learners and persons.*
- *Students will be able to function at high cognitive levels, not just at the
  lower levels expected on standardized tests.*
- *Students will be good problem solvers and decision makers, will be compe-
  tent in group processes, and will be accountable for their own behavior.*
- *Students will be self-directed learners.*
- *Students will have concern for others.*

*Naturally, local parental and community input was instrumental in estab-
lishing such laudable goals, but it was the central administration which saw to
it that they were implemented and achieved. Johnson City's central administration is charged with making sure that all instructional processes are fully
supported with curriculum, personnel, organization, and school regulations
that can work to achieve the desired outcome. For instance, since students are
taught to assume responsibility for their own learning process, the attendance
policies were revamped to reduce the chance that frequent absences would
undermine that responsibility. Today, all special needs students are mainstreamed into regular classrooms, which receive additional support both for the
teacher and the student.*

*Teachers are given a tremendous amount of responsibility as well, along
with the risk-free opportunity to develop programs that work for them in their
classrooms. Staff development is given high priority and is seen as a means of
shared decision making on all levels. Parents are called upon to participate in
their children's learning process and support their local schools. More than 98
percent of the Johnson City school parents rate the system as outstanding.
That's a remarkable turnaround in a town where the founding father, shoe
magnate George F. Johnson, used to go into the schools a generation ago and
persuade high school students to forget all that nonsense and come to work in
his shoe factory.*

The most powerful tool of any local management council is the budgetary power allotted to it by the central administration (personnel and
curricular power are next). By law, the district school board cannot
delegate fiscal responsibility, and it must answer to the state authority
for all schools under its jurisdiction. Normally a school principal receives
a discretionary fund of about 10 percent of the total school budget —
everything else must be "purchased" from the central administration.
But SBM councils can legally receive a lump-sum equivalent to a much
greater percentage of their total budget to spend as they see fit (within
established parameters, of course). The only expenses that cannot be

handled at the local level are capital expenses, which involve the building itself, and those established by district-wide collective bargaining for union contracts.

Even with attempts to use existing central structures in innovative ways, accountability is an unresolved issue of the SBM concept. A large part of this problem is administrative. While school boards and school administrations get their authority from the state boards of education, the local management unit has no legal status. The power vested in the local SBM council is therefore limited by law as well as by design. When a school wants to create a computer lab and the central administration says there is no money for such a lab, the lab will not get built. Even if the school goes out and raises the money from its community, it may have to contend with legal restrictions governing the imbalance in community resources.

Another problem, though, is more personal. However well-intentioned, it is difficult for those in power to cooperate fully in a venture that will result in their eventual loss of power. Education administrators have been trained to see themselves as decision makers having the ultimate authority over all school issues. It's not a malignant role, simply one they have been educated to perform. Making the change from a management model to a service-provider model does not come easily to many administrators, and relinquishing power to people perceived as "nonprofessionals" (i.e., parents and even teachers) often creates a real stumbling block to effective local management.

ALLOWING FOR VARIETY

Once an SBM council has been formed and its parameters defined, it must ask itself what its goals are. Does the council have a mandate to make basic changes in the way the school is run? In what is taught? In the student body? What particular issues need to be addressed, and what are their priorities? The answers to questions such as these distinguish one school from another because they depend on the particular needs of the school community.

Anne Henderson and Carl Marburger of the National Committee for Citizens in Education write "There may be as many forms of SBM as there are schools using it, ranging from fairly authoritarian to laissez-faire. What [each SBM council] looks like varies with what it was set up to do and which problems it is supposed to resolve." Schools that are having problems with tailoring programs to the variety of learning needs of the students may choose to develop SBMs that have strong instructional leadership. Schools that feel their students are not being prepared for the technological future may concentrate only on creating a computer-based curriculum. Schools that are experiencing disciplinary problems may look to parents and community members for advice and leadership.

Most SBM councils are developed to reduce the inefficiency of a central bureaucracy and provide for freedom of choice among the schools, which may need to serve a widely disparate population in a variety of ways. The degree of autonomy experienced by each SBM system depends largely on the way the central administration has allowed it to be structured. Sometimes SBM systems are designed to achieve decentralization but not reduce administrative power. This is particularly true in large urban areas where individual school councils would be impossible to monitor. Such a situation was encountered in New York City, where the huge public school system was divided into many districts, each with its own community school board serving a number of local schools.

When New York City Public Schools Chancellor Joseph Fernandez heard that Brooklyn's Community School Board 17 had $2 million in unspent federal funds and nearly a quarter of a million dollars in mislaid funds, he sent in trustees to manage the embattled local district council until the mess could be straightened out. School officials, parents, and teachers were relieved. "I didn't know what funds I had or would be getting," reported the head of one school's early-childhood intervention program. "It's hard when you go into a classroom and face thirty-five children and you have nothing to offer them, and yet you know there is money for a cartload of supplies."

Financial mismanagement was at the root of the problem in the Brooklyn community, which serves over 28,000 students. The district board had overestimated the number of students it would be serving and hired too many teachers. It had spent $200,000 on computers that auditors couldn't find. Yet even those who applauded the chancellor's action in appointing a guardian from central administration were wary of what it might mean to the decentralization program that had given the community so much autonomy over its schools. According to some SBM proponents, the problem was that the decentralization program had been vaguely designed and the community school board had not been provided with enough training to enable them to handle the huge fiscal responsibility involved in running the schools.

The president of the local parents council knew something had to be done about the problem with Community School Board 17, but doubted that intervention from the chancellor's office was the answer. "We feel every time you supersede a board, that takes away power from the parents. It takes away decentralization." The community school board vice president accused Chancellor Fernandez of acting to deliberately undermine the decentralization program.

Fernandez countered that he could not sit by and watch children go without necessary programs because of mismanagement. He noted that he had intervened only in the board's fiscal operations, leaving their other powers intact.

In rural areas, decentralization brings its own problems. While small school systems may not choose decentralization to streamline a large bureaucracy, the differing needs of far-flung schools within a rural system demand that each operate in accordance with its own needs.

In January 1989, Greensburg, Louisiana, was forced by a court order to consolidate its seven schools into three. The school district, St. Helena Parish Schools, served a largely poor African-American rural population, and parents mourned the loss of the small school communities. ''Dealing with fallout from the consolidation and restoring community support for the public schools'' became the primary goal of Myrtle Wofford, the district superintendent.

Armed with a federal equity grant received through the Louisiana State Department of Education, community members, teachers, and administrators went on a retreat designed to reduce tensions and come up with answers. A sense of common purpose emerged to replace the lost community identities. Leadership teams were formed to help the newly consolidated schools deal with the change and improve academic performance in the district.

''The leadership teams became a group with a special sense of excitement and energy,'' says Shirley McCray, a math teacher at the new middle school. ''We were being guided and coached into actions based on parish information. That was a big change for us, and we became leaders and innovators.''

While parents did not hold active seats on the school's leadership councils, they did participate in defining new parameters. They also faithfully attended parent education sessions at night, an unusual record for rural school systems with widely distributed families. Teachers and administrators learned that curricular improvements would not work without parental support and community involvement. Each leadership team collected data on staff, site, student, and community needs, approved mission statements, and developed campus action plans to guide the schools' activities in attaining those goals.

Even in systems where SBM takes the form of a single council managing a single school and answering to a centralized administration, there is a great variety in the kinds of restructuring that results. While financial and legal limitations prevent some SBM councils from realizing their dream schools, local school councils have achieved dramatic changes. They have established year-round calendars to allow students to proceed at their own pace and make more efficient use of buildings and personnel. They have created magnet programs, accelerated programs, and alternative programs within their own buildings to provide incentives and options for students and teachers. They have eliminated or changed the grade structure, the grading system, and the one-grade classroom and instituted team teaching, collaborative learning, and learning contracts. In short, they have done whatever they felt was most likely to increase their children's academic performance and social stability.

EDUCATING A NEW MANAGEMENT TEAM

Educator Thomas Timar jokes that "finding the center of control over schools is like nailing Jell-O to the walls." Changing the power structure of any institution is a revolutionary idea, and one that is bound to encounter many pitfalls and much resistance. Indeed, even the best-designed SBM program can falter when power sources conflict.

In spite of a dramatic record of success, local school management is not easy to achieve, and even harder to maintain. Problems can emerge district-wide because of a failure to develop guidelines, to provide training, to respond to local council needs, to move personnel where appropriate, and because of a lack of oversight and follow-up.

Building principals can undermine SBM programs by failing to build staff support, by insisting on veto power, by agenda-setting, or co-opting council members. The principal's main concern may be for social cohesion, not social change, and he or she may resist any efforts to make substantive alterations in the existing program in order to contain conflict at local levels or avoid conflict with the central administration. Principals can also be a *source* of conflict, especially if they have been denied tenure by parents.

Councils themselves may err by giving too much power to the principal, by taking on too much or too many issues at once, by submitting to one faction, or by neglecting to set up ground rules for operating as a group. But by far the greatest difficulty for local council members who are not educators (i.e., parents, students, or community members) is that they are not prepared to tackle the technical details or the significant burden of leadership. Often this initial reluctance is exacerbated by a central administration less than willing to provide such essential support.

In December 1989, the Illinois General Assembly passed a law in the hope of reversing the dismal achievement record of Chicago's 420,000 public school students. The legislation was designed in 1986 with the help of Citizens United for Responsible Education (CURE), a multiracial group of parents, educators, and community activists who lobbied untiringly for its effective passage. Approval was given a boost after an acrimonious monthlong teachers strike in the fall of 1987 convinced many citizens and legislators that dramatic changes were the only recourse.

The Chicago School Reform Law was designed with several key features:

1. *The shift of major decision-making authority from a central administration to the school level.*
2. *The establishment of local school councils to be composed of six parents elected by the community, two teachers, and two community members-at-large.*
3. *The majority control of the local school councils was given to parents and community residents who were not employees of the school system to reduce the chance of parents being influenced by professionals, who had more inherent power by virtue of their knowledge of the system and their networking abilities.*
4. *Local school council powers included hiring a principal, designing a three-year school improvement plan, and developing a school-based budget.*
5. *Tenure for principals was abolished and their jobs became dependent on the approval of the local school councils, based on their implementation of the councils' school improvement plan over a three-year period.*
6. *Increased decision-making powers for teachers on school-wide policies as well as curriculum content and methods of instruction.*
7. *Reductions in size and limitations on the authority of the central administrations, shifting from daily management to service provision for the local schools.*
8. *Additional funds for local schools and increased authority over how those funds should be spent.*
9. *Increased opportunity for school choice.*
10. *Monitoring of the program by an outside independent authority.*

Certainly the most controversial aspect of the Chicago reform plan lies in the power delegated to parents, and in the means by which they achieved that power. The plan came under immediate fire by critics who charged that the election process was open to easy manipulation and that few parents would be interested in applying for the slots. In fact, participation in the council elections was extensive — 17,000 parents ran for the 5,400 council seats in 512 schools, and 98 percent of the schools had enough candidates to fill every seat, including those on the ''minority'' school councils, which skeptics worried would go unfilled.

Also criticized (mostly by educators) was the decision to give parents majority power. But the plan's designers felt strongly that community members were more likely to raise basic issues about the inadequacies of the school than were staff, and that they were more likely to know the community's needs and to have access to its resources. The concept seems to have paid off already. One school council got a court order to have an abandoned building near the school (long a haven for drug-dealing) demolished. Another enlisted two neighborhood policemen to volunteer their security services before and after school.

To be sure, there are major problems with the reform. The biggest has to do with lack of support for the councils by the central administration. Councils report that they received conflicting or false information, that they couldn't use their own school buildings to meet and couldn't get purchase requests filled. They also reported a woeful lack of training services to deal with the huge managerial problems they faced. Training sessions offered by the central administration were either perfunctory, poorly planned to conflict with work schedules, or beside the point.

As one council member wrote in her journal, ''The parents and community members on our council are family-oriented, hardworking immigrants who have a sincere desire to better the educational opportunities for their children and their neighbors' children. What I see is a lack of information, a lack of awareness of the responsibilities involved. They are intelligent people who will have little trouble grasping concepts once they are presented. But there is so much they need to know.''

The lack of information and management training is currently being remediated by several outside agencies; councils are learning how to work together as well as how to design a school budget and translate the technical language of school professionals. But there are other doubts about the efficacy of the parent-dominated system. Some education researchers worry that the parent-majority structure of the councils refutes the concept of partnership that is so essential to strong coalition building. They feel that improvements cannot be implemented by a professional staff who feel they are held hostage to parental input.

Is the Chicago reform plan simply replacing one bureaucracy with another? In its design, it represents an interactive model of management rather than a hierarchical one. But the reality of the program may become less than that, especially if local councils are left to their own devices without the technical assistance and resources necessary to make the improvements they so desperately want to make.

The law calls for the establishment of professional personnel advisory committees made up of local teachers to help each council translate its goals into workable programs for the school. But unless the goals set by the council are reasonable, no amount of implementation will make them effective. To their credit, most local councils have avoided the stalemates and acrimony expected by many critics, and have concentrated, in the first year of their reign, on smaller, doable projects that will help them hone their management skills as well as their vision.

In late 1990, the Illinois Supreme Court declared the reform plan unconstitutional. A suit had been filed by several school principals who charged that the legislation had denied them tenure and was therefore illegal. However, the court ruled against the school system on another issue. It said that by using a weighted electoral system to elect school council members (votes can be cast for *parent-members, for example, only by citizens who are themselves parents of that school), the one-person, one-vote rights of nonparents had been violated. The state legislature promptly went to work to design a new voting procedure, so the entire reform plan is not jeopardized by the ruling.*

It is far too early to rate the success of the Chicago experiment. But a November 1990 poll of local council members reported that 74 percent saw improvement in their schools already (the figure is even higher — 84 percent — for African-American council members). Their schools were already operating better, and they expected the improvement to accelerate as they gained experience.

"It's not perfect," says education professor William Ayers at the College of Staten Island. "But 6,000 citizens sit down once or twice every month to look at the school's problems and worry about how to correct them." Something good must come of that.

Problems such as those encountered in Miami, where parents were not given enough control, and Chicago, where they were given too much, are part of the same syndrome — a lack of planning on the part of those designing the SBM program. Including active parental and community input at the program-design level might be one way to forestall such conflict. And those conflicts are by no means confined to large urban school systems. Smaller systems have perhaps even greater need for careful planning, since it is easier for them to assume homogeneity than it would be for those systems in a large city.

But even a coalition-built SBM program will probably encounter similar pitfalls during the early stages of its existence. It is nearly impossible to establish an entirely new system of management without allowing for the practical education of the new bureaucracy. Even those systems that provide comprehensive training through workshops and booklets find their SBM councils faced with dilemmas they have no skills to solve. The central administration must provide ongoing service support for all SBM councils in addition to comprehensive training in practical management, advocacy skills, and group decision making before the first SBM council meeting gets under way.

Parents need not assume that only the nonprofessional members of councils require training. Teachers and administrators also need to get an education — in how to deal with their council-mates, how to listen and work collaboratively, and how to work in new ways with the central administration. Several cities with SBM programs make provisions for joint training of staff and nonstaff council members, allowing each to learn from the other as the whole group learns the ropes. Retreats — intensive workshops held at a neutral site where all members of the group can interact both formally and informally — are an increasingly popular method of addressing both the practical goals of the council and the subtler communication needs of the members.

The ropes are complicated in a school system. Budget issues, personnel and building management, and program implementation are not skills picked up in a single weekend seminar. Functioning within the maze of state and federal regulations is also very tricky, and more than one SBM council has found its prized programming strangled in a legislative noose because members were not informed of program requirements.

While advice from the central administration is invaluable to any council, peer education can sometimes be equally effective. Other SBM councils are more likely to have encountered the technical snafus so common to local management. The best-intentioned administrative training program may leave out crucial information simply because the administration has never had to deal with the kinds of problems that might come up in local schools. SBM systems in California, Florida, and Michigan have learned to rely on council networking as an effective way to foil mistakes before they happen rather than having to execute emergency measures after they have.

One danger that lies in training SBM council members to be effective participants in the new bureaucracy is that they themselves will become bureaucrats. Instead of being part of the solution, they would then become part of the problem. So far this has not been a significant problem for SBM councils, whose agendas for change are still fresh in everyone's mind. But the danger of being co-opted by existing administrators, who have prevent-change agendas, is very real.

It can be hard to maintain one's perspective when suddenly confronted with unaccustomed power and welcomed to the inner circle. Several SBM councils have encountered a disappointing loss of fresh energy and vision when members became "tools" of the central administration rather than agents for change. Naturally, parents are not the only council members at risk for such co-opting. Teachers, in fact, may find themselves even more vulnerable because they know so much of the educational jargon, and because they are dealing with the people responsible for their paychecks. Administrators come under the same kinds of pressure.

There is no power without knowledge. Both must be acquired carefully, and successful SBM councils establish some means of keeping their agendas attuned to the needs of the school community. Parents who serve on SBM councils and who participate in helping school systems adopt SBM programs must insist that they are not given one without the other.

The Parent Action Committee of Direct Action for Rights and Equality (DARE) is a citizen advocacy network based in Providence, Rhode Island, that concentrates on helping parents deal with public school issues. It is located in the inner city and services mostly poor, minority families, many of whom experience language or cultural barriers when they encounter school officials.

DARE is not an SBM program, but it operates from the same philosophy — that the power to create change comes from knowing how to work effectively with the system. By providing training and advocacy for parents trying to maneuver their way through the local school system, DARE enables parents to have a more direct and effective impact on their children's education and their school's quality.

One of the most encouraging and successful aspects of DARE's parent action program is its use of peer support to empower parents. The Parent Advocate Training Program has two goals: (1) to increase knowledge of school policies and procedures, and (2) to develop parents' skills so they can address issues more effectively. The Parent Action Committee provides direct support, sending skilled advocates to a school if, for instance, a family feels their child has been unjustly suspended or is being tracked into a vocational program because English is not his or her primary language.

The Parent Action Committee of DARE addresses general school issues as they affect DARE's target population. Issues they are currently confronting include lack of discipline, lack of minority teachers, shortages of textbooks and unfair allocation of materials, and a lack of parental-involvement opportunities.

These problems are being handled not only by training parents to advocate for themselves and each other but also by providing informational sessions and grouping parents with similar concerns together for more effective advocacy. DARE operates training sessions with titles like ''Speak and be Heard,'' ''What Are Your Rights as a Parent?'' and ''Exercising Your Rights.''

DARE is not only concerned with public school issues. The organization's mission is to take action on behalf of Providence's low-income and minority families (who also make up a majority of the staff, trainers, and volunteers) to improve their social and economic conditions and to educate them about sources and solutions. DARE works with other local groups as part of the Human Rights Organization Project, and with other Providence groups who are concerned with public school quality and equality.

THE SCHOOL BOARD'S NEW ROLE

As we have seen, the relationship of the SBM council to the central administration is integral to the success or failure of any SBM program. But what about the school board of education? School boards (aka school committees or school trustees) are the equivalent of city councils. They are charged with overseeing and operating the school system and setting policies that guide their schools. To a large extent, individual school boards are answerable to their state boards of education, who determine grade-level requirements, graduation requirements, and school attendance mandates. But most local boards have broad power to determine curriculum guidelines, negotiate personnel contracts, and establish disciplinary procedures.

There are 97,000 school board members in the more than 15,000 school districts nationwide. Over 97 percent of them are elected rather than appointed by other city officials; most have two- or three-year terms in office. Some localities have statutes limiting the number of times a member can run for reelection. Only 22 school boards in the country pay their members salaries — another dozen offer small stipends. The pay ranges from $10 per meeting to $25,000 per year. One third of all board members are women, 3.5 percent are African American, less than 1 percent are Hispanic, and only a handful are of Asian descent. In Massachusetts and Rhode Island, school boards are called school committees.

Of the vast majority of school board members elected to their positions, most are elected at large by members of the community. Some members from larger cities run from a specific district or neighborhood. Many boards hold staggered elections, so the membership of the board changes annually even though members hold office for several years. Eligibility for school board membership is deliberately nonexclusive to allow anyone with an interest the possibility of election. Board members must be residents of their districts, must be able to read and write, and must have no other proprietary interest in the school system.

Nonelected board members are usually appointed by the highest-ranking city official — the mayor or city manager. Appointed members may serve longer terms than elected officials and tend to be more professionally oriented — former schoolteachers or active parents with an education background. The appointment system is coming under fire in several areas where it exists because, critics charge, it opens the system up to charges of nepotism and tends to politicize the board. Supporters of the appointment system retort that it is the election system that politicizes the school board, with members acting to preserve their candidacy rather than in the best interests of the students.

In Boston, Massachusetts, an elected school committee has been the norm for decades. Eleven members of the thirteen-member committee are elected from Boston's neighborhoods, and two hold at-large seats, each for two-year terms.

But as the city's schools suffer under the burden of decreasing scores and increasing dropout rates, sentiment has risen for a change in the system. The city's mayor has long been in favor of changing over to a smaller, appointed committee, and in November 1990 Boston voters narrowly defeated a nonbinding referendum asking for just such a change in the school committee system.

The mayor and other proponents of change argue that the current committee is too unwieldy, too mired in politics, and incapable of making key decisions in a timely fashion. Committee members now spend so much time protecting their seats that they don't have time to concentrate on education issues. Innovations or changes in the system that might become a threat to elected officials are routinely denied acceptance.

Opponents of change refute the efficacy of an appointed committee to make the necessary changes in the system. They point out that disenfranchising voters will do more harm than good, and point to similarly sized cities like Philadelphia to prove that appointed boards do not necessarily help troubled urban systems. Granting appointment powers to the mayor would place too much power in one person's hands. ''I have a lot of problems with the school system,'' says Citywide Parent Council director Hattie McKinnis, ''but not enough to give up my right to vote.''

In large cities, school board members work full-time in highly visible positions. They are responsible for handling high-level contract negotiations, multibillion-dollar budgets, and politically sensitive crises. Small rural boards have members who work other jobs, meet biweekly or when the need arises, and must pay for their own secretarial work. Most school board members function somewhere in between those two extremes, but must get intricately involved in their systems, both on a policy-making level and on a practical day-by-day basis.

Over three quarters of all school boards must operate within the fiscal limitations set on them by the city or town but independently of other city services such as the police force or hospital. That means the board can allocate as it sees fit only the money distributed to it by city officials, who arrive at their own general budget figures and distribute funds to all city services. If the school system needs more money than the city management is willing to provide, the school board members must go directly to the voters and ask for it.

The board gets its information about how much to ask for in terms of money by holding budget hearings in which the school department and the public can argue for needed funding. The school superintendent is responsible for submitting a final budget to the school board, which then votes on it depending on the money it has received from the city or town. The board decides on how the money it receives from the city or town is spent.

None of this changes when the school system adopts an SBM policy.

The local school board is still answerable to the board of education, and the SBM council is answerable to the local school board for its legal status. Any SBM decision that affects the policy goals or fiscal restrictions of the school board is subject to board approval, just as any centrally mandated decision from the school system administration would be. The school board acts likewise as a system of checks and balances on the central administration or the SBM council.

What does change is that the school board is now directly answerable to the community on two sides — to the electorate who put the members in office and to the local school councils who fulfill school board mandates as well as their own agendas. This dual responsibility means that school board members must become even more tuned-in to the needs of the school communities they represent.

The concept of the elected school board (as opposed to the school board appointed by an elected official) is uniquely American and was always intended to increase community representation in public education. But with the increasing complexity of school systems and the increasing demands on them from all sectors, school members are in danger of losing sight of their populist mandate. SBM programs could ensure that school boards remain accountable to their constituencies by allocating some of their power to local councils and by forcing boards to maintain close and constant contact with their local councils.

It has also become a more viable avenue for advocacy by parents who take issue with the school board status quo. In 1982, school board campaign consultant Cipora Schwartz wrote a book, *How to Run a School Board Campaign and Win,* outlining the process by which citizens could mount campaigns for their local boards. The popularity of the book, which is published by the NCCE, attests to the growing commitment of parents to affect their children's education by becoming part of the system.

''I was a parent activist for ten years before I became a school committee member,'' recalls Janet McAliley, member of the Dade County, Florida, school committee, whose positions are full-time. ''Most board members are parents and they establish issues. But who is the parent who represents parents?''

McAliley's question is one that many parents are asking themselves as school boards become more and more involved in and identified with the central administration. The fact is, the vast majority of all school board members are themselves parents, or are parents of graduates of the school system they represent.

But does the very act of representing parents imply that sooner or later the committee member will lose touch with his or her constituency? McAliley acknowledges that, once involved in school management issues on a daily basis, things are rarely as clear-cut as they seem to parents on the "outside." The board has to balance many differing points of views, including those of other parents with conflicting perspectives. "You can't fully appreciate issues until you spend hours in meetings with all sides."

One solution, according to McAliley, is to insist that parent involvement remain a high-priority issue that stays before the committee. And the committee must use its broadened perspective as a reminder to listen to all points of view. "We have to listen, not just to the loudest speakers with the most radical positions, but to hear the voices that aren't speaking. And we have to ensure that we maintain ultimate accountability by remaining accessible to all parents."

Still, the practical aspects of running a school system take a lot of attention and a lot of time to learn. McAliley has been on the Dade County board for many years. She points out that no committee member currently has children in the system.

There is the danger that the length of time invested in learning about operations may weaken the link between a school committee member and his or her constituency. For this reason, several school systems have adopted regulations limiting the number of consecutive terms a committee member may serve. It also prevents elected members from using their positions as springboards to broader public office.

But limiting terms may mean a lack of professionalization, and the depoliticization of the school committee office is a two-edged sword. An effective school board needs efficiency and sound management solutions. It also must be accountable to parents, to personnel, and of course, to all students and to the fiscal system.

That's a lot to put on anyone's plate. Aside from limiting terms of office, what else can parents do if they are considering a run for the school committee as an effective solution to school problems? Karen Voci, a Providence, Rhode Island, parent activist who ran on a reform slate with several other parents, joined with her peers to sign a paper reminding them of their mandate and insisting that, if they do become co-opted by their role, they will be reminded and asked to resign. "It seems hard to imagine that it would ever happen," said Voci, "but we have to consider that we could lose sight of our goals, which are to make changes that will have a positive effect on students, not on school board members."

School boards, even those with members who are committed to improving their community's schools, can become unwieldy and members can lose sight or lose hold of their initial good intentions. How can you ensure that such a problem doesn't befall your local board? You can, of course, run for office yourself and apply Karen Voci's fail-safe principle of accepting a reminder from those closely involved, such as parents and parents groups. You can advocate for limited membership on the board so that members do not become entrenched. You can have one professional educator or town official on the board to act as a mediator when opposing camps conflict. You can elect neighborhood members to represent your local constituencies as well as at-large members to provide a broader perspective.

You can advocate for "sunshine" laws that open school board meetings to the public. This doesn't mean that the public gets due notification and can attend some meetings. It means that anyone who wants to can attend all but the most sensitive of meetings, and anyone who chooses to speak can do so for the record. The only exception is union contract negotiations, and even so, some states are experimenting with parental input and trilateral bargaining techniques.

Perhaps most importantly, you can connect local elections to local, state, and federal legislative actions, ensuring that your school board will act in the broader interests of your community at the legislative level as well as remaining focused on local school-based issues. Statistics show that only 10 percent of the general electorate votes in school board elections. The other 90 percent needs to be made aware of the tremendous effect public school systems have on cities and towns even for those residents who are not directly involved in them. Parents can point out that good schools raise the tax base, provide long-term security in the form of a better educated citizenry, and reduce the drain on local social services. It is crucial that the whole community contributes to the process.

In Lakewood, Colorado, the Jefferson County School District developed a district-wide policy addressing the relationship of school employees to parent groups. Written by members of the local school board, it is notable as a system-wide affirmation of the strongest values underlying an SBM program and its assumption that parents and community members are not petitioners for school board favors but equal partners in the education process.

Adopted in 1988, the manual reads, in part:

> *The Board endorses the creation of parent organizations such as PTAs and PTOs and local School Advisory Councils as appropriate means of achieving effective and maximum feasible involvement of parents and guardians of students in the affairs of our schools. The Board expects all staff members to work closely and in harmony with the officers and directors of all parent organizations in pursuit of the following goals:*
>
> *1. To involve parents and school personnel in a cooperative and sustained system of activities that will increase the educational opportunities of the children both in school and at home.*

2. *To improve school-home relationships by enabling parents and school personnel to (a) define their relationship to each other; (b) define their roles as they pertain to the children served by the schools; and (c) identify family needs and resources, including those of the community, as well as school needs and resources.*
3. *To provide teachers and administrators with opinions and viewpoints that will lead to a better analysis of the needs of students and more relevant programming.*
4. *To sustain parental interest through a program of training and consulting services.*
5. *To develop the skills needed by school personnel to function effectively in a working relationship with parents and other community members.*

GETTING THE COMMUNITY TO PITCH IN

An effective school-based management program should really be a community-based management program. Not only should it include members of the community on the decision-making council, but it should try as hard as possible to incorporate community resources into the school program. Not only would the school benefit from the input of local businesses, social service agencies, and civic agencies, but community institutions would benefit from involvement in the schools as well. It would pay off for them in potential employees, customers, clients, and voters, just as the investment would pay off for the schools in terms of human expertise, valuable materials, and cold, hard cash.

Involving communities in local schools works even in systems where the community is not the neighborhood. In systems with school-choice programs, for instance, your children may attend a school across town. But the allegiance of the local computer-software firm or the civic theater group needn't be based on geography. The community is defined by the people who participate in it: If your office can provide scrap paper for the third grade or you know of a computer programmer who wants to volunteer to work with the sixth grade, you have the makings of a school community.

The federal government, pressed for funds with which to improve the nation's public schools, insists that the private sector must pick up the tab. With SBM, local businesses are getting a unique opportunity to do more than donate funds — they can donate human services, resources, and, most importantly, management skills to help local councils solve local school problems.

Unfortunately, the liaison between businesses and schools is not always a positive one. We saw in Chapter 8 that the concept of the school as a marketplace has been enthusiastically supported by corporate leaders who feel that educators aren't doing a good enough job of teaching tomorrow's workers. The response of many educators has been that schools are not meant to produce workers, they are meant to produce thinkers.

It may very well be, with members of the local business community serving on an SBM council as parents or community representatives, that a curriculum developed to ensure qualified workers is part of the school's mandate. But if the school's academic goals differ from the goals of a local business offering help, conflicts may result. It's a good idea to make sure that the resources provided by the local community are in keeping with the goals of the school.

High school youths in Germany have for years benefited from a unique apprenticeship program that plugs them in, from the tenth grade onward, to their local businesses. The aim is not just to create part-time and summer jobs, as do the many work-study programs in the United States, but to foster a long-term commitment for full-time employment after high school and college.

High school students and local businesses pair up for three-year paid apprenticeships in which the student assumes increasing levels of responsibility as he or she acquires the necessary skills. Classroom instruction provides general academic skills as well as a curriculum that integrates work-study experience.

In Germany, nearly 400 businesses offer blue-collar and white-collar jobs to the apprentices, who make up more than 70 percent of the total high school population. In fact, one of the leading executives of the German National Bank was an apprentice-program graduate rather than a college graduate. The program is unique because of its broad base of involvement, and because it does not target only those students who would be expected to go into factory work or manual labor. In Germany, early tracking determines which students will be offered which kinds of jobs. As applied in this country, the system would have to be more open-ended, allowing any student the opportunity to invest in any kind of job training.

All over the country, SBM programs are proliferating as rapidly as school-choice programs. In fact, the two concepts — and often a combination of them — are frequently touted as The Answer to troubled American public schools. There is no doubt that both are uniquely American solutions, depending as they do on the democratic principle of ''more voice for more people.''

That does not, of course, mean that they are the only answer, but merely that they are the most promising commonly used alternative. Parents and parent coalitions all over the country have proven that there are many more answers — as many, in fact, as there are questions.

HOW TO: Avoid the Pitfalls of School-Based Management Programs

1. All Aboard, Please — Unless everyone is involved in the SBM program from the very beginning, the system is wide open to sabotage. It's easy for a superintendent to say to School A, "I'm going to help you out by instituting SBM." But if School A wasn't consulted first the likely response will be one of resentment rather than one of eagerness. Staff and parents who are resistant to change will be much less so if they are included in the initial decision-making process about what kind of SBM program it is going to be.

2. The Shared Decision-Making/School-Based Management Confusion — Many superintendents and school boards make the error of thinking that school-based management consists only of principals sharing their authority with school teams. But the central administration must be ready to relinquish some of its authority as well, rather than just dividing up the authority that has already been relegated to the principal. SBM turns the school principal into the chief executive officer of the building, and no CEO should operate without a board of directors.

3. The Project Mentality — SBM is not a project with a limited lifespan. It is an ongoing process, and unless team members are aware that SBM is a process, not a product, the effort will not be effective. In addition, personnel who are involved on the SBM council must be given the time to do their new jobs properly. The SBM council representative who is also the third-grade teacher will not be able to devote his or her attention to council meetings while holding parent conferences. A change in the school structure will have to be made to accommodate the new roles of SBM members.

4. Sacred Cows and Dirty Linen — New teams are often reluctant to change the core of the school; instead they chip away at the edges. In addition, insiders such as principals and teachers may not feel comfortable with changes.

5. The Repainting-the-Lunchroom Syndrome — Training should help team members go beyond the "norm of civility" that prevents them from attacking any substantive issues and instead concentrating on small, finite projects that are certain not to ruffle any feathers. Choosing this sort of project, good for starters, can become a rut for members who are uncomfortable with their newfound power.

6. Fuzzy Lines of Authority — One of the biggest stumbling blocks encountered by SBM councils is the lack of technical information about how things are done and what is legally and/or fiscally doable. Districts that are serious about empowering schools must not only provide an authoritative source of such information; they must also set up a process for seeking waivers of board regulations, union contract provisions, even state requirements.

7. Big Man on Campus — Principals tend to dominate SBM teams, using them as a venue for listening to ideas, comments, and complaints and then acting unilaterally. Collaborative planning is not shared decision making, and steps must be taken to ensure that the building principal does not undermine the effectiveness of the management team with the force of his or her power.

8. Great Ideas Come from Nowhere — The presence of an SBM council does not mean that all the necessary solutions to school problems are going to come from the council. Old patterns are hard to break, and council members will need to get plenty of support from central administration as well as by communicating with other councils.

9. The New Elite — Once people become a member of a group, they begin to form an allegiance to it. Unfortunately, the result is that council members, who are supposed to represent their schools, end up representing their own SBM group's interests or those of the central administration. When this happens, the team becomes just another part of the bureaucracy and is no longer effective as a local managing agent.

10. Time to Do It — Change always takes a lot longer to accomplish than council members expect. Plan on steady effort for at least five years before tangible results are visible (i.e., higher test scores, lower dropout rates). Also plan on providing coverage time for council members, like teachers, who have other responsibilities. And make sure meetings are held when the greatest number of members can regularly attend.

(from *Network for Public Schools*, April 1990)

C H A P T E R *10*

Drawing Conclusions,
Making Commitments

E'VE examined the structure of our local school systems and learned many of the technical terms we'll need to communicate with school personnel. We've looked at our many options for advocacy as individuals and as members of a community-based group. We've explored the school issues of most concern to parents as well as some of the major trends in current school reform. And we've read about scores of groups who have successfully undertaken to improve their local schools by advocating for changes in everything from the kind of math textbook used to the structure of the school district itself.

What can we do with all this information? As our investigation into effective academic techniques has taught us, acquiring skills and knowledge by reading a book is one thing; putting those skills and that knowledge to use is another matter altogether. We need to find ways to apply what we know to our own situations by examining what needs to be done in our own schools and determining how we can best go about doing it.

Chances are that most parents are already involved in school improvement on the local level and need only the stimulation and suggestions provided by resources such as this book to accelerate their involvement. Other parents may have to start at the beginning and work on a small scale — perhaps even alone at first — to implement small changes that might be the precursor of more broad-reaching actions. Every parent has an agenda; it remains only to act on that agenda, using effective skills and knowledge, and to form coalitions with others who share our concerns.

But getting more actively involved in improving our own schools is only part of our mission as parent-advocates. We must look beyond our own neighborhoods and our own personal concerns to get involved in improving public education in a larger arena. We must think beyond the immediate issues confronting our schools and consider the long-range effects of our efforts to improve all schools. We must begin to act in concert with others who share our vision, and work to create coalitions of groups who can together shape a new vision of effective American public education.

WHAT DOES THE FUTURE HOLD?

"Currents of Change for Public Schools in the 80's and 90's," a recent issue of the National Committee for Citizens in Education's quarterly *Network* newsletter, was devoted to assessing the state of American public schools. Determined through extensive research, outreach, and the NCCE's valuable telephone hotline, their assessment was that the 1980s, with all the hue and cry for reform that the years produced, was not a decade of great change. Nationwide, gains for educationally disadvantaged students were slight — dropout statistics declined by only 2 percent and reading and math scores increased only marginally for African-American students and not at all for Hispanic students. State-wide reforms such as higher salaries for beginning teachers, increased funding, and higher graduation requirements were achieved only when those reforms were politically comfortable to enact. Recommendations for changes that more directly affected the basic structure of our schools were usually diluted, often beyond real usefulness.

And the 1990s? Despite this mediocre record, the NCCE is hopeful that the present decade will bring an acceleration in several areas. They predict that:

- School-based management and parent choice will provide opportunities to involve parents and create close-knit, responsive learning communities.
- Dropout prevention efforts will begin earlier, even extending to early-intervention programs that help build self-esteem and positive learning experiences for preschoolers.
- The importance of family and parent involvement to school achievement will be nationally ratified as it was with the passage of the federal Family-School Partnership Act.
- Employers will help reconnect families to schools by establishing programs like work-site enrollment and by granting parent release time to attend school functions and by allocating corporate resources to local schools.
- Educators will reach a consensus on the best ways to teach children.

That's an optimistic forecast according to some public school critics. They predict instead that since not nearly enough has been done to save them, our schools are headed for swift and certain failure if we do not put our noses to the grindstone — and fast. Said president Ernest Boyer of the Carnegie Foundation for the Advancement of Teachers in 1990, "We are absolutely running out of time. I am convinced that we have perhaps a decade — and I may be optimistic — to make school improvement the universal experience, and to have some confidence in the public mind that the system is working."

Educators have argued education policy for as long as schools have taught children. A decade ago, parents were forced to listen to the debate from the sidelines, like spectators at a tennis match. These days, though, parents are much more likely to pick up a racquet and take a good shot at the ball. And increasingly, educators, businesspeople, and legislators are willing to accept parents as serious players on the field. As the NCCE's Anne Hallett says, "The challenge of the 1990s is to make sure all parents are respected, all cultures are valued, and all parents and citizens set the agenda for the education of our youth."

Clearly, parent advocacy doesn't *always* work. Parents report efforts that are in vain, ignored, or undone by school administrators and elected officials. School boards can act to protect themselves and their employees before they act in the best interests of the children, especially in grievance cases. Changes in administrative or elected personnel can negate long-range efforts in one sweep. The "local machinery," as one parent calls it, can move inexorably over all efforts at school improvement, making parents feel helpless and hopeless about the prospects for change.

Then, too, parents can be wrongheaded, shortsighted, and selfish about their goals. They can press for changes that represent only their own interests, which can, in turn, give all parent-advocacy efforts a bad name. "I walked away from my PTO," complains another parent. "They were so busy arranging things for their own precious kids — putting their names at the top of waiting lists for special programs and pressing the principal for special attention — that it just seemed pointless to identify myself with them. I prefer to act on my own."

Parents can rebut these charges by continuing their own well-balanced and well-meaning efforts at improvement while disassociating themselves from others who might be acting selfishly. The stereotype of the pushy parent, or the educationally ignorant parent, remains to be overcome, and only our persistent commitment to positive reform will prevail. And when discouraged by the failure of their efforts to accomplish their goals, parents should remember the words of one parent who worked for six years to get a biased testing policy abolished in her school district: "By the time the board finally got around to reviewing and then revising the test, my son had already graduated from high school! But I was so proud that I had made a difference. And he was so proud of me. He said, 'Hey, Mom, at last you graduated, too! Congratulations!' "

There have, to be sure, been brilliant individual efforts, and there is much that is good about the trends in education today. There is very little argument about the positive effects of good school-based management programs, for instance, and government support for school choice has made it a national priority. Elements of effective teaching — collaborative learning, hands-on investigation, active inquiry, personally meaningful assignments, problem solving and idea generating, intellectual risk taking, and individual or small-group work — are becoming accepted by teachers and administrators alike. But so far not much headway has been made toward instituting real educational reform, and not much change has been seen in the performance of our children or our schools.

Clearly, the ball is in our court.

A PARENTS' PROPOSAL

As leaders of education reform on the home front and in the national arena, parents will have an inestimable impact in coming years. But what is the parents' agenda, and in what areas will parents choose to make the greatest changes? As yet, there has been no effort to build a nationwide, grass-roots agenda determined and developed by parents and based on a strong coalition of common goals. Certainly efforts should be made to provide an umbrella organization under which parents could establish such an agenda.

Until then, however, perhaps we can begin to define the parameters of our goals based on what we have learned about the interests and efforts of parents across the nation. Every parent, and every parent group, has a unique agenda, but there are several similar themes to current parent-advocacy efforts. These themes can be applied to a parents' proposal for reform on three fronts, each of which addresses a basic issue in public education and each of which presumes that parents will work as leaders in partnership with educators, legislators, and community members to solve the problem in their own way.

TEACHING THE NEW BASICS

Today's schools engage only a narrow slice of an individual's capacity to learn, and they often work only for the student who is comfortable in the prescribed track, absorbing the prescribed kinds of information. We need to mobilize a potent variety of forces to enact far-reaching and elemental changes in the current curricula. We need to see to it that our schools adopt a curriculum that includes basic skills acquisition as well as preparation for a changing, shrinking world, and which is taught by the most effective methods for maximum assessable results.

There is no room for nostalgia in the New Basics curriculum. It used to be enough to say to a child, "a good education will get you a good job"; that is no longer true. Furthermore, in a more homogeneous society, it was easier to determine what course of study was applicable to most students; that, too, is no longer a simple truism. The perils of nostalgia, however, run deeper than that. Our own hidden agendas about our children and our own harkening back to the bucolic images of our youth (real or romanticized) can lead to dangerous misperceptions about the realities of growing up today. In an essay entitled "New World, New Kids, New Basics," Leroy Hay writes, "It is wishful thinking to assume that a return to the basics of the past will lead to kids who dress more neatly, play softer music, show more respect, and stay childlike and innocent."

Nor is there room in our new curricula for empty experimentation or the naive assumption that children, given greater academic freedom, will make sound academic choices. *A Nation at Risk* charged that the American public school curriculum has been diluted and homogenized beyond recognition, and that there appears to be no central purpose or mission to the education agendas of most school systems.

We need to work with school personnel to establish curricula that meet the changing needs of today's students — needs that include a broad multicultural component, strong computer skills, and the development of critical thinking — without sacrificing competency, accuracy, and literacy. The concept of curricular functionalism, as proposed by educator Diane Ravitch, comes closest to describing the needs of today's students. Ravitch points out that there is "a close correlation between a course of study and what one does as an adult. We must meet the needs of the society and the child, both of which are constantly changing." Even the way we teach basic skills like reading, writing, and arithmetic has been forever changed by computers, television, and interactive electronics. We can't pretend those things are not there, nor can we ignore the inroads they have made against literacy.

We must expand the concept of basic education to include that which is necessary, not only as a foundation for further learning but also for human development. While they need the same three R's we did when we were in school, our children will also need some coping skills that we did not, and a global awareness that includes language as well as knowledge of cultural mores other than our own.

Making such dramatic changes in what our children learn and how they learn is a huge task, but in most schools it is already being entertained, if not yet implemented. Creating the New Basics is not a task that we could — or should — undertake alone. But we need to participate, to guide professionals toward a curriculum that is meaningful for our community and effective for our children. We need to make schools aware of their own resources to help achieve these curricular upheavals, and commit ourselves to working with our children and our children's teachers to accelerate the change.

A strong, relevant curriculum is only part of what makes a school effective. We need to work for schools that are focused on broader issues as well. Educator Ron Edmond conceived of the concept of "effective schools" as being schools that worked in spite of the problems that all schools encounter, and regardless of what those problems were. Edmonds and his colleagues looked at small rural schools, at poor inner-city schools, at well-funded suburban schools, and at independent schools. Effective schools — and they exist all over the country — turned out to have several common characteristics. Parents working for curriculum and teaching reform can use these common elements as a guideline for improving their own schools. Effective schools have

- focused school goals and a strong sense of the school's mission;
- strong instructional leadership;
- an emphasis on basic skills acquisition;
- a positive, orderly school environment that is not authoritarian;
- frequent monitoring of student, teacher, and school progress;
- strong parent and community involvement.

Will what works for Hispanic students in a northeastern inner city work for Native American students in the rural Southwest? Even more important, can we hold both sets of children — and all other children who attend our schools — accountable for a common curriculum? The debate over a national curriculum rages on unresolved, and parents will have much to say on the subject in the coming years. Certainly there is mounting pressure to provide all children in America with the best possible education, regardless of who they are, where they live, or how they learn. But that honorable conviction raises questions of equity and quality. In our effort to see that everyone gets the same education, how can we avoid having everyone end up with the lowest-common-denominator education — universal mediocrity?

The debate over a national curriculum extends into a debate over national standards. Should every high school child have to complete the same curriculum to be considered for graduation? How will we test all those students, and by what criteria will we judge them to have succeeded? How will we deal with school systems where there are inadequate resources to provide students with the necessary teachers and materials for them to succeed?

These are questions that parents need to raise among themselves, with their school personnel, and in their communities. Their answers will, in the end, determine national policy, and that policy will, in turn, determine our children's educational future. ·

BECOMING PARENTS OF THE AMERICAN COMMUNITY

In addition to working to improve our children's educational opportunities, we need to look beyond our own front doors. The solutions to personal education problems can spawn institution-wide reform. We must make the leap from awareness of our local problems to the awareness that the same problems affect others in the state, in the region, and nationwide. In doing so, we will discover that our own solutions can have repercussions that affect the broader community as well as our own children's lives.

We must also recognize the formidable power of numbers to persuade, whether those numbers are amassed as calls to the principal, turnout at a school board session, signatures in a letter-writing campaign, or votes at the election ballot. Making the leap from the personal sphere to the political arena does not require greater effort than we made on our own behalf, but it does require that we sustain that effort for a long time — sometimes for years — before we can hope to see results. Fortunately, the energy generated by working in a group of like-minded individuals can more than replenish what each member spends.

We can be confident that if we are concerned about special education, or school discipline, or budget imbalances, or administrative irresponsibility, then other parents in other communities share those concerns. We must connect with those other parents, and pool our resources so we can help each other be more effective in our own advocacy efforts. Not only will our own causes and those of our "network" of groups be furthered by our mutual work, but our joint power could affect even those children whose community has not advocated in their behalf.

We have to think locally, regionally, statewide, and nationally. And we must look beyond our own borders as well, not just as advocates, but as parents of children who will someday be citizens of a polyglot society with many close connections to the international community. More than us, our children will need global survival skills if they are to compete in the global economy.

If there are no more comfortable distances between "us" and "them," between our safe, well-known families and the stranger, riskier world of other cultures, there is also no longer a distance between school and home, or between schools and businesses, or schools and government. Where once each stayed politely out of the others' domain, now each has become dependent on the other for survival. We have begun to realize that we must cooperate because to remain separate is foolish and to battle over responsibility dangerous. If we all invest in the human capital provided by education, we will all reap benefits for our children and our society.

So we must be comfortable working together and overcome the formidable barriers to mutual cooperation, even if it means facing un-comfortable truths about ourselves. We need to be able to deal with perspectives other than our own in a constructive fashion — not neces-sarily to embrace them, but certainly to consider them and to acknowl-edge that they, too, have value for those who hold them. We must share resources, information, and skills and be willing to exercise flexibility to achieve the goal that best meets all of our needs.

As we broaden our geographic perspective, we must also broaden our temporal perspective and learn how to think long-range, as well as short-term. Getting one incompetent teacher replaced is a short-term goal; overhauling the teacher evaluation system district-wide is a long-range goal. The battles we fight on the home front today may be win-nable on the national front next year.

Politics often makes for strange bedfellows; education reform for even stranger ones. Conservatives find themselves meeting liberals on the same side of issues like bilingual education and local governance, tuition tax credits and vouchers, home schooling and freedom of speech. The same provisions that make it possible for some parents to get outdated textbooks taken off classroom shelves allow others to have allegedly obscene books taken off the library shelves; the same freedom that allows us to teach a multicultural perspective may allow others the opportunity to teach a fundamentalist or even racist perspective.

We must acknowledge the limitations of such a democratic system even while we take advantage of the great freedom it allows us to determine our fate and the fate of our children. Parents will find that they disagree with each other as much as they disagree with teachers, administrators, or legislators. We need the courage to reach a consensus about what is intolerable in our schools, and to determine what must change. We need a willingness to acknowledge that the solutions will differ from one group to the next, from one moment to the next. Our mandate is to find the best possible solution for the greatest number of children at any given time.

LEARNING HOME LESSONS

An old Chinese proverb contends that one parent is worth a thousand teachers, and few teachers would disagree that the power of the parent far outweighs any classroom effort. The best lessons we can pass on to our children are the ones we teach them by example. Our advocacy efforts are a great lesson in hard work and caring, and we must never forget that *how* we go about advocating teaches our children as much as *what* we advocate for.

We share some basic assumptions about ourselves and our schools. One is that the environments of home and school are complementary; that is, they share the same values. This is no longer the case. In fact, says educator Sarah Lawrence Lightfoot, school and home sometimes work against each other, leaving the child hostile and confused and diluting the efforts of both home and school.

We can't work to make those environments homogeneous again (for many Americans, they never really were). In fact, some dissonance may be helpful in broadening the child's perspective about the world. But we must strive for greater equality of power and greater continuity of communication between the home and school environments. We can work to make our schools aware that the variety of home environments experienced by our children are equally valid, and equally deserving of attention in the education process.

Another assumption is that all parents are not equally invested in raising — or equally able to raise — their children. Some parents (particularly disadvantaged and minority parents) are perceived as needing help in knowing how to be parents. It is certainly true that some parents are unable to take care of their children, and equally true that some parents need support, training, and resources in order to do a better job. But while parents are not always literally blamed for a lack of parenting ability, this condescending attitude seems to enlarge the distance between parents and schools, and keeps parents in a subordinate role.

The deficit theory implies that the poor child will constantly need to play catch-up in school to make up for a lack in the home. We need models of parent involvement that assume family strengths, not family deficits. Dorothy Rich of the Home and School Institute has pioneered the use of many such models. "We are not assuming that the low-income family has fewer meaningful experiences than the middle-class child," she says. "All parents have the intrinsic ability to teach their children."

Parents of children who are not disadvantaged need to spend some time thinking about the parents of children who are. If middle-class parents can be cowed by school authorities, impoverished single parents can be thoroughly intimidated. Parents who have advocacy skills need to extend their skills to parents who do not. Parents of all children need to learn how to work together to show their children that cooperative efforts can overcome barriers, and that heterogeneity (of culture or of ideas) is more often the solution than the problem.

PARENTS CAN LEAD THE WAY

Frank Newman, president of the Education Commission of the States, tells a wonderful story: "American educators are like a bunch of zoo-keepers who went out and woke up all the lions and said, 'Hey, it's feeding time!' Now the lions are up and moving around, and the zoo-keepers say, 'Oops, we were wrong — we still have an hour and a half to go.' That's a bad time to be around the lion cage."

Parents are the lions in Newman's scenario — along with legislators, businesspeople, and community activists who have been warned that our schools are in trouble. And we are impatient, and sometimes angry, about our children's imperiled education. But Newman's witty analogy fails to take into account the fact that we lions are perfectly capable of feeding ourselves if necessary, and that we will certainly do what is needed to care for our young.

We can't do it alone, of course, and chewing up our educators is not the answer. But parents and communities have always been the source of change, although all too often our work is piecemeal and defensive, like putting a Band-Aid on a wound when surgery is indicated. Let's look briefly back over our options. We need several key ingredients to make parent advocacy work, on a small scale or a large, as individuals or in groups:

1. We need practical skills:
   - organizational ability (to put an effective group together)
   - information-gathering (compile as much material as possible on a subject)
   - publicizing (let as many people as possible know about the issue and what should be done about it)
   - lobbying (talk to everyone who is connected with the issue and let them know your position)
   - negotiating (be ready to offer alternatives, and be flexible about suggestions from the other side)
   - networking (let other groups know about your activities)

2. We need administrative support:
   - written policies about parent involvement; clear guidelines about the extent of that involvement
   - two-way communication and mutual respect without attempts to co-opt or usurp parent input
   - two-way education (school personnel need to learn from parents as well as the other way around)
   - training in school structure to help parents understand the language of school administration
   - training in management to handle the mechanical details of running a school system
3. We need access:
   - to information
   - to resources
   - to support
   - to funds
4. We need a partnership approach:
   - to work toward parity of power, not just in an advisory capacity
   - to build coalitions with professionals (especially with teachers) as well as other parents
   - to work for a change in the way we perceive schools and the way schools perceive families — as institutions that have equal power and resources, and which can mutually benefit from cooperation
5. We need to learn to think like advocates:
   - Children at risk are consistently shortchanged in the quality of the programs and services they receive.
   - Failures of the schools or the children are not inevitable.
   - Quality programs and services will not be provided unless advocates ask for them.
   - One important key for improving educational programs is to change the formal policies that shape what happens in the schools.
   - Educators and legislators will not carry out their policies in a way that will benefit children unless advocates monitor and prod them to do so.
6. We need to replace outdated perceptions with new ones.
   Old ideas include these:
   - Home and school are separate.
   - Educators are trained professionals with all the answers.
   - The principal is the most effective decision maker.
   - School officials are best equipped to handle problems.
   - Problems usually begin at home.
   - Using parents undermines the authority and effectiveness of school.

- Schools should stay out of family business.
- Parents must meet the school schedule.

New ideas include these:
- Schools and homes share responsibility.
- Educators and parents have complementary expertise.
- Collaborative teams make the best decisions.
- Parents can help solve school problems.
- Problems are a product of interaction between conflicting environments.
- Parents and community involvement are necessary.
- Schools should assume some responsibility for child welfare.
- Parents and schools must meet halfway.

THE CONTINUUM OF INVOLVEMENT

Not every parent can ride a white horse into the schools to rescue them. Not every parent should. Author Michael Williams agrees that "it may take years to create in a school the ethos that parents are not only welcome, but desperately needed. Apathy of parents is a legacy of the 'one-best-system' theory which holds that there is only one right and good way to educate a child, and that professionals are the only people who know such a way."

Each parent does what he or she is comfortable with, and schools need to provide parents with a variety of ways to get involved. All involvement is good, but more is not necessarily better for everyone, although more total involvement is certainly better for the school. The parent who can come to a classroom conference and speak eloquently about the needs of his or her child is advocating just as strongly as the parent who can organize a write-in campaign to oust an inept school superintendent.

According to Nancy Honig of California's Quality Education Project, parenting is a continuum, and advocacy (of any sort) is at the highest level, the most difficult to achieve. As for the continuum of involvement, that is up to the needs and abilities of the parent. Dade County assistant superintendent Frank Petruziello spoke of "searching for the right balance for parent input into the public education enterprise. It lies somewhere between the good old punch-and-cookie days of the PTA and giving them complete control."

Still, it is clear that token representation of parents in school life is no longer defensible from any perspective. Educator Joyce Epstein's classic division of the five types of parent representation is worth repeating here because it reminds us that all parents are effective when they are involved in their child's behalf:

1. basic obligation of parents — the responsibility to ensure health and safety
2. basic obligation of schools — communication between school and home
3. parent involvement at schools (volunteers)
4. parent involvement in learning at home
5. parent involvement in governance and advocacy

We all have the freedom to move up and down that ladder of involvement at a pace that is comfortable to us and consistent with the needs of our children. To broaden that perspective so that a community of children is affected (whether it's locally, regionally, or nationally) is to move along the continuum from Epstein's fifth level and get involved in changing our society at every stage.

The time to act in our own communities is at hand. We need to use our existing skills for information gathering, communication, networking, and negotiation, along with our newly acquired knowledge about our own school and the most effective means of initiating change. And we need to apply our efforts to the broader community so that all children benefit from our efforts and so the position of parents as powerful participants in the American public school system is firmly entrenched in the American mind.

We need to do it not by fitting into the existing system but by sitting down together to create a new system; not haphazardly but with careful preparation, consideration, and training; not peripherally but with adequate financial support, administrative support, and resources; not by reacting but by initiating; not as angry individuals but by creating a strong political base; not by acting alone but by seeking out coalitions and opportunities for collaboration at every turn.

With effective parent intervention and guidance, American public schools of the next century will not be centers of mediocrity, pumping out students with minimal mass-produced knowledge and outdated concepts of their position in the world. They will not suffer from economic atrophy or from hostile corporate takeovers. They will not be dangerous places that alienate and batter our children's egos and sever their connections to our family values.

They will instead provide an environment of variety and quality in which all children can learn to the best of their potential in an atmosphere of united efforts on their behalf by parents, teachers, administrators, and communities. They will offer children basic skills as well as specialized training to meet future challenges with interest and ability. They will produce citizens with a strong self-image and an even stronger ability to think critically and solve problems creatively. They will foster a worldview that is outward looking but inward sustaining. They will acknowledge the variety of American experience without sacrificing a high standard of achievement.

And parents will lead the way.

HOW TO: Use Successful Advocacy Methods

Designs for Change, the Chicago-based education research group that has been instrumental in the Chicago reform project, published *Standing Up for Children: Effective Advocacy in the Schools*, an excellent handbook on advocacy. The group observed the efforts of fifty-two advocacy groups around the country, and extracted twenty-one elements that characterized effective advocacy methods. While Designs for Change focused largely on at-risk students, we can broaden their methods inventory to include advocacy for all children.

Area I. Building and Maintaining a Strong Organization

1. strong leadership for the project
2. staff dedication to improve services for substantial numbers of children
3. attention to maintenance activities to keep group going by defining responsibilities, maintaining clear internal communication, et cetera
4. sustaining needed funds

Area II. Developing a School-Improvement Strategy

5. developing a cycle of intervention and analysis to establish a clear experience-based strategy
6. clarity of strategy
7. focusing on central issues that determine quality of services
8. envision a clear solution in terms of improved services
9. focus on changing a subsystem of the education system that shapes services to a particular group of children
10. focus on bringing about a major policy change
11. focus on implementation

Area III. Gathering Comprehensive and Accurate Information

12. documenting problems and solutions
13. gathering information about the educational system

Area IV. Building Support

14. using the media effectively
15. developing a support network
16. building a committed constituency

Area V. Intervening to Improve Schools

17. intervening at multiple levels
18. competent use of multiple tactics
19. carrying out specific intervention tactics competently
20. bargaining approach to intervention
21. persistence

Resources

A Better Chance
419 Boylston Street
Boston, MA 02116
(617) 421-0950

Advocacy for minorities

Advocates for Children of New York
24-16 Bridge Plaza South
Long Island City, NY 11101
(718) 729-8866

American Federation of Teachers
555 New Jersey Avenue NW
Washington, DC 20001
(202) 879-4400

*Provides explanations and serves as a
monitoring agency for all school programs
that receive federal funds*

Appalachian Educational Laboratory
P.O. Box 1348
Charleston, WV 25325
(304) 347-0400

Boston College Center for Corporate
   Community Relations
36 College Road
Chestnut Hill, MA 02167
(617) 552-4545

*A nationwide data base for business-
education partnerships*

Center for Law and Education
955 Massachusetts Avenue
Cambridge, MA 02139
(617) 876-6611

*A group of lawyers and advisers who
concentrate solely on education advocacy
and legal rights issues around public
schools. While they generally get involved
at the administrative level, CLE lawyers
will accept phone calls from parent groups
and even individual parents who feel that
their children's legal rights are being
violated in the public schools.*

Center on Parent Involvement
Johns Hopkins University
3505 North Charles Street
Baltimore, MD 21218
(301) 338-7570

*Research and policy-related analysis on
school issues, directed by noted education
researcher and parent-advocacy supporter
Joyce Epstein*

Children's Defense Fund
122 C Street NW
Suite 400
Washington, DC 20001
(202) 628-8787

*The nation's leading child advocacy
organization; conducts research,*

evaluation, and legislative lobbying on a
variety of children's issues

Cities in Schools
401 Wythe Street
Suite 200
Alexandria, VA 22314-1963
(703) 519-8999

Citizens for Educational Freedom
927 South Walter Reed Drive
Suite 1
Arlington, VA 22204
(703) 486-8311

Advocacy lobby that tries to influence the
collection and expenditure of education tax
dollars

Coalition of Advocates for Students
100 Boylston Street
Suite 737
Boston, MA 02116
(617) 357-8507

Coalition of Essential Schools
Brown University
Box 1969
Providence, RI 02912
(401) 863-3384

Committee for Education Funding
505 Capitol Court NE
Suite 200
Washington, DC 20002
(202) 543-6300

The Coop
Municipal and School Business
   Officials Cooperative Exchange
135 Beaver Street
Waltham, MA 02154
(617) 891-1999

Consultancy to improve business
management capabilities of school
personnel

Council for Basic Education
725 Fifteenth Street NW
Washington, DC 20005
(202) 347-4171

Promotes an emphasis on academic
disciplines in the schools

Council of the Great City Schools
1413 K Street NW
Suite 400
Washington, DC 20005
(202) 371-0163

Education Commission of the States
707 Seventeenth Street
Suite 2700
Denver, CO 80202
(303) 299-3600

Legislative advisory agency made up of
representatives of educators from every
state

Education Funding Research Council
1611 North Kent Street
Suite 508
Arlington, VA 22209
(703) 528-1000

Provides information on fund-raising and
other methods of assessing financial
resources for public schools

Education Leadership
Association for Supervisory Curriculum
   Development
1250 North Pitt Street
Alexandria, VA 22314
(703) 549-9110

Education Priorities Panel
70 Lafayette Street
7th Floor
New York, NY 10013
(212) 571-0718

Coalition of twenty-five major parent and
civic organizations

Education Writers Association of America
1001 Connecticut Avenue NW
Suite 310
Washington, DC 20036
(202) 429-9680

Federation of Children with Special Needs
95 Berkeley Street
Suite 104
Boston, MA 02116
(617) 482-2915

Harlem Parents' Union
271 West 125th Street
Suite 407
New York, NY 10027
(212) 662-4888

Home School Legal Defense Association
P.O. Box 159
Paeonian Springs, VA 22129
(703) 478-8585

Home and School Institute
Special Projects Office
1201 Sixteenth Street NW
Washington, DC 20036
(202) 466-3633

Advocates for parental involvement in the academic process by providing parents with simple, affordable educational tools and ideas

Institute for Responsive Education
605 Commonwealth Avenue
Boston, MA 02215
(617) 353-3309

The IRE's publication A Citizen's Notebook for Effective Schools *is an invaluable tool for parents who want to get a general feel for what's being done all over the country to improve schools. It*

contains a vast array of research and resource information and presents it in an efficient and easy-to-read way. It includes a reading list and research briefs as well as a sampler of local school improvement projects around the nation. It also provides the names of fifty-five ''people who can help''—individuals who can offer advice to parents in their area who are looking to implement school improvements.

Kettering Foundation
200 Commons Road
Dayton, OH 45459
(513) 434-7300

Learning Disabilities Association of America
4156 Library Road
Pittsburgh, PA 15234
(412) 341-1515

Merrimack Education Center
101 Mill Road
Chelmsford, MA 01824
(508) 256-3985

Consultants to twenty-two Merrimack Valley cities and towns on school issues

National Association of Federally Impacted Schools
444 North Capitol Street NW
Suite 405
Washington, DC 20001
(202) 624-5455

Provides explanations and serves as monitoring agency for all school programs that receive federal funds

National Association of Partners in Education
209 Madison Street
Suite 401
Alexandria, VA 22314
(703) 836-4880

National Center for Effective Schools
Research and Development
1025 West Johnson Street
Madison, WI 53706
(608) 263-4272

National Center for Education Statistics
U.S. Department of Education
555 New Jersey Avenue NW
Washington, DC 20208
(202) 219-1828

Information Services (800) 424-1616

National Center on Education and the
Economy
39 State Street
Suite 500
Rochester, NY 14614
(716) 546-7620

National Committee for Citizens in
Education
900 Second Street NE
Suite 8
Washington, DC 20002
(202) 408-0447
(800) NET-WORK

*Since 1973, the NCCE has acted as an
advocate and monitoring agency for school
reform. The Baltimore-based group offers
information and resources to parent groups
through its toll-free Helpline and Access
Clearinghouse. A bimonthly publication,*
Network for Public Schools, *provides
parent-group subscribers with information
about education-related issues around the
country as well as a listing of current
groups from all over the nation and
information about what they are doing in
their local districts. The NCCE is currently
involved in research and advocacy about
school choice; early dropout prevention;
middle-school improvement; effective
school-based management programs; single
parents dealing with schools; opening
school records and school committee
meetings to public access; and providing*

*greater opportunities for non-English-
speaking students and their families.
Parent groups or individuals may join the
NCCE for $25 a year and receive* Network
*for free. NCCE membership ensures that
parent groups will receive updated
information about education issues as well
as support from the NCCE to pursue their
own school improvement agendas.*

National Coalition for Parent
Involvement in Education
801 North Fairfax Street
Suite 209
Alexandria, VA 22314
(703) 683-6232

*A broad-based coalition of parent and
school groups organized under the auspices
of the NEA to encourage parent-school
cooperation*

National Community Education
Association
801 North Fairfax Street
Suite 209
Alexandria, VA 22314
(703) 683-6232

National Council for Better Education
101 North Alfred
Suite 202
Alexandria, VA 22314
(703) 739-2660

*Group seeking to return control of
education to parents and locals through
"the exposure of the National Education
Association as a tool of the radical left"*

National Education Association
1201 Sixteenth Street NW
Washington, DC 20036
(202) 833-4000

National Information Center for
Children and Youth with Disabilities
P.O. Box 1492
Washington, DC 20013
(703) 893-6061

National Parent Center
National Coalition of Title I/Chapter 1
  Parents
Edmonds School Building
9th and D Streets NE
Washington, DC 20002
(202) 547-9286

National PTA
700 North Rush Street
Chicago, IL 60611
(312) 787-0977

     or

1201 Sixteenth Street NW
Washington, DC 20036
(202) 822-7878

National School Boards Association
1680 Duke Street
Alexandria, VA 22314
(703) 838-6722

Parent Educational Advocacy Training
  Center
228 South Pitt Street
Room 300
Alexandria, VA 22314
(703) 836-2953

The Parent Institute
P.O. Box 7474
Fairfax Station, VA 22039-7474
(703) 569-9842

Publishes the newsletter Parents Make a
Difference

Parent Involvement Center
Chapter 1 Technical Assistance Center
RMC Research Corporation
400 Lafayette Road
Hampton, NH 03842
(603) 926-8888

Parent Involvement in Education
  Program
San Diego County Office of Education
6401 Linda Vista Road
San Diego, CA 92111-7399
(619) 292-3500

*Offers resources and advice to local
community groups and publishes the
newsletter* Communicating with Parents

Parents United for the DC Public
  Schools
1400 I Street NW
Suite 450
Washington, DC 20005
(202) 289-4988

Parents Union for Public Schools of
  Philadelphia
311 South Juniper Street
Room 602
Philadelphia, PA 19107
(215) 546-1166

Quality Education Project
2110 Scott Street
San Francisco, CA 94115
(415) 921-8673

*Provides parents with education seminars
and management help for parent
organizations*

Research for Better Schools
444 North Third Street
Philadelphia, PA 19123
(215) 574-9300

Southwest Educational Development
  Laboratory
211 East Seventh Street
Austin, TX 78701
(512) 476-6861

*A regional center that conducts research
and training as well as providing technical
assistance to area school systems*

United Parents Association of New
  York
70 Lafayette Street
7th Floor
New York, NY 10013
(212) 619-0095

*A coalition of more than 350 groups
involved in the city's public schools*

U.S. Department of Education
400 Maryland Avenue SW
Washington, DC 20202
(202) 708-5366

Information Services (800) 424-1616

Work and Family Research Council
845 Third Avenue
New York, NY 10022
(212) 759-0900

Bibliography

Access: The Information Clearinghouse About Public Schools. "Education Block Grant — Chapter 2." Columbia, MD: National Committee for Citizens in Education, n.d.

————. "School Board Improvement and Effective Schools: A Perfect Match for Bottoms-Up Reform." Columbia, MD: National Committee for Citizens in Education, 1988.

Ad Hoc Committee on Parental Involvement. "Strategies for Increasing Parental/ Family Involvement in Schools." Dade County, FL: Dade County Public Schools, 1990.

Adler, Mortimer J. "The Paideia Proposal." In Gross, Beatrice and Ronald, eds. *The Great School Debate: Which Way for American Education?*

Albert, Linda. *Coping with Kids and School.* New York: Ballantine Books, 1984.

Anderson, Beverly, Richard Stiggers, and David Gordon. "Educational Testing: Facts and Issues (A Layperson's Guide to Testing in the Schools)." Washington, DC: National Institute of Education. U.S. Department of Education, 1982.

Appolloni, Tony. "Self Advocacy: How to Be a Winner." National Information Clearinghouse for Children and Youth, 1984.

Bane, Mary Jo. "On Tuition Vouchers: An Essay Review." In Harvard Educational Review, *Education and the Legal Structure.*

Bastian, A., et al. *Choosing Equality.* Philadelphia: Temple University Press, 1986.

Bennett, William J. "James Madison Elementary School: A Curriculum for American Students." Washington, DC: U.S. Department of Education, 1988.

————. "James Madison High School: A Curriculum for American Students." Washington, DC: U.S. Department of Education, 1987.

Berger, Eugenia H. *Parents As Partners in Education: The School and Home Working Together.* St. Louis: C. V. Mosby Co., 1981.

Berger, Michael L. *The Public Education System* (American Government Series). New York: Franklin Watts, 1977.

Berla, Nancy, and Susan H. Hall. *Beyond the Open Door: A Citizen's Guide to Increasing Public Access to Local Schools.* Columbia, MD: National Committee for Citizens in Education, 1981.

Bowsher, Jack E. *Educating America: Lessons Learned in the Nation's Corporations.* Chicago: Wiley & Sons, 1989.

Brandt, Ronald S., ed. *Partners: Parents and Schools.* Alexandria, VA: Association for Supervision and Curriculum Development, 1979.

Brickell, Henry, and Regina Paul. *Time for Curriculum: How School Board Members Should Think About Curriculum / What School Board Members Should Do About Curriculum.* Alexandria, VA: National School Boards Association, 1988.

Bridges, Edwin M. "The Identification, Remediation, and Dismissal of Incompetent Teachers." Burlingame, CA: Association of California School Administrators, Foundation for Education Administration, 1984.

Brofenbrenner, Uri. "Who Needs Parent Education?" *Teachers College Record,* vol. 79, no. 4 (May 1978).

Brown, Martha C. *Schoolwise: A Parent's Guide to Getting the Best Education for Your Child.* Los Angeles: Jeremy P. Tarcher, 1985.

Buskin, Martin. *Parent Power: A Candid Handbook for Dealing with Your Child's School.* New York: Walker & Co, 1975.

Carlson, Dennis. "Teachers as Political Actors: From Reproductive Theory to the Crisis of Schooling," *Harvard Educational Review,* vol. 57, no. 3 (August 1987).

Cavazas, Lauro F. "Educating Our Children: Parents and Schools Together." Report to the President. Washington, DC: U.S. Department of Education, 1989.

Cenedella, Joan. "The Parent-Teacher Conference." New York: Bank Street School, 1989.

Center for Law and Education. "Congress Institutes Major Changes in Chapter 1 and Other Elementary and Secondary Education Programs." Cambridge, MA: Center for Law and Education, 1988.

_____. "Providing Effective Legal Services on Education Issues." Cambridge, MA: Center for Law and Education, 1989.

Children's Defense Fund. "It's Time to Stand Up for Your Children: A Parent's Guide to Advocacy." Washington, D.C.: Children's Defense Fund, 1979.

Citizen Action in Education. Biannual newsmagazine of the Institute for Reponsive Education.

Coffee, Glenn and Beverly. *Effective Schools for Poor Children: A Parent Handbook.* Cambridge, MA: Center for Law and Education, 1982.

Coleman, James S., and Thomas Hoffer. *Public and Private High Schools: The Impact of Communities.* New York: Basic Books, Inc., 1987.

Comer, James P. *School Power: Implications of an Intervention Project.* New York: Free Press, 1980.

_____. "Educating Poor Minority Children," *Scientific American.* vol. 259, no. 5 (November 1988).

Committee on Policy for Racial Justice. *Visions of a Better Way: A Black Appraisal of Public Schooling.* Washington, DC: Joint Center for Political Studies Press, 1989.

Cross, Patricia. "Wisdom from Corporate America." In Gross, Beatrice and Ronald, eds. *The Great School Debate: Which Way for American Education?*

Cutwright, Melitta. *A National PTA Talks to Parents: How to Get the Best Education for Your Child.* New York: Doubleday, 1989.

Daresh, John. "The Pre-service Preparation of American Educational Administrators." Paper prepared for the British Educational Management and Administration Society Annual Meeting, 1989.

Davies, Don, ed. *Schools Where Parents Make a Difference.* Boston: Institute for Responsive Education, 1976.

Davis, Bertha, and Dorothy Arnoff. *How to Fix What's Wrong with Our Schools: A Toolkit for Concerned Parents.* New York: Ticknor & Fields, 1983.

Della Dora, Delmo. "Parents as Partners in Curriculum Development." In Brandt, Ronald S., ed. *Partners: Parents and Schools.*

Dersh, Rhoda E. *The School Budget: It's Your Money, It's Your Business.* Columbia, MD: National Committee for Citizens in Education, 1979.

Designs for Change. "Quietly Making History: Facts about Chicago School Reform." Chicago, IL: Designs for Change, 1990.

Digest of Educational Statistics. 25th ed. National Center for Education Statistics. U.S. Department of Education, Office for Education Research and Improvement, 1989.

"Education, Participation and Power: Essays in Theory and Practice," *Harvard Educational Review.* Reprint Series no. 10, 1976.

Educational Visions Seminar. "Progressive Federalism: New Ideas for Distributing Money and Power in Education." In Gross, Beatrice and Ronald, eds. *The Great School Debate: Which Way for American Education?*

Elam, Stanley M. "1989 Gallup Poll," *Phi Delta Kappan* (September 1989).

Epstein, Joyce L. "How Do We Improve Programs for Parent Involvement?" *Educational Horizons* (Winter 1988).

Epstein, Joyce, and Henry Becker. "Parent Involvement: A Survey of Teacher Practices," *The Elementary School Journal,* vol. 83, no. 2 (1982).

Esmay, Judith. *Collective Bargaining and Teacher Strikes: The Expanding Role of Parents and Citizens.* Columbia, MD: National Committee for Citizens in Education, 1978.

Feistritzer, Emily C. *On Being a Teacher: A Report of Teacher Education and Certification.* Washington, DC: National Center for Education Information, 1984.

Fernandez, Happy. "Parents Organizing to Improve Schools." Columbia, MD: National Committee for Citizens in Education, 1985.

Finn, Chester A., Jr. "The Drive for Excellence: Moving Toward a Public Consensus." In Gross, Beatrice and Ronald, eds. *The Great School Debate: Which Way for American Education?*

Foglia, Ed. "Let's Make All Schools Choice." *Los Angeles Times,* March 21, 1989.

Frith, Terry. *Secrets Parents Should Know About Public Schools.* New York: Simon & Schuster, 1986.

Gabler, Mel and Norma. *What Are They Teaching Our Children?* Wheaton, IL: Victor Books, 1985.

Glenn, Charles Leslie. *The Myth of the Common School.* Amherst, MA: University of Massachusetts, 1988.

Gordon, Ira. "Effects of Parent Involvement on Schooling." In Brandt, Ronald S., ed. *Partners: Parents and Schools.*

Graham and Parks School. "Handbook for Teachers." Cambridge, MA: Graham and Parks Alternative Public School, n.d.

Groller, Ingrid. "School Prayer: Americans Express a Change of Attitude," *Parents* (September 1989).

Gross, Beatrice and Ronald, eds. *The Great School Debate: Which Way for American Education?* New York: Simon & Schuster, 1985.

Hamer, Irving, Charles Cheng, and Melanie Barron. *Opening the Door: Citizen Roles in Education Collective Bargaining.* Boston: Institute for Responsive Education, 1979.

Harrison, Charles. *Public Schools U.S.A.: A Comparative Guide to School Districts.* Charlotte, VT: Williamson Publishers, 1988.

Harvard Educational Review. *Community and the Schools.* Cambridge, MA: Harvard Graduate School of Education, 1969.

_____. *Education and the Legal Structure.* Cambridge, MA: Harvard Graduate School of Education, 1971.

Hay, Leroy E. "New World, New Kids, New Basics." In Gross, Beatrice and Ronald, eds. *The Great School Debate: Which Way for American Education?*

Henderson, Anne. *The Evidence Continues to Grow: Parent Involvement Improves Student Achievement.* Columbia, MD: National Committee for Citizens in Education, 1987.

Henderson, Anne T., Carl L. Marburger, and Theodora Ooms. *Beyond the Bake Sale: An Educators Guide to Working with Parents.* Columbia, MD: National Committee for Citizens in Education, 1986.

Hess, Hannah S. *The Third Side of the Desk: How Parents Can Change the Public Schools.* New York: Scribners, 1973.

Hoachlander, E. Gareth, and Susan P. Choy. "Work-Based Attendance: A New Approach to Expanding Parental Choice in Education," *Phi Delta Kappan* (September 1984).

Honig, Bill. *Last Chance for Our Children: How You Can Help Save Our Schools.* Reading, MA: Addison-Wesley, 1985.

Hopfenberg, Wendy S., et al. "Towards Accelerated Middle Schools for At-Risk Youth." Stanford, CA: Stanford School of Education, 1990.

Hostrop, Richard, ed. *Outstanding Public and Private Elementary Schools in the United States.* Palm Springs, CA: ETC Public, 1989.

"How to Tackle School Reform," *Time* (August 14, 1989).

Hubbell, Ned S. "Some Things Change, Some Do Not!" In Brandt, Ronald S., ed. *Partners: Parents and Schools.*

Institute for Contemporary Studies. *Parents, Teachers and Children: Prospects for Choice in American Education.* San Francisco: Institute for Contemporary Studies, 1972.

James, Betty Harris. "Parental Involvement: Asking the Real Questions." Charleston, WV: Appalachia Educational Laboratory, 1989.

Jones, Philip and Susan. *Parents Unite! The Complete Guide for Shaking Up Your Children's School.* New York: Wyden Books, 1976.

Kappelman, Murray, and Paul Ackerman. *Between Parents and School.* New York: Dial Press/James Wade, 1977.

Karnes, M. B., and R. Zehrbach. "Parental Attitudes and Education in the Culture of Poverty," *Journal of Research and Development in Education* (1975).

Kearns, David T., and Denis P. Doyle. *Winning the Brain Race: A Bold Plan to Make Our Schools Competitive.* San Francisco: Institute for Contemporary Studies, 1988.

Kidder, Tracy. "Alone in a Little Room: from *Among Schoolchildren,*" New England Monthly (September 1989).

Kirp, David L. "The Poor, the Schools, and Equal Protection." In Harvard Educational Review, *Education and the Legal Structure.*

Kozol, Jonathan. *On Being a Teacher.* New York: Continuum Books, 1981.

Krasnow, Jean. *Building Parent-Teacher Partnerships: Prospects from the Perspective of the Schools Reaching Out Project.* Boston: Institute for Responsive Education, 1990.

Laughy, Linwood. *The Interactive Parent: How to Help Your Child Survive and Succeed in Public Schools.* Kooskia, ID: Mountain Meadow Press, 1988.

Leitch, M. Laurie, and Sandra S. Tagari. "Barriers to Home-School Collaboration," *Educational Horizons,* vol. 66, no. 2 (Winter 1988).

Levine, James A. "How Schools Help Families," *Good Housekeeping* (September 1989).

Lieberman, Myron. *Privatization and Educational Choice.* New York: St. Martin's Press, 1988.

Lightfoot, Sarah Lawrence. *Worlds Apart: Relationships Between Families and Schools.* New York: Basic Books, 1978.

Lueder, Donald C. "An Evaluation of the Tennessee Parent Involvement Program: Twelve Exemplary Parent Involvement Models." Nashville: Center of Excellence, Tennessee State University, 1987.

Lurie, Ellen. *How to Change the Schools: A Parent's Action Handbook.* New York: Vintage, 1970.

Marburger, Carl L. "Who Controls the Schools?" Columbia, MD: National Committee for Citizens in Education, 1978.

————. *One School at a Time: School-Based Management, a Process for Change.* Columbia, MD: National Committee for Citizens in Education, 1988.

McGarry, Daniel D. "The Story of Citizens for Educational Freedom and Their Quest for Justice and Liberty," *Educational Freedom,* vol. 23, no. 1 (Fall–Winter, 1989–90).

McKenzie, Floretta Dukes. "An Education Program for 'Oz.' " In Gross, Beatrice and Ronald, eds. *The Great School Debate: Which Way for American Education?*

McLaughlin, Milby, and Patrick Shields. "Involving Low-Income Parents in the Schools," *Phi Delta Kappan,* vol. 69, no. 2 (October 1987).

Moore, Donald, et al. *Standing Up for Children: Effective Child Advocacy in the Schools.* Chicago: Designs for Change, 1989.

Morrison, George S. *Parent Involvement in Home, School and Community.* Columbus, OH: Charles E. Merrill Co., 1978.

Murray, Ann. *Parent Power in the Schools*. Chelmsford, MA: Merrimack Education Center, 1974.

Nathan, Joe. "Results and Future Prospects of State Efforts to Increase Choice Among Schools," *Phi Delta Kappan* (June 1987).

National Center for Education Statistics. "Education Partnerships in Public Elementary and Secondary Schools." Washington, DC: U.S. Department of Education, 1989.

National Center on Education and the Economy. "High Expectations: What Rochester's Students Should Know and Be Able to Do." Rochester, NY: National Center on Education and the Economy, 1990.

National Committee for Citizens in Education. *Network for Public Schools*. Columbia, MD. Bimonthly newsletter.

_____. "Parents *CAN* Understand Testing." Columbia, MD: National Committee for Citizens in Education, 1980.

National Committee for Citizens in Education. "A Nation at Risk." In Gross, Beatrice and Ronald, eds. *The Great School Debate: Which Way for American Education?*

National Institute for Parent Involvement in Education. *Forging Education's Future: Family-School-Community*. Charlotte, NC: National Coalition for Parent Involvement in Education, 1989.

National School Boards Association. "First Teachers: Parental Involvement in the Public Schools." Alexandria, VA: National School Boards Association, 1988.

Nazario, Thomas A. *In Defense of Children: Understanding the Rights, Needs, and Interests of the Child*. New York: Scribners, 1988.

NEA Research/Gallup Opinion Polls. "Public and K–12 Teacher Members." West Haven, CT: National Education Association, Spring, 1987.

Northeast Regional Exchange. "The National Reports on Education: A Comprehensive Analysis." In Gross, Beatrice and Robert, eds. *The Great School Debate: Which Way for American Education?*

Oppenheim, Joanne. *The Elementary School Handbook: Making the Most of Your Child's Education*. New York: Pantheon, 1989.

O'Shea, Suzanne. "The Rights of Parents to Determine Their Child's Curriculum." In Brandt, Ronald S., ed. *Partners: Parents and Schools*.

Pantridge, Margaret. "Private Lives, Public Schools," *Boston Magazine* (September 1989).

Paulu, Nancy. "Improving Schools and Empowering Parents." Washington, DC: U.S. Department of Education, 1989.

Peterson, Sally. "A Practicing Teacher's Views on Bilingual Education: The Need for Reform." Washington, DC: National Bilingual Conference, 1989.

Pierce, Neal. "Chicago School Reform Could Spark New City Politics," *Nation's Cities Weekly* (May 1, 1989).

Pine, Gerald, and Asa Hilliard III. "Rx for Racism: Imperatives for America's Schools," *Phi Delta Kappan*, vol. 71, no. 8 (April 1990).

Pizzo, Peggy. *Parent to Parent: How Self-Help and Child Advocacy Groups Can Help You Get Better Schools*. Boston: Beacon Press, 1983.

Ravitch, Diane. "Why Educators Resist a Basic Required Curriculum." In Gross, Beatrice and Ronald, eds. *The Great School Debate: Which Way for American Education?*

Rhetts, Paul Fisher. "Finding Out How Parents Feel About Local Schools." Columbia, MD: National Committee for Citizens in Education, 1984.

Rich, Dorothy. *Megaskills: How Families Can Help Children Succeed in School and Beyond.* Boston: Houghton Mifflin, 1988.

————. "Parents as Educators of Their Own Children." In Brandt, Ronald S., ed. *Partners: Parents and Schools.*

Rich, Dorothy, et al. "Building on Family Strengths: The 'Non-Deficit' Involvement Model for Teaming Home and School," *Educational Leadership* (1979).

Rioux, William (and staff of NCCE). *You Can Improve Your Child's School: Practical Answers to Questions Parents Ask Most About Public Schools.* New York: Simon & Schuster, 1980.

Rotberg, Iris C. "Some Legal and Research Considerations in Establishing Federal Policy in Bilingual Education," *Harvard Educational Review* (May 1982).

Schimmel, David, and Louis Fischer. *Parents, Schools and the Law.* Columbia, MD: National Committee for Citizens in Education, 1987.

School Council Assistance Project. "Ten Guides for School Advisory Council Activities." Columbia, SC: University of South Carolina, 1990.

Schwartz, Cipora O. *How to Run a School Board Campaign and Win.* Columbia, MD: National Committee for Citizens in Education, 1982.

Sinclair, Robert L., ed. "A Two-Way Street: Home-School Cooperation in Curriculum Decision-Making." Boston: Institute for Responsive Education, 1980.

Slaughter, Diana, and Edgar Epps. "The Home Environment and Academic Achievement of Black American Children and Youth: An Overview," *Journal of Negro Education,* vol. 56, no. 1 (1987).

Sleeter, Christine E., and Carl A. Grant. "An Analysis of Multicultural Education in the United States," *Harvard Educational Review* (November 1987).

Snider, William. "Parents as Partners: Adding Their Voices to Decisions on How Schools Are Run," *Education Week,* (November 21, 1990).

Sobol, Tom and Harriet. *Your Child in School: Kindergarten Through Second Grade.* New York: Morrow, 1988.

Stedman, Laurence C., and Marshall S. Smith. "Weak Arguments, Poor Data, Simplistic Recommendations." In Gross, Beatrice and Ronald, eds. *The Great School Debate: Which Way for American Education?*

Steinberg, Lois. "The Changing Role of Parent Groups in Education Decision Making." In Brandt, Ronald S., ed. *Partners: Parents and Schools.*

Sussmann, Leila. *Tales Out of School: Implementing Organizational Change in the Elementary Grades.* Philadelphia: Temple University Press, 1977.

Swap, Susan McAllister. "Comparing Three Philosophies of Home-School Collaboration," *Equity and Choice* (Spring 1991).

Thomas, M. Donald. "Your School: How Well Is It Working?" Columbia, MD: National Committee for Citizens in Education, 1982.

Timpane, P. Michael. "Educational Experimentation in National Social Policy." In Harvard Educational Review, *Education and the Legal Structure.*

Turner, Joseph. *Making New Schools: The Liberation of Learning.* New York: David McKay Co., 1979.

Tyack, David, and Elisabeth Hansot. "Hard Times, Then and Now: Public Schools in the 1930s and 1980s." *Harvard Educational Review* (February 1984).

U.S. Department of Education. *The Condition of Education.* Washington, DC: National Center for Education Statistics. U.S. Department of Education: Office for Education Research and Improvement, 1989.

————. *Making Sense of School Budgets: A Citizen's Guide to Local Public Education Spending.* Washington, DC: U.S. Department of Education, 1989.

————. *What Works: Research About Teaching and Learning.* 2d ed. Washington, DC: U.S. Department of Education, 1987.

Walker, Ron, et al. *Education for All People: A Grassroots Primer.* Boston: Institute for Responsive Education, 1980.

Webster, William G. *Effective Collective Bargaining in Public Education.* Ames, IA: Iowa State University Press, 1985.

Weinberg, Richard L., and Lynn Goetsch. *Parent Prerogatives: How to Handle Teacher Misbehavior and Other School Disorders.* Chicago: Nelson-Hall, 1979.

Westin, Jeane. *The Coming Parent Revolution: Why Parents Must Toss Out the ''Experts'' and Start Believing in Themselves Again — An Action Plan for Strengthening the Family.* Chicago: Rand McNally, 1981.

Weston, Susan Perkins. "Choosing a School for Your Child." Washington, DC: U.S. Department of Education, 1989.

Williams, Michael R. *Neighborhood Organizing for Urban School Reform.* New York: Teachers College Press, 1989.

————. "Neighborhood Organizing for Urban School Reform," *Equity and Choice* (Fall 1989).

Wilson, Bruce L., and Gretchen B. Rossman. "Collaborative Links with the Community: Lessons from Exemplary Secondary Schools," *Phi Delta Kappan* (June 1986).

Zeldin, Shepherd. "The Implementation of Home-School-Community Partnerships: Policy for the Perspective of Principals and Teachers," *Equity and Choice.* vol. 10, no. 10 (Spring 1990).

Zerchykov, Ross. *A Citizen's Notebook for Effective Schools: A Sourcebook of Research Briefs and Local School Improvement Projects.* Boston: Institute for Responsive Education, 1984.

————. *School Boards and the Communities They Represent: An Inventory of the Research.* Boston: Institute for Responsive Education, 1985.

Many thanks to:

Nancy Berla of the National Committee for Citizens in Education for her unceasing assistance and support;

John Cawthorne and the students of the Wheelock College Summer Certification Program for helping me think like a parent, a teacher, and a true advocate for all children;

The National Committee for Citizens in Education for providing information and inspiration to me and to parent-advocates everywhere;

Amanda Peters for wading bravely through my bibliographic morass and putting it in order;

and to Leana and Julia, for graciously agreeing to watch television in the afternoons so I could finish up my work.

Index